The Handbook of Tennis

The Handbook of Tennis

PAUL DOUGLAS

Foreword by John McEnroe

New York: Alfred A. Knopf 1993

A DORLING KINDERSLEY BOOK

Project Editor   David Lamb
Art Editor   Pauline Faulks
Editor   Miren Lopategui
Designer   Debra Lee

Managing Editor   Jackie Douglas
Art Director   Roger Bristow

Library of Congress Cataloging-in-Publication Data

Douglas, Paul
    The handbook of tennis/Paul Douglas. – Rev. ed.
        p. cm.
    Includes index.
    ISBN 0-679-74062-7: $20.00
    1. Tennis.   I. Title.
GV995.D66   1992
796.342'2—dc20   91-58566
                                        CIP

Manufactured in Hong Kong
Published March 29, 1982
Revised and updated, First American Paperback Edition, July 1992
Second Printing, October 1993

THIS IS A BORZOI BOOK
PUBLISHED BY ALFRED A. KNOPF, INC.

Contents

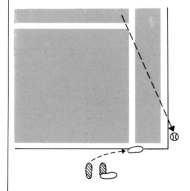

Foreword

I met Paul Douglas during the 1981 Wimbledon championships and was impressed by his approach to tennis coaching. Mainly I liked it for two reasons: one, he really emphasizes the importance of getting your basic game on a sure footing, of mastering the essentials of sound technique and good strokeplay. Also – and this is not as usual as people may think – he encourages you to make use of good technique to develop your own strengths. A lot of players I know haven't made it to the top because they were coached into being robot performers and they weren't allowed to play their natural game.

Now in this terrific all-round coaching book Paul Douglas has set out his teaching method, and I really believe it will help players at all levels to improve their game. Every chapter, whether covering strokeplay or strategy, is tremendously well illustrated, and if you are playing competitive tennis there is solid advice on getting yourself into good physical and mental shape. I would really recommend this book to young players who aren't lucky enough to have the help of a coach – *The Handbook of Tennis* is a terrific alternative.

Good luck.

John McEnroe

Introduction

The sport of tennis has been played for hundreds and hundreds of years, but the game as it is known today is little more than a century old. By mid-nineteenth century many were experimenting with new versions of the old game of "real" or "royal" tennis, but the immediate ancestor of lawn tennis was the game of "Sphairistike," invented by Major Walter Clopton Wingfield and first played by him in 1873 on a grass court in Wales. "Sticky," as it was first known, or "lawn tennis," as it became, was an immediate success and was soon being played on hourglass-shaped courts and lawns all over England. In 1875 the All England Croquet Club set aside one of its grounds specifically for the new game, and the Marylebone Cricket Club, the governing body of the old games of "real" tennis and rackets, drew up a code of rules.

The first Wimbledon Championships
In 1877 the All England Croquet Club formally changed its name to the All England Croquet and Lawn Tennis Club and held the first tennis championships in July 1877. The referee was Henry Jones who, with a two-man committee, devised the rules for the tournament using a revolutionary scoring system. Players were required to change ends after each set, matches were the best of five sets, and advantage sets were played only in the final. If a game reached 5-5 in earlier rounds, the outcome of the next game decided the set – like present-day tiebreakers. The shape of the court was also changed from hourglass to rectangular, with measurements similar to those of today. Thus, despite some subsequent adjustments, the basis of present-day tennis was created in 1877 by Henry Jones.

Players were not seeded – opponents were chosen by draw – and twenty-two men entered that first championship. (In 1919 the number of entrants for men's singles was limited to 128.) The first lawn tennis champion was Spencer Gore, who employed the tactic of an intimidating net attack against his opponents. At that time the net was 5ft high at the posts and only 3ft 3in at the center. It

Ernest (left) and William Renshaw

Laurie (left) and **Reggie Doherty**

Maud Watson   Blanche Bingley   Lottie Dod

Arthur Gore (Wimbledon champion 1901, 1908, 1909)   **Anthony Wilding** (Wimbledon champion 1910-13)

was lowered to its present height of 3ft 6in at the posts in 1882. Volleying was still largely unknown; it would be many years before a continuous serve and volley attack over five sets of match play would prove tactically successful.

During the 1880s Wimbledon was dominated by the British Renshaw brothers, Ernest and William, who influenced tennis development by setting new and higher standards of stroke and match play and who kindled increased public interest in the sport. William Renshaw, seven times Wimbledon's Singles Champion, demonstrated the smash as a most decisive stroke and was the first exponent of a "rising ball" style of play.

Two other brother teams succeeded the Renshaws. Herbert and Wilfred Baddeley won the doubles title four times in the 1890s. Between 1897 and 1906 the Doherty brothers, Reggie and Laurie, won the singles championship a combined total of nine times and surpassed the Renshaw record by capturing the doubles eight times.

Early United States Championships
In 1881 the United States Lawn Tennis Association was founded and held its first championship at Newport, Rhode Island. (The tournament moved in 1915 to Forest Hills where it remained through 1977, when it was relocated to its present site, the National Tennis Center in Flushing, New York.) The first winner was R.D. Sears, a young Harvard graduate, who successfully defended his title six consecutive times, an accomplishment that has never been equaled. Sears also teamed up with Dr. James Dwight, a founder of the USLTA, to win the national doubles title five times. Another Harvard athlete, Robert Wrenn, won the singles title six times during the 1890s and was one of the earliest members of the U.S. Davis Cup team. Between 1901 and 1911, William Larned won the title seven times and was ranked in the top ten for 19 years (1892–1911).

International contests
By 1900 tennis had become truly international, and in 1912 the International Lawn Tennis Federation was created in Paris. In August

Champions in contrast
Few in the history of tennis can be discussed on equal terms with America's Maureen Connolly and Australia's Rod Laver.

Maureen Connolly was first spotted in Balboa by Wilbur Folson, who encouraged her to change from her natural left-handed style to that of an orthodox right-hander. Further tutelage from coach "Teach" Tennant developed her basically Eastern style of play to the highest of groundstroke standards. "Little Mo" won the US Singles Championship in 1951, at the age of 16, and took the first of her three successive Wimbledon championships in 1952. In 1953 she became the ladies' first Grand Slam winner.

Rod Laver, coached by Charlie Hollis and Harry Hopman, won the first of his two Grand Slams almost 10 years later, in 1962, beating Roy Emerson in the Australian, French and American championship finals and Marty Mulligan at Wimbledon. In the same year he also won the Italian and German championships, dominating the tennis world with his attacking Continental style of play, which featured aggressively struck topspin strokes and vicious slices of penetrating fierceness. His topspin services were almost unreturnable.

Maureen Connolly

Rod Laver

1900 the first Davis Cup match was held between Britain and the United States at the Longwood Cricket Club, Boston, in order to promote international competition. The first match was inaugurated by U.S. team member Dwight Davis, who donated the cup and, with M. Whitman and Halcombe Ward, defeated the British team. The format is best of five matches: one doubles and four singles contests, with each team limited to four players. For many years only a few countries participated, and the cup was the exclusive possession of Great Britain, France, Australia and the United States (between 1937 and 1973 American and Australian domination was total). In recent years, with the entry of professional players into cup play, the Davis Cup match has become a major event involving more than 50 countries.

Women champions

In 1884 a women's singles event was played at Wimbledon for the first time, and thirteen women competed. The champion was Maud Watson, a vicar's daughter, who defeated her sister Lilian in the final. Between 1884 and 1900 there were only five champions, including Maud Watson, who held her title in 1885, and Lottie Dod, who became champion for the first time at age 15. In 1899, the doubles championship was initiated. The greatest women's champion in the years before World War I was Mrs. Lambert Chambers, who played in no less than 11 Wimbledon finals, winning seven.

The U.S. Tennis Association inaugurated women's championships in 1887. The tournament was held in Philadelphia until the move to Forest Hills. The first players to dominate the championship were Juliette Atkinson, who won the title three times (1895, '97, '98), and Bessie Moore, who won it four times (1896, 1901, '03, '05). Hazel Hotchkiss, a Californian, won the singles, doubles and mixed doubles titles three years in a row (1909, '10, '11) – a unique achievement. In 1915, Molla Bjurstedt Mallory, a Norwegian, won the first of her eight titles. The woman player with the most successful singles record was Helen Wills Moody. Between 1923 and 1933 she

Bill Tilden

Fred Perry

12

Suzanne Lenglen

Jean Borotra

played in 9 singles championships, winning seven titles and finishing as runner-up twice. In 1923 the internationally acclaimed Wightman Contest between American and British women was launched and continued until 1990.

American and French domination

The 1920s was a golden age for tennis. Never before had there been so many first class tennis players. Pre-eminent among them was a man who many consider to be the greatest player of all time, "Big Bill" Tilden. In 1920 Tilden defeated Australian Gerald Patterson to win the championship after playing eight singles matches in a tournament that had not yet introduced seeding; he won again in 1921. From 1920 through 1925 he did not lose a singles match in six Davis Cup challenge rounds and six U.S. Championship finals. Even in defeat, Tilden was remarkable: his loss to René Lacoste in the finals of the 1927 U.S. Championship and Henri Cochet in the semi-finals at Wimbledon the same year are regarded among the classic matches in all tennis history.

The year 1924 was the beginning of a six-year period of French domination of the men's singles at Wimbledon; until 1929 the "Four Musketeers" – Jean Borotra, Henri Cochet, René Lacoste and Toto Brugnon – ruled. Among the women, Suzanne Lenglen of France and Helen Wills Moody of the United States dominated during the 1920s and 1930s respectively, although tough opposition was provided by such players as Elizabeth Ryan, Mrs. Mallory, Kitty McKane Godfree, Lili de Alvarez, Helen Jacobs, and Dorothy Round. The 1930s ended with Alice Marble becoming champion in 1939.

In 1930 Tilden broke the French hold on the men's events, beating Borotra in the semi-finals, and went on to defeat Texan Wilmer Allison, who had, remarkably, reached the finals although unseeded. In the 1930s other great players emerged: Ellsworth Vines, Don Budge of the United States; Fred Perry of Great Britain; Jack Crawford of Australia and Gottfried von Cramm of Germany. In 1938 Don Budge

Champions in contrast

Although their styles of play were very different, Bjorn Borg and Billie Jean King showed how determination and total dedication can achieve greatness in sport.

Bjorn Borg made his Davis Cup debut in 1972 at the age of 15, and by 1976 was Wimbledon Champion, a title he held for five successive years. This was a particularly noteworthy achievement since he was really a clay court player. Under the direction of Lennart Bergelin he became the most feared counter-hitter from the baseline. His two-handed backhand, with its exaggerated looping action, was hit with enormous power and spin. He achieved a higher percentage of first service winners than most of his contemporaries.

Billie Jean King, a natural net player, was first encouraged to develop her groundstoke play by coach Clyde Walker. Her basically Eastern style of play was the perfect model of a sound technical game that could be adapted to any court surface. She used a Continental grip which allowed wrist snap and racket face angle control and was the key to her superb serve and overhead play. Her six wins at Wimbledon were only a small part of over 50 major titles won during her career.

Billie Jean King

Bjorn Borg

became the first player to win the Grand Slam by winning the Australian, French, Wimbledon and U.S. championships in the same year. Despite opposition, the first professional tournament was staged in 1926 at Madison Square Garden, and players such as Tilden, Lenglen, Perry and Budge were among the first to set the trend of turning professional.

Modern times

During World War II there were no Wimbledon championships; the chief tournaments were in the United States. After 1945 Australian and American players continued their domination of tennis. Double-handed play became a common feature on the courts, matches became much longer, and in 1970 the then controversial tiebreaker method of scoring was introduced for the first time.

Leading players of the post-war period included the Australians Frank Sedgman, Lew Hoad, Fred Stolle, Ken Rosewall, John Newcombe and Rod Laver, who dominated tennis for a decade from the late 1950s. Other great players included Jaroslav Drobny of Czechoslovakia, and the American Pancho Gonzales, who, in 1969, at the age of 41, played and defeated Charlie Pasarell in a remarkable 112-game match lasting five hours 12 minutes. In the 1950s and '60s a number of brilliant women champions emerged, including Louise Brough, Doris Hart, Maureen Connolly, Althea Gibson (the first black woman to achieve international tennis prestige), Maria Bueno, Margaret Court, Billie Jean King, Evonne Goolagong Cawley, and Virginia Wade.

In 1968, the British Lawn Tennis Association voted to open Wimbledon to professionals, initiating the "Open Era", as the other Grand Slam tournaments followed, and the eventual abolition of the amateur-professional distinction. This step was a crucial factor in the successful development and expansion of women's tennis, which had never been able to support a professional tour. National titles and major tournaments, no longer restricted to amateurs, quickly attracted the best tennis

Jack Kramer

Frank Sedgman

Lew Hoad

Ken Rosewall

Angela Mortimer (Wimbledon champion 1961)

players and became major sports events that drew huge crowds, extensive press coverage, and eventually international television exposure. With the advent of open tournaments, Rod Laver, who had achieved the Grand Slam in 1962 as an amateur player, repeated this remarkable feat as a professional in 1969.

During the 1970s and 1980s the United States again moved to the forefront of men's tennis with such players as Stan Smith and Jimmy Connors. After years of foreign domination, the Americans regained control of the U.S. Open. Connors won on three different surfaces: on grass in 1974, on clay in 1976, and on the hard courts of Flushing Meadow in 1978, 1982 and 1983. John McEnroe won the U.S. Open for three consecutive years, 1979-1981 – the first player to perform this feat since Bill Tilden in the 1920s – and again in 1984. In the 1970s the top player in the world was Bjorn Borg of Sweden. He first won the Wimbledon title in 1976 and successfully defended it four times until he lost to McEnroe in the 1981 final. After Borg retired, Connors and McEnroe dominated major tournament tennis, repeatedly meeting in finals and playing closely-fought classic matches.

Borg's outstanding success led the resurgence of European players. Czechoslovakia's Martina Navratilova and Ivan Lendl were soon dominating the tennis world. After many frustrating attempts, Lendl finally won the U.S. Open in 1985, and defended his title for the next two years. Navratilova triumphed at Wimbledon nine times – for six consecutive years in the 1980s – and at the U.S. Open four times. The Chris Evert/Martina Navratilova rivalry for the top spot spanned more than a decade and is thought to have been the best in the history of women's tennis.

In France too there was a reawakening of the patriotic fervor started by Max Ducugis in 1903, with the emergence of Yannick Noah, Henri Leconte, and Guy Forget. The three players (with Noah as coach) surprised the U.S. team to win the Davis Cup in 1991. In 1985 Germany's Boris Becker, at 17, became the youngest

World champions in the making

1989 saw the retirement of Chris Evert; 1990 saw the emergence of the greatest child prodigy since Lottie Dod, when Florida's Jennifer Capriati made her professional tennis debut at 13 years of age. For every champion whose career is ending there is a host of young "champions in the making", all of them determined to become their country's best player, the next Wimbledon champion or number one in the world rankings. The fact that champions come from many nations helps to keep the competitive spirit kindled.

Potential champions eager to emulate the success of players like Steffi Graf, Boris Becker, and Monica Seles include Anke Huber, Andrea Sternadovia, Amy Frazier, and Barbara Rittner among the women, and André Agassi, Sergi Bruguera, Goran Ivanisevic, Malivai Washington, Niklas Kulti, and Thomas Enqvist among the men.

Michael Chang and Arantxa Sanchez-Vicario, the youngest players ever to win a Grand Slam event when they took the French titles in 1989, have already established themselves as likely world champions of the future.

Jennifer Capriati

Michael Chang

ever and first unseeded men's singles champion at Wimbledon; he won again in 1986 and 1989. With the sport dominated by such players as Germany's Steffi Graf and Michael Stich, Spain's Arantxa Sanchez-Vicario, Sweden's Stefan Edberg, Argentina's Gabriela Sabatini, and the United State's Pete Sampras and Jim Courier, no one country rules.

In 1972 the Association of Tennis Professionals – representing the players – was formed, and in 1990 the ATP Tour took control of all non-Grand Slam men's tournaments. In women's tennis, the Federation Cup was launched in 1963, and in 1921 the Virginia Slims tournaments. The Women's Tennis Association was founded in 1973, and has worked ever since to gain more exposure – and equal prize money – for the women's tour.

In 1988 tennis returned to the Olympics, when Steffi Graf and Miloslav Mecir won the gold medals, and in 1990 the $8 million Grand Slam Cup was launched. The most prestigious and coveted championships remain the Grand Slam events – the U.S., French, and Australian opens, and Wimbledon – while the Davis Cup and the Federation Cup are still the major international team competitions.

Chris Evert Lloyd

Increased attention to player fitness and training methods and advances in the technology of rackets and balls and court surfaces have contributed to power tennis, a game that is fast and hard, a game dominated by the scorching serve. Some worry that strength and technology are overtaking other elements, such as deftness and strategy. They link high-impact tennis with shoulder and elbow injuries. Debate swirls about the need for speed limits, perhaps through adjustment of the rules (such as eliminating the second serve).

The sport continues to evolve and to attract larger audiences and bigger money. Through the 1960s and 1970s tennis enjoyed the fastest growth in participation of any sport, and in 1990 there were more than eighteen and a half million players in America.

John McEnroe

Fundamentals

Choosing your equipment

Tennis equipment is not as expensive as that of some other sports. Rackets are an initial expense, but well-made rackets will last for years. Although clothes and shoes can also be expensive, tennis balls are the costliest items, as they need constant replacing.

Rackets

Rackets can be bought complete, or as frames for which you can buy stringing separately (see p.270). The type of racket that you buy will, to a large extent, depend on the level of your game. As a beginner, an aluminum racket of medium flex will be useful; as you improve, you will find that you benefit from using a stiffer-framed composite or graphite racket. Power players require stiff frames and touch players more flexible ones.

When choosing your racket, consider carefully its weight, balance and grip. Always take a few practice swings to ensure that the racket does not drag on your wrist. Generally speaking, very young players should start with mini and cadet then junior rackets; women with light rackets from around 335g (11^1/$_2$oz), and men with medium rackets from 350g (12oz) upwards. Try supporting the frame across your extended finger at the point of balance – 34cm (13in) from the butt of the handle. As a rule, the racket should be of an even balance or slightly light towards the head – remember that all rackets will feel heavier when you are actually hitting the ball.

The wide-bodied design of the modern tennis frame has helped to reduce racket weight, and the general specification of tennis rackets is now "Light" (see table).

There is also a choice of grip numbers. These normally correspond to the different racket weights and grip circumference (listed right). Wrap your hand around the grip with the butt of your palm on the butt end or cap. If the end of your thumb nail goes past your second finger nail, then the grip is too small.

Grip Coverings

Grip coverings are usually made of leather, but many players prefer a more absorbent grip, or one of a finer leather. Whatever your needs, you will find that there is a full range of overgrips available, which can be wrapped on top of the existing grip. These overgrips do not last very long, but they are not as expensive as the standard grips, and can be replaced. With the overgrip your racket handle may feel fractionally larger than before and you may have to take this into consideration when buying your racket.

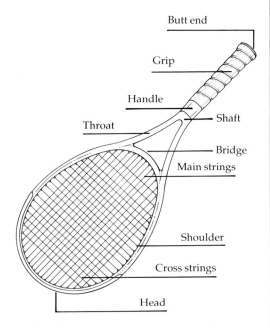

Stringing

The lengthwise strings on a racket are known as main strings, and the widthwise strings as cross strings. Rackets are normally strung with synthetic materials because it is much cheaper than gut, is not affected by moisture, and does not wear out as quickly through friction as gut does. Tournament players, however, still tend to

Spec.	Weight Approx.	Grip No.	Grip Size	
			Cm.	In.
Superlight	330g	0	10.2	4
Light	From	1	10.5	4^1/$_8$
Light	335g	2	10.8	4^1/$_4$
Light	to	3	11.1	4^3/$_8$
Light	360g	4	11.4	4^1/$_2$
Light		5	11.7	4^5/$_8$

Light/medium and medium rackets will be a little heavier and have a grip range from 2–5, as above.

prefer gut because it provides a more sensitive feel. Any racket can be strung to the tension that you require, but as a general rule stiff frames can be strung more tightly than flexible ones. The novice player should select a medium tension (p.274). Racket manufacturers usually recommend specific tensions for their frames, and, unless you are getting professional advice, you would be wise to follow these recommendations. Stringing your racket too tightly simply shortens the life of both frame and strings.

Checking stringing On a racket that has already been strung, check that the strings are parallel by making sure that the interwoven pattern of the strings is uniform. Check the tension be pressing your thumbs into the corners of the stringing: all four should feel identical. When you press in the center you should feel that extra "give" when compared to the tension in the corners. Check your stringing regularly by holding the racket head up to your ear and plucking the main string near the racket throat. If strung tightly, it will make a resonant "pinging" sound.

Trebling Trebling at the top and at the throat of tennis rackets has virtually disappeared. It was woven to give a rough surface on the one side and a smooth surface on the other, so that players, when spinning up, could call "rough" or "smooth". Nowadays, players simply flip a coin.

Balls
Always try to play with either officially tested approved tennis balls (see p.279) or those made by well-known manufacturers. Good balls can be expensive, but purchasing cheap ones of poor quality is a false economy. When you buy balls that are not supplied in pressurized cans, drop them on the floor to see if there is any life in them. New balls that do not bounce adequately are of little use to anyone. As soon as a ball goes soft or its nap wears out, its characteristics of flight and bounce will change dramatically. Most tennis balls are pressurized, but there are pressureless balls available (see p.275).

Clothing and accessories
Tennis clothing should allow freedom of movement without hampering your stroke-making. There is a very wide range of clothes to choose from – favor those made from easily washable fabrics.
Socks with thickly cushioned soles and heels absorb perspiration and provide extra support.

With thinner socks, try wearing two pairs at a time for a more cushioned effect when you are playing on very hard surfaces. Alternatively, wear a small bandage or elasticized ankle sock under your playing sock (see p.264).
Elasticized terrycloth wristbands can be used to wipe perspiration from your forehead and palms and can also stop perspiration from running down your arm into your hand. There are also dual-purpose wristbands which are strong enough to act as wrist supports (see p.264).

Shoes
Tennis shoes are among the most advanced items of tennis equipment. There are shoes with soles to suit every type of court surface, so unless you can afford to buy several pairs at a time, get a pair that is suitable for the surface that you will be playing on most. If you play quite regularly on different surfaces, select shoes with all-court soles, or a cross-trainer type suitable for a variety of games and sports. All-court soles normally have a herringbone patterned sole. Indoor courts may require a smooth-soled shoe if injuries are to be avoided. Rubber-pimpled soles are best for grass court play – but there may be "pimple" regulations at your club so check this before choosing. Shock absorption is a feature of all good shoes, as is the use of air cushions and air balls that return energy as well as absorbing shock. When choosing your shoes, comfort is the top priority. Ample arch support is very important. Shoes should lace well down towards the toe and should not need to be pulled up too tightly for a snug fit. The cut of the upper must not cause blistering or soreness around the ankle, and heel protectors must be softly cushioned and angled so as not to damage the Achilles tendon,

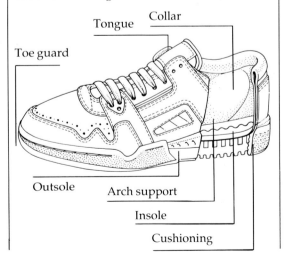

Collar

Tongue

Toe guard

Outsole

Arch support

Insole

Cushioning

HOW TO PLAY THE GAME

Tennis can be played as an individual contest between two players (singles), or a team game between two pairs of players (doubles). Each match is composed of a series of points which form a game; a number of games which form a set; and, finally, a number of sets which form a match. Major men's championships are played on a best of five sets basis; other matches and all women's matches, on a best of three basis.

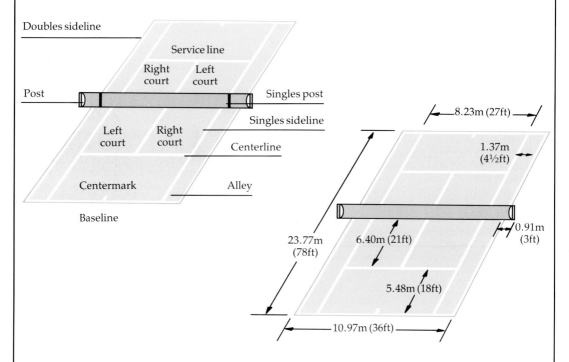

In or out

During play, the lines bounding the court, or part of the court, are considered to be areas of play, so that if part of the ball touches the line the ball is still in court. Only when the whole of the ball bounces beyond the line is it considered out of court. The three diagrams below illustrate the different demarcations for the singles player, the doubles player, and those which come into play for the server. In tournaments the final decision rests with the umpire and linesmen.

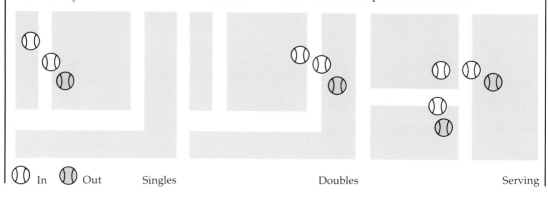

⓪ In ⓪ Out   Singles   Doubles   Serving

Starting a singles match

The decision as to who shall serve in the first game can be made by spinning the racket (see p.23) or tossing a coin. Whoever wins the spin or toss decides whether to serve or receive, selects an end or requests his opponent to make the choice.

The players then take up their respective positions at opposite ends of the court and take some time (five minutes in tournament play) warming up their strokes in preparation for the match.

Serving

The server must always begin from the right, or first, court and must stand behind the baseline within the imaginary extentions of his center-mark and sideline. The server must put the ball in the air by hand in any direction, and then strike it with the racket before it hits the ground. The ball must cross the net before bouncing within the service court diagonally opposite him. When the point has been decided, the server then serves from the left court into his opponent's left service, or second (advantage), court. The receiver can stand where he likes at the other end of the court in order to make a return stroke but may not volley the service or let the ball bounce a second time before hitting the ball.

Jeremy Bates

Singles court

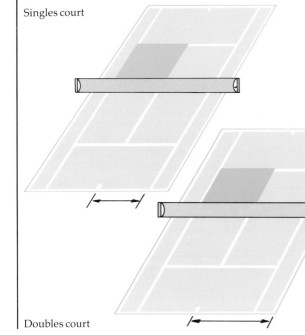

Doubles court

Footfaulting

A footfault occurs if either foot touches the baseline or the court within the baseline before the ball is struck; also, if part of your foot extends beyond the imaginary extension of the centermark as shown below. Footfaulting is shown in detail on page 102.

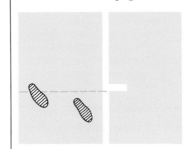

The server's right heel, above, has gone past the centermark extension, causing a footfault.

Scoring a game, set and match

During a game the server's score is always called first to avoid confusion. Four points in a row to either player win the game outright and can be scored in any of the variations shown in the chart below. When the score is deuce, either player must win two consecutive points to win the game. The first point won after deuce is an advantage point; whenever the player with the advantage loses the next point the score reverts back to deuce.

A set is decided when one of the players (pair in doubles) wins six games. If the score reaches 5-5 then one player or pair must win two games in a row in order to win the set 7-5. This is an advantage set (ending with a two game lead).

Apart from major championships and Davis Cup matches for men, when the best of five sets are played, all tournaments have a best of three set rule for both men and women players. The winner's score is always recorded first, so that a best of three set match might read 6-4, 6-3, or, perhaps, 6-2, 3-6, 6-4. Advantage sets could prolong a match indefinitely were it not for the tiebreaker system (see below).

Server wins four points	Receiver wins four points	Both players win points
15-0 (Fifteen - love)	0-15 (Love - fifteen)	1 point each 15-15 (Fifteen all)
30-0 (Thirty - love)	0-30 (Love - thirty)	2 points each 30-30 (Thirty all)
40-0 (Forty - love)	0-40 (Love - forty)	3 points each 40-40 (Deuce)
Game to server	Game to receiver	Server or receiver must now win two consecutive points; alternate scoring reverts the score to deuce.
Love game	Love game	

The tiebreaker

The tiebreaker scoring system is used when the score reaches six or eight games each, in all but the final set where the normal advantage set would be played. It is, however, used in the final sets of some indoor matches and certain tournaments. The basic scoring system is as follows:

1 The first player (or pair) to win seven points wins the tiebreaker and that set if he leads by a margin of two points (7-0 up to 7-5). If the score reaches 6-6 the tiebreaker continues until one of the players wins by two points. Numerical scoring is used.

2 The player whose turn it is to serve serves for the first point. His opponent serves for the next two points, then each player serves alternately for two consecutive points till the tiebreaker is decided.

3 The first point of the tiebreaker is played from the right court with the service then alternating as in the normal scoring system.

4 Players change ends after every six points and at the end of the tiebreaker.

5 The tiebreaker counts as one game for the ball change, but if this change is due at the beginning of the tiebreaker it is delayed until the second game of the following set.

6 The player (or pair) who served first in the tiebreaker must receive service in the first game of the following set.

Special doubles match rules

For doubles, the server can take up any position behind the baseline between the centermark and doubles sideline.

After the spin and call, the serving team decides which of the two players is to serve first, once determined, the order cannot be changed until a set has been completed. The other pair decide which one will serve in the second game. The first server's partner serves in the third game and the remaining player who has not yet served serves in the fourth game. The order then reverts back to the beginning and continues until a set is won. If a player realizes he is serving out of turn in the middle of a game the player who should be serving must do so immediately. The existing point score stands and any faults served also count.

Receiving players must decide in which court to receive service for their first receiving game because receiving courts cannot be changed until a set has been played. A player receiving in the wrong court must continue until the end of the game before reverting to the correct position.

The role of the umpire, referee and linesmen

The main role of the umpire is to see that fair play and the Rules of Lawn Tennis (see p.279) are observed. He is also duty-bound to keep an accurate record of the score at all times; this includes calling faults and points and announcing the score after each game and set, and at each changeover. He is required to check the height of the net before play and also during the match if he thinks it may have altered.

During a match the umpire's decision is final on all questions of fact, and any player who expresses disapproval can be disqualified. He may order any point to be replayed, even to the extent of overruling the linesmen. If he is unsure of a rule he should refer it to the referee, who can overrule the umpire's decision if he sees fit.

The main role of the referee is to run the tournament for the management committee. An appointed referee has the power to appoint linesmen, umpires and other court officials. He is not a second umpire, but has the final decision on any point of law referred to him by an umpire or by a player.

In championships and tournament play, linesmen are qualified umpires in their own right who may also be called upon to act as netcord or footfault judges. They are situated around the court in seats positioned well back from the playing area and looking along the lines they have been appointed to judge. The maximum number of linesmen allowed is eleven; the minimum re-

quired is six linesmen per match, in which case the service linesman moves to a vacant seat opposite the service line at the other end of the court on the even games. The full quota of linesmen and court officials in championships is as shown in the diagram below. The linesman's specific duty is to call faults and decide points relating solely to his own line and in any instance where he may be unsighted the umpire should fulfil his duty. Helpful guidelines for linesmen are as follows:

Service line Do not watch the ball in flight. Watch a point halfway between the center line and the sideline for the far service court and a third in from the sideline for the near one.
Center line Watch a point on the line about a foot towards the net from the service line.
Baseline When you realize a ball is about to land near your line look at the line ahead of the ball to see exactly where it lands. Try to anticipate volleys and deep smashes.
Sideline Watch the ball till just before it lands, then look quickly towards the line. If it is a service sideline watch a point on the sideline about a foot towards the net from the corner of the service line and the sideline.

Call "out" or "fault" clearly, then signal by extending your arm in the direction of the ball.

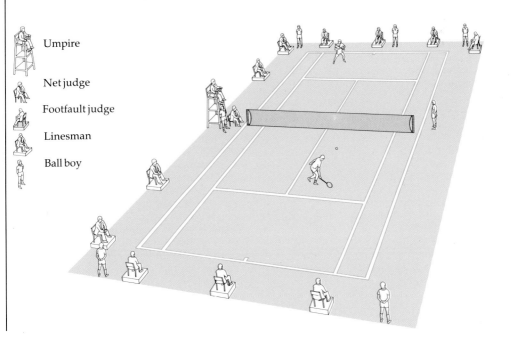

Umpire

Net judge

Footfault judge

Linesman

Ball boy

Defining strokes

The word "stroke" in tennis is used to describe the refined action of the racket hitting the ball. This action can take the form of swinging, throwing or "punching", depending on whether you are hitting groundstrokes, serving or volleying. To qualify as a stroke the action must have long contact or a feeling of "staying with the ball" so that maximum control is achieved.

Sound stroke-making is the basis of all good tennis. If you are capable of hitting the ball consistently, with pace and accuracy, towards whichever part of the court you aim, then you will be a relaxed and confident match player. There are three main types of stroke, and each has its own variations of stroke within that type.

The groundstroke

Groundstrokes are basically swinging strokes which are used to hit the ball after it has struck the ground. They are mainly used in the backcourt and in the area between the baselines and their respective service lines, as shown in the diagram below. There are many types of groundstrokes, but the two main ones are the forehand drive (top right), hit with the front or palm of the hand facing the oncoming ball; and the backhand drive (bottom right), hit with the back of the hand facing the approaching ball. Returning service and baseline rallying are an important part of the overall function of these strokes.

Forehand

Backhand

Target area

Moving area

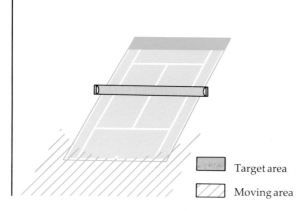

The service

Every point in tennis is started by one of the players serving a ball from behind his baseline, over the net and into the service court of his opponent diagonally opposite. This serve is a free hit at the ball (with another being permitted if the first attempt should fail) and is played with an overarm throwing action. Once released, the ball must be struck before it can bounce and must be sent over the net before bouncing within the lines of the appropriate service court.

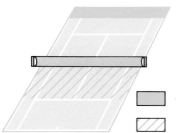

A Singles serve

B Doubles serve

The volley

This is a stroke played against the ball before it bounces. It is usually played in the forecourt during rallies and often above net height. The purpose of the volley is to make your opponent hurry his next shot, and to win the point by getting close to the net and "punching" the ball into an empty part of the court.

Target area

Moving area

Defining shots

Whereas a stroke is the action of hitting the ball, the word "shot" is used to describe the shape of the ball's flight through the air and off the court. The diagrams below show how each stroke produces a characteristic shot. These shots can be played in different situations on court when they are named by their use, as shown on the opposite page.

First and second flights

The first flight of the ball is its trajectory as it comes over the net towards you; its second flight occurs after it has bounced on your side of the net. The diagram, right, shows the typical trajectories of a tennis shot in which the ball has bounced, though these will vary according to the amount of spin which is applied to the ball.

Shapes of tennis shots

Groundstroke Hit from behind the centermark of the baseline to the opposite baseline. First and second flights are shown right.

Service Hit from behind the server's baseline into the service court diagonally opposite. The first flight stops short of the service line, and the ball bounces to produce a second flight.

Volley When hitting a volley, the ball has only one flight. No second flight is involved because the racket intercepts the ball before it bounces, resulting in a much shorter shot.

Lob In the diagram, right, a lob is shown clearing the net by a large margin to land just short of the opposite baseline. The high, arcing trajectory of its first flight causes the ball to rise quite steeply off the ground after the bounce, to produce a relatively high second flight.

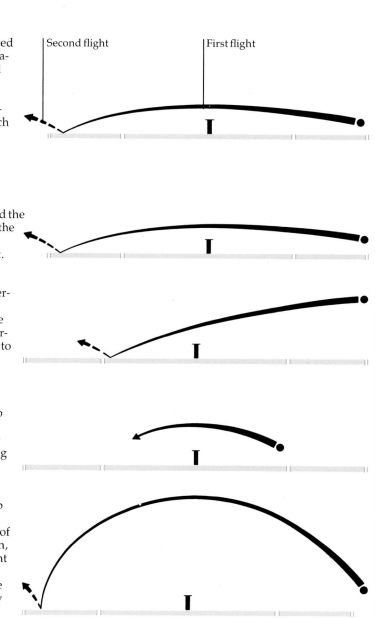

Second flight

First flight

Types of shot

The different types of shot you are likely to encounter in match play are described below. They are mainly named for their tactical uses and match-play effect. In some cases, the actual stroke and its effect are the same thing, and so their name covers both. Examples are the chip shot and the drop shot, where the names are explicitly descriptive of their function.

Most shots, however, can be produced by different strokes, so one speaks of, for example, a topspin forehand crosscourt shot, or a sliced backhand approach shot.

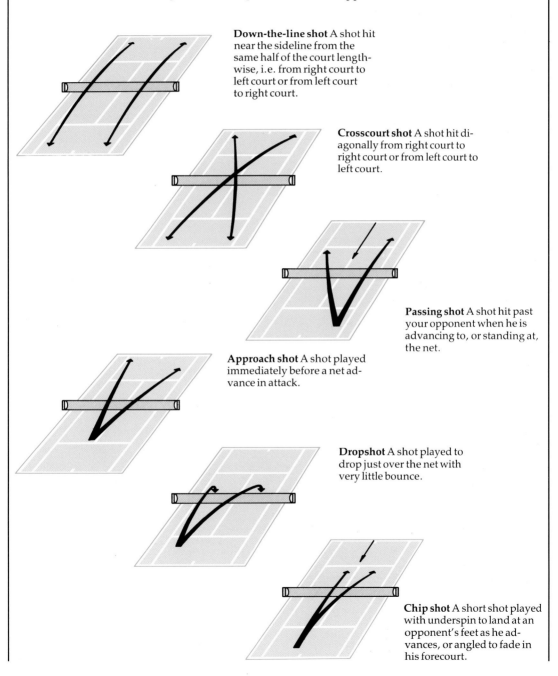

Down-the-line shot A shot hit near the sideline from the same half of the court lengthwise, i.e. from right court to left court or from left court to right court.

Crosscourt shot A shot hit diagonally from right court to right court or from left court to left court.

Passing shot A shot hit past your opponent when he is advancing to, or standing at, the net.

Approach shot A shot played immediately before a net advance in attack.

Dropshot A shot played to drop just over the net with very little bounce.

Chip shot A short shot played with underspin to land at an opponent's feet as he advances, or angled to fade in his forecourt.

31

Starting to play

Once you have chosen your tennis equipment and are familiar with the scoring system, and with the distinction between strokes and shots, you can progress to learning the basics of playing tennis: footwork, timing, how to hit the ball, which grip to use, and how to apply spin. All of these are described on the following pages.

Ball sense

The Lawn Tennis Association defines ball sense as "the ability to react naturally to a moving ball in order to perform a simple skill".

Everyone has ball sense to some degree. This can sometimes become apparent at a very early age – some children are so gifted that they can keep a gentle rally going against a wall at the age of 18 months. Parents who wish their children to develop a keen interest in the game should not be discouraged, however, if ability seems to be lacking at first, but should continue to encourage their children to play tennis, and should also introduce them to other moving ball games whenever possible.

You can judge how much ball sense a person has by throwing a ball to them and watching how they react. Good ball sense can be developed through the exercises described below.

Stage 1
1 Toss ball into the air. Catch it. Repeat 20 times.
2 Bounce the ball. Catch it. Repeat 10 times.
3 Bounce the ball hard. Wait till it falls towards the second bounce before catching it.
4 Repeat 1. This time turn a full circle on the spot before catching the ball.
5 Throw the ball against a wall. Catch it. Repeat 20 times.

Stage 2 (with a partner)
1 Throw a ball back and forth and catch it with both hands without letting it bounce.
2 Repeat 1, catching the ball with the playing hand only.
3 Throw the ball back and forth letting it bounce on the ground between you, and catch it waist high with both hands, as it falls from the top of the bounce.
4 Repeat 3, using only the playing hand to catch the ball.

Stage 3
1 Bounce the ball first to your partner's right, then to the left. He catches it after the bounce and then bounces it to your right or left so that you have to move quickly to catch the ball before it bounces a second time.
2 Bounce the ball short as well as to the side so that your partner has to move forwards quickly to recover the ball. Vary this exercise by throwing fast, slow, short and long balls so that maximum development can be achieved.
3 With your partner facing away from you, call out and then bounce the ball towards him for him to turn around and catch; he will have to react sooner with this exercise. Bounce balls to the right and left for each other too.

Stage 4 (with a racket)
1 Bounce the ball up into the air off the racket strings. Keep the ball bouncing.
2 Bounce the ball down on to the court off the racket strings. Keep the ball bouncing.
3 Bounce the ball up into the air off the strings, then turn your racket so that the next bounce comes off the other surface of the strings. Keep alternating the racket face between hits, getting used to altering the angle of the racket face while strengthening the wrist.
4 Bounce the ball down on to the court off the edge of the racket head. Keep it bouncing.
5 Bounce the ball up into the air off the opposite edge of the racket head. Keep it bouncing.
6 Practice 1 to 5 in turn, seeing if you can reach pre-set targets. For example, in exercises 1 and 2, try to keep the ball bouncing 10 times, then try for 20; in exercise 3, try for 6 and then 12 repetitions; in exercises 4 and 5, try for 5, 10 and then 20 repetitions if possible.

7 As a final aid to developing your ball sense and testing your progress, perform all of the exercises while moving about. When you are proficient try exercise 8, which introduces acquiring the "feel" of a spinning ball.
8 Bounce the ball up into the air off the racket strings. When the ball falls, deflect it upwards by cutting sharply across the bottom of the ball with the strings from right to left. Keep deflecting it upwards each time it falls. When you can keep it going, reverse your action from left to right across the bottom of the ball. Finally, try alternating every hit.

Basic actions

There are three basic actions in tennis: swinging, throwing and punching, all of which are used to a greater or lesser degree no matter what stroke you are playing. Once you have learned these actions you will be able to relate them to whatever new forms of stroke play you learn. The three actions, together with their basic uses in tennis, are described below.

Swinging The swinging action is a long flowing movement made against the ball normally when players are in their backcourt or behind their service lines.

Throwing The throwing action consists of bending the elbow before fully extending the arm. The throw is used to propel the racket against the ball when serving at the start of a point from behind the baseline, or when playing a smash.

Punching This action is a short, sharp movement, which is used against the ball when playing it in the air, usually in the forecourt when there is very little time to do anything else. It is mainly used when volleying.

Throwing

Swinging

Punching

Positioning to the ball

In order to position your body in relationship to the ball so that perfect timing and control result, you must know, as you move into the hitting area, exactly where and when your racket head should make contact with the ball. Perfect positioning can be achieved regularly if you follow the three-point procedure which is described below.

The ball's height

Groundstrokes	Falling ball met between knee and waist height
Volleys	Ball met before the fall, when possible between waist and shoulder height
Services	Falling ball met in the center of the strings at the full extension of the racket arm

The ball's distance from the body

Groundstrokes	Racket arm's reach in sideways-on position, a comfortable distance away
Volleys	Slightly closer to the body than in groundstroke play
Services	Racket arm's distance overhead

The ball's relationship to the body

Groundstrokes	Forehand – opposite leading hip Backhand – ahead of leading hip
Volleys	Well in front of the body
Services	In front of the body

Palming the ball

A good way to develop your basic timing, particularly if you are a beginner, is to practice hitting the ball with the palm of your hand. Try to keep a rally going against a wall or over the net with a practice partner, and get used to hitting the ball between knee and waist height a comfortable distance away.

Short tennis

This is a particularly useful game (see p.276) for young players, as it is an excellent stepping stone to the more advanced game. Short tennis is played to most normal lawn tennis rules on a Badminton court measuring 13 meters (42ft) by 5.8-6 meters (19ft) with the net 0.78 meters (2ft 7in) high. The service can be underarm or overarm and should change every two points. The first player to reach 11 points wins the game.

Moving to the ball

Good approach footwork should be measured and controlled, allowing you to line up your shoulders and feet to the ball's flight so that you are correctly balanced to play the ball (your weight should be poised on the rear foot, ready to be transferred on to the front foot to coincide with the forward swing). Basic approach footwork should move you forwards into the hitting area (the part of the court where the moving ball can be hit successfully) from a position behind and parallel to the flight of the ball, as shown below. This basic footwork will have to be adapted when returning wide balls, or balls directed at the body.

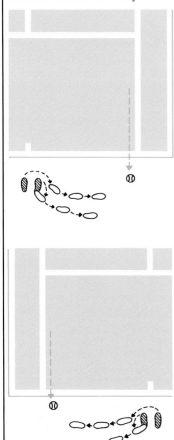

Stepping across to the ball
When returning a wide ball – either a service or a volley – the front foot will have to be placed well across, as shown in the diagram below, so that the ball can be reached. Any transference of weight into the shot will now have to be through rotation of the upper body. Providing weight transference and footwork are combined correctly, balance will be maintained.

Using an open stance
In certain emergency situations there may be no time to use normal footwork: examples are when returning fast services and in close volleying encounters at the net. In such situations open stance footwork (which can involve moving towards the ball with the foot closest to it, as shown in the diagram below) may be the only solution (see also p.245).

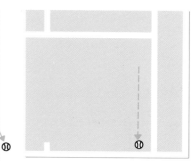

Improving your timing

Basic timing is dependent on being correctly positioned to hit the ball at the right time. Positioning can be improved by judging the two flights of the ball correctly. A common mistake made by inexperienced players is to concentrate on the first flight, and to rush towards the ball, subsequently finding themselves too close to play the ball. To be correctly positioned to hit the ball you must try to judge where the second bounce would occur, by watching the first flight of the ball as it leaves your opponent's racket. Position yourself just ahead of where you think the second bounce will take place, weight ready to be transferred as you swing your racket forwards.

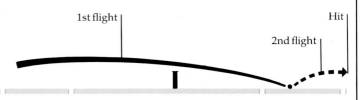

1st flight | Hit | 2nd flight

Practicing on your own
Drop the ball to the right and slightly in front of your body, as you take your racket back. Try to hit it between knee and waist height as it falls from the top of the bounce. Repeat 10 times on each side, then try alternating between right and left. Then try bouncing the ball instead of dropping it.

Practicing with a partner
Have your partner stand on the other side of the net and feed balls underarm to your right side, and practice adjusting your positioning and timing so that you can hit them at the right time. Repeat 10 times on each side. Switch roles with your partner and practice alternating sides. Then progress to a rally.

Using your weight

Good timing is not just a question of hitting the ball with the racket at a particular moment, it also has a great deal to do with transferring your bodyweight correctly so that it coincides with the swing of the racket. The extent to which you transfer your weight will decide the exact pace of your shot. Correct footwork and racket work must be combined with this forwards movement of bodyweight for the perfect timing of a pace-making stroke.

Watching the ball

The simplest way of improving your control is to watch the ball more closely. Watching the ball properly means looking at it all the way on to your racket strings. If you do this correctly, even the fastest travelling ball will seem to slow up for you to hit comfortably. The last 3-4 feet of the ball's flight before it is hit are particularly vital for good timing and control; if you take your eye off the ball during this crucial period to see what your opponent is doing you will almost certainly mis-hit the ball or spoil your shot completely. Keep your head down and focus your eyes on the ball the way a photographer focuses his camera lens on his subject to get a perfect picture. In fact, it will be a physical impossibility to watch the ball at the split second of impact with the racket strings – you will automatically find yourself looking ahead of the ball. Nevertheless, feel as if you are watching the ball right on to the strings.

Timing racket head speed

If you are mistiming the ball it will probably be because you are swinging at it too soon: when a player prepares too late it often results in him snatching quickly at the ball and playing it a fraction of a second too early. This is caused by not allowing for the variation in racket head speed during stroking.

When you take a positive swing at the ball, the racket will gather momentum throughout the stroke, reaching maximum speed over the last 3-4 feet of the swing, and if you do not take this into account you will hit the ball before you intended to. If you pause or ease up at the end of your preparation, or at the height of your take-up when serving or smashing, it should correct your timing. The varying speeds at which the racket head should travel when playing a drive and a service are shown below. Maximum racket head speed should be reached just prior to the hit. The rhythm of all your strokes should enable you to achieve this controlled acceleration from preparation into the hitting zone.

Forehand drive

Speed increasing

Speed decreasing

Service

Preparing for your stroke-making

An important part of the preparation for stroke-making is adopting the correct stance. There are two preparatory stances when playing tennis: the service stance, adopted before serving, and the ready position, which is used as the starting point for all your other strokes. Both of these positions are described below.

Ready position

When adopting the ready position you should face your opponent with your feet shoulder-width apart, knees slightly bent, and your weight poised over the balls of your feet. Try to stand midway between possible forehand and backhand strokes so that you can turn and prepare for either equally well. Hold the racket with the forehand grip, and support the racket throat with your non-playing hand: this will make it much easier for you to change grips between strokes. Keep your elbows clear from your body and fix your gaze on what is happening at the other end of the court. Some players prefer to crouch down slightly when they are at the net or returning service because it brings their eyes closer to the ball's flight path. Always return to the ready position between strokes as it will provide the best basis for your next stroke.

Service stance

When adopting the service stance, you should stand just behind the baseline with your body almost sideways to the net and your feet shoulder-width apart, knees slightly bent with your weight poised over your rear foot ready to be transferred as you begin placing the ball up. Hold the racket out in front of you with your serving grip and aim it in the direction you intend to send the ball; place the ball against the middle of the strings with your non-playing hand. A sideways stance will allow power to be initiated through the legs and applied over a long range. The tossing arm and side can be braced against the build-up of the throwing action. The basic, or flat service is delivered from an almost sideways position, which should become more accentuated as you apply more spin to your serve.

Basic baseline position

Basic service stance

Holding the racket

Eleven basic grips and their variations are shown below from the three styles which have developed in lawn tennis – Eastern, Continental and Western. The Eastern and Western grips were first classified on the East and West coasts of America and were developed on the contrasted court types of the two areas. The Continental grip and its variations may have originated in Britain but have produced a style which is generally looked upon as European and Australian. It is likely that you will find a change of grips between backhand and forehand the best way of playing powerful, controlled strokes, as required by the Eastern style of play. One-grip tennis – the Continental style – requires wrist strength and timing which the beginner does not as a rule possess. I recommend a style of play using Eastern grips for groundstrokes and the Continental grip for serving and volleying, as described on pages 40 and 41. The slants and planes of the racket grip (shown right) help you to locate your hand exactly according to the "V" between your thumb and first finger.

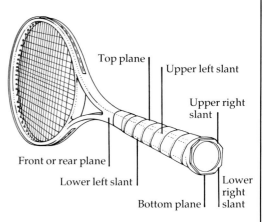

Top plane

Upper left slant

Upper right slant

Front or rear plane

Lower left slant

Bottom plane

Lower right slant

History of grips

The Eastern forehand and backhand grips originated on the clay courts of the Eastern United States. These produced a bounce which consistently placed the ball at about waist height. A powerful stroke could best be achieved by "shaking hands" with the racket. The Eastern grips fulfil this requirement perfectly and can also be used effectively for higher and lower balls. The Continental grip developed on early grass courts and on the soft clay courts of Europe, where the ball often stayed low, and a flexible grip with the palm more on the top of the handle could be used to play the ball effectively on the forehand and backhand. The full Continental forehand grip, which is almost an Eastern backhand, encourages sliced drives and does not promote strong forehand play. The forehand and backhand Western grips tend to be ineffectual against low, wide balls.

Eastern grips

1 Full forehand The "V" formed by the thumb and first finger is positioned to the right of center of the top plane of the racket, with the palm and the large knuckle of the forefinger on the rear plane. Your thumb and fingers should be wrapped around the handle with the pad of your second, third and little fingers gripping the front plane. Your first finger is spread slightly up the handle.

2 Modified forehand The "V" between the thumb and forefinger is positioned in the center of the top plane, and the fingers are not as far up the front plane as for the full grip.

3 Full backhand The "V" is in the upper left slant and the thumb is placed diagonally across the rear plane. First finger knuckle on upper right slant.

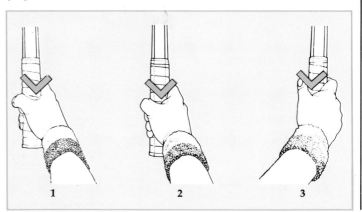

1   2   3

Continental grips

4 Modified forehand "V" left of center on the top plane, palm towards the top plane and large first finger knuckle on, or on the bottom edge of, upper right slant. Thumb around front plane.

5 Full forehand "V" in center of upper left slant and thumb wrapped around front plane. Large first finger knuckle near the top edge of the upper right slant.

6 Modified backhand "V' as in the equivalent forehand grip. Palm towards the top plane with first finger knuckle on, or on the bottom edge of, upper right slant. Thumb across or wrapped around rear plane.

7 Full backhand "V" as in the equivalent forehand grip, but thumb is placed diagonally across rear plane as for Eastern backhand.

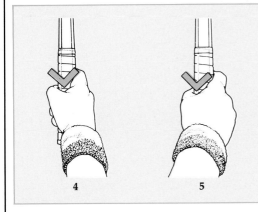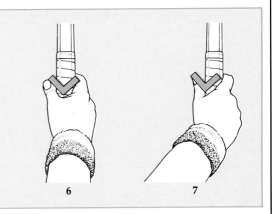

Western grips

8 Forehand and reverse topspin service "V" on, or on the lower edge of, the upper right slant. The palm is positioned towards the bottom plane, with the wrist behind the rear plane, and the pad of the first finger on the front plane; the large knuckle is placed on the lower right slant of the racket grip.

9 Backhand and reverse slice service The "V" is moved down behind the rear plane and the racket head turned over so that the ball can be struck with the same face of the strings as with the Western forehand.

Double-handed grips

10 Double-handed forehand The playing hand uses the Eastern forehand grip – the butt of the hand rests above and against the thumb of the supporting hand. The supporting hand, below, is positioned between the Continental and Eastern backhand grips with the thumb around the rear plane.

11 Double-handed backhand The playing hand is positioned between the Eastern and Continental backhand grips; the supporting hand nestles above, in an Eastern forehand grip, to provide a firm-wristed stroke.

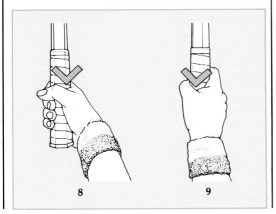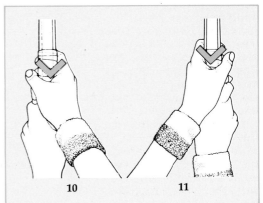

Choosing your grips

The majority of players are best suited to an Eastern style of play and should start by using the Eastern forehand grip for serving and overhead play, and the Eastern forehand and Eastern backhand grips to play groundstrokes and volleys, simply changing from forehand to backhand as required. As your game develops, some modifications are necessary to help you improve. You will have seen on page 38 there is a modified version of the Eastern forehand grip, and you may wish to consider its use as explained below. Your game will be strengthened by developing the use of the modified Continental grip exclusively for serving, volleying and overhead play. The Eastern grips will help you to develop solid, pace-making groundstrokes, and the modified Continental grip will give you a combination of power and spin in your serving together with control in your volleying.

Groundstroke play

The Eastern grips (the full and modified forehand grip and the backhand grip) are best employed in groundstroke play. You must decide which of the two forehand grips to use. You can make this choice in consultation with your coach or adviser on the basis of the grip which best suits your natural attributes and best complements your overall style of play.

The positioning of the palm along the handle in the full Eastern forehand grip will promote a feeling of control and firmness allowing you to hit powerful and deep strokes from the back court. The modified forehand grip, on the other hand, approaches the more free-wristed Continental grip and will provide more flexibility than the full Eastern grip. Although it provides the best combination of firmness and freedom, and is totally versatile in approach and forecourt play, it may apply fractionally less power than is provided by the full forehand grip.

The grip you choose, therefore, will depend on the type of game you prefer (see p. 194). If you favor a baseline game, the full Eastern grip would be preferable, whereas if you are more inclined towards all-court play, combining approach and serve and volley play with your groundstroke game, the modified grip will be more suitable to your style of play.

Since the backhand is naturally the defensive side, there is a great need for having the strongest and most reliable grip possible if any form of attacking or counter-attacking is to be undertaken. The Eastern backhand grip is the answer to most of the problems faced by players on this side. The thumb diagonally across the rear plane provides a firmness and power similar to that of the full forehand grip.

Serving and overhead play

Although a number of grips can be used for serving, the modified Continental grip is by far the most successful grip for this purpose. The main requirements when playing from a stationary position behind the baseline, and aiming for the smallest area on the court (all prerequisites of serving) are a great deal of control, accuracy and power. The grip used must allow maximum use of the wrist, which can be combined with weight transference to present either a full racket face to the ball for power, or an angled face for spin. The flexibility, control and speed offered by the modified Continental grip make it ideal for good serving and for overhead play.

Volleying

Sound groundstroke play at any level demands some change in grips between forehand and backhand play, however slight. In volleying, where the time factor becomes critical, one grip has to suffice during a quick exchange at the net. Since it is advisable to volley with your serving grip when involved in serve and volley play, it makes sense to progress to playing serves, volleys and smashes with the same grip. The best grip for all three is undoubtedly the modified Continental grip. Beginners who have become used to volleying with their groundstroke grips should make the transition when they adopt the modified Continental grip for serving.

You will find it easier to volley on the backhand with the modified Continental grip than on the forehand, and may, therefore, prefer to play the first volley after a forehand approach shot with the very similar modified Eastern grip, and then make the slight change when a backhand volley is required.

Controlling the racket

Accurate racket control is an essential part of stroke refinement, and should be practiced before perfecting other details of stroke play. It involves ensuring that the racket head follows through the hitting zone correctly, and checking that the racket face is correctly positioned to achieve the effect you require. These two controls are described below.

Racket head control

Racket head control means checking that your racket head follows correctly through the hitting zone, throughout the swinging, throwing and punching actions. The drawings, below show the definite paths the racket should be taking just before and immediately after the hit. The hit itself occurs near the mid-point of the hitting zone in each case.

Basic swings

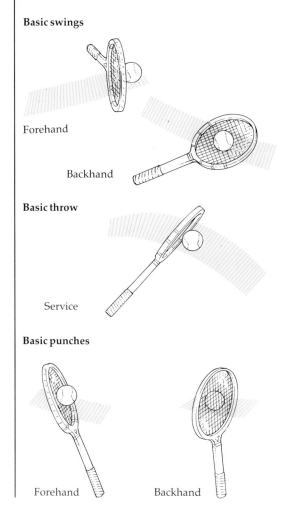

Forehand

Backhand

Basic throw

Service

Basic punches

Forehand   Backhand

Racket face control

The angle of your racket face directly influences your control of the ball at the hit and over its subsequent flight path as you follow through. The exact angle at which the racket face meets the ball will to a large extent depend on circumstances, such as your distance from the net, the height at which you strike the ball, how the ball has bounced, and the degree of spin applied, together with your physical height and strength and the grips and strokes you employ. Considerable control is possible by either opening the racket face (tilting it back with the bottom edge leading) or closing it (tilting it forwards with the top edge leading). The three basic racket face positions, together with their different effects on the ball, are described below.

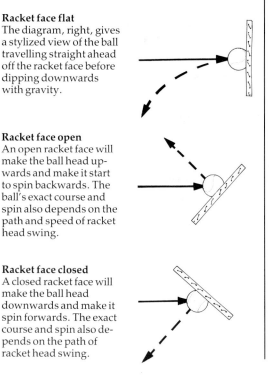

Racket face flat
The diagram, right, gives a stylized view of the ball travelling straight ahead off the racket face before dipping downwards with gravity.

Racket face open
An open racket face will make the ball head upwards and make it start to spin backwards. The ball's exact course and spin also depends on the path and speed of racket head swing.

Racket face closed
A closed racket face will make the ball head downwards and make it spin forwards. The exact course and spin also depends on the path of racket head swing.

Understanding spin

The flight of a ball and the way it bounces will be greatly affected by the amount of spin applied at the hit. The spin will, in turn, be affected by whether the ball meets the court surface or the strings of a tennis racket. Topspin, underspin and sidespin – the three main types of spin – together with their effects in different situations, are described below. Before considering these, however, it will first be useful to consider the flight of a non-spinning ball and how it bounces off a court or a racket.

Ball without spin

The three diagrams below show the flight of a non-spinning ball, and how it bounces off the court and your racket. When in flight, it will be slowed down by air resistance, and forced downwards by gravity. It will bounce off the court surface at an angle almost equivalent to its approach and off the racket strings at almost the same speed and angle to its approach.

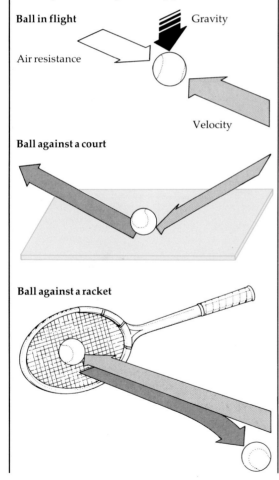

Ball in flight

Gravity

Air resistance

Velocity

Ball against a court

Ball against a racket

Ball spinning in flight

Spin applied to a ball will cause it to rotate; its flight path will vary according to the type of spin applied. The three main types of spin – topspin, underspin, and sidespin or slice – together with their effects on the ball, are described below.

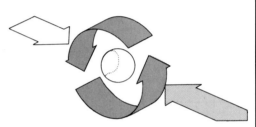

Topspin The top surface of the ball rotates against air resistance creating increased friction and so pressure forcing the ball downwards.

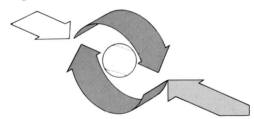

Underspin The reverse occurs than with topspin, and the ball is lifted and kept up for longer than if it had no spin by increased pressure below the ball.

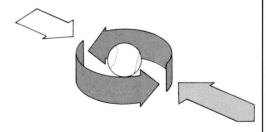

Sidespin Whichever side rotates against air resistance will force the ball to swerve to the opposite side.

Ball bouncing off the court

The way a ball bounces off a court when travelling with spin will be affected by many factors, such as the amount of power applied in the stroke, the height from which it approaches, and the type of spin used. The type of court surface on which the ball is hit may also make a considerable difference. The typical bounce and flight path of balls hit with topspin, underspin and sidespin are described below. In most cases, the practical outcome of hitting a ball with topspin or underspin will be very different from what you might expect.

Topspin

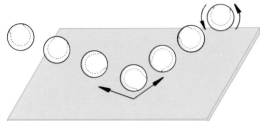

Practice In practice, the height from which a topspun ball approaches and the power behind it, cause the ball to approach at a very steep angle, bouncing higher and further than a drive hit without spin.

Theory The diagram, left, shows the theoretical path of a topspun ball. The ball dips downwards, grips the court surface and bounces off low, at a smaller angle than its angle of approach.

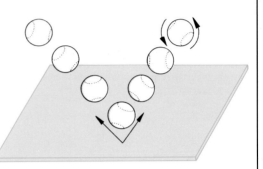

Underspin

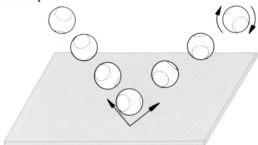

Practice The diagram, right, shows how, when an underspun ball is in fact hit with power and approaches at a low angle, its spin causes the ball to skid and it will bounce lower than expected.

Theory The diagram, left, shows the theoretical path of an underspun ball. The ball grips the court surface and bounces off high at a greater angle than its angle of approach.

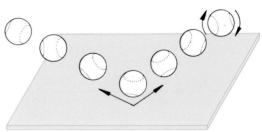

Sidespin

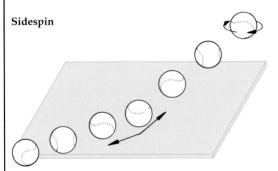

Theory and practice In the case of a ball hit with sidespin, theory and practice are the same. The diagram, left, shows the approach of a sidespin shot. The spin in this case is clockwise and it causes the ball to curve from right to left from the receiver's viewpoint. After bouncing the ball carries on spinning in the same way as it continues to curve to the left.

Ball spinning off a racket

After learning how a ball with different types of spin travels through the air and bounces off the court, you will be ready to consider how spin affects the ball as it bounces off the racket face, providing that no strong counter-force is exerted against it. In the case of topspin and underspin, the ball will continue to spin with the same rotation as it leaves the racket. But when you have hit the ball the effect of its spin will be changed, topspin becoming underspin and vice-versa. In the case of sidespin, the angle at which the ball leaves the strings will also differ from its angle of approach, as it changes from right-hand spin to left-hand spin and vice-versa. A sound knowledge of these effects is essential if you are to learn how to counteract your opponent's spin. With experience you will be able to adjust your aim and racket face angle automatically to compensate for your opponent's shots.

Sidespin

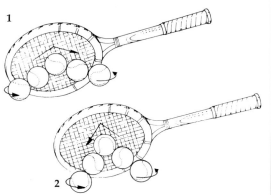

1 Ball approaches from right with counterclockwise spin. It will leave the face further to the left than you would expect.

2 Ball approaches from left with counterclockwise spin. It will leave the face less sharply to the right than expected.

Topspin

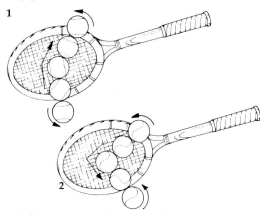

1 Ball rebounds up off racket. After biting the strings, the ball will rotate with underspin and it will leave the racket higher than expected.

2 Ball rebounds down off racket. The racket strings will bite and the ball will rebound higher than expected, again with underspin.

Underspin

1 Ball rebounds up off racket. It will leave the racket with topspin after biting the strings, and will rebound lower than expected.

2 Ball rebounds down off racket. It will come off the strings with topspin and will leave the racket lower than you might expect it to.

Combining spin

When a ball is hit with topspin, underspin or either sidespin, the axis about which it rotates is unlikely to be exactly horizontal or perpendicular to the court surface. It is more likely to be somewhere between these two "pure" axes and combines, for example, topspin and sidespin. The diagrams, right, shows the two pure axes of topspin and underspin and both left and right sidespins, together with a typical combining axis.

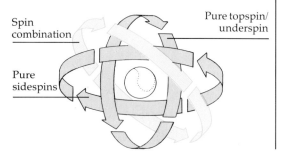

Spin combination

Pure sidespins

Pure topspin/ underspin

Strokes

GROUNDSTROKES: Forehand drive

The forehand is a good starting point for the beginner as it is played on the side of your body which seems most natural for hitting. Most players are more aggressive on the forehand side and it is this aggression that you must harness to produce a reliable attacking stroke during matches.

Essentials of the stroke
A sound grip and a firm-wristed swing from the shoulder are essential for a controlled stroke. The Eastern forehand grip is recommended (as shown opposite) for the beginner as it will itself encourage a firm wrist. Moving your feet so that you get into a sideways position parallel to the flight of the ball is also fundamental. From this position you can hit the ball with the most control and

power, swinging the racket across the front of the body from hip to hip. Transferring your weight on to your front foot will put your bodyweight into the stroke.

How to perfect the stroke
The sequence below shows the basic forehand drive played from the back of the court. When copying it, concentrate on your footwork, stepping in with your front foot and keeping far enough from the ball to extend your playing arm when swinging.

As with all tennis strokes there are features of the forehand which are especially vital. These key elements, such as the loop, the hitting zone and the follow through, are described in the next few pages so that you can give them particular attention when

Playing the stroke

Prepare as early as possible by taking the racket back level with or slightly below the hitting height and turning your shoulders until your non-hitting shoulder is pointing at the ball. To start the forward swing at the ball you must form a loop with the racket head, letting the elbow of the hitting arm relax so that the forward swing starts from below the hitting height. Step in with your front (left) foot to transfer your weight forward and into the hit. Watch the ball right on to the strings.

1

2

3

Footwork

To position yourself sideways to the flight of the ball, turn on your right foot and step in with your left foot.

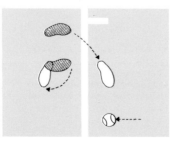

1 Take up the ready position (see p.37) behind the centermark of the baseline.

2 Start to turn on your right foot, moving your weight on to it. Let your knees bend as you release your non-playing hand from the throat of the racket face.

practicing and perfecting your stroke. In a match you will have to use your forehand in all sorts of difficult situations, each depending on the speed and direction of your opponent's shot.

Eastern forehand grip

The Eastern forehand grip (see p.38) will give you good control in your forehand play because it encourages a firm-wristed swing. The palm is positioned well on the side of the grip lending a feeling of power to the stroke.

Distance from the ball
You must extend your hitting arm at the hit. If you have to hit the ball with your elbow bent when using the Eastern forehand grip you are too close to the ball and will lose power and control.

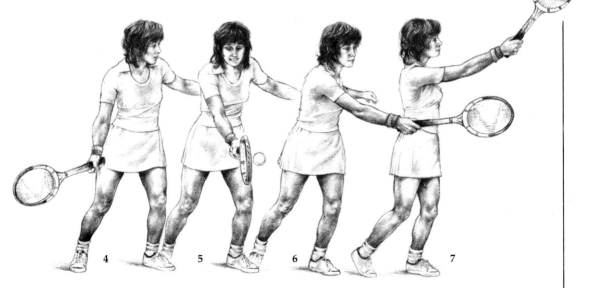

4   5   6   7

3 Take your racket back, turning your shoulders. Relax your hitting elbow and form a loop with the racket head.

4 Step in with your front (left) foot as you swing the racket head up to meet the ball. Tighten your grip keeping your wrist firm and racket head level with your wrist.

5 Hit the ball opposite your leading (left) hip as your weight moves forward over your bent left knee. Keep your head down and watch the ball.

6 Lift the racket head through in the direction of the shot.

7 Finish the stroke about head high with your racket arm straight.

Your right leg will swing through allowing your body to turn towards the net as you regain the ready position.

Improving your stroke

To improve the effectiveness of your basic forehand it will help you to study the key elements of the stroke as shown below. Particularly note the overall shape of the stroke with the forward swing rising slightly through the hitting zone. Try to develop the feel of lift in the forward swing as this will impart the minimum of topspin (see p.42) to the ball required to keep it from flying beyond your opponent's baseline when hitting the ball hard in attack.

Using the Eastern forehand grip means keeping the wrist particularly firm through the forward swing of the racket. When you first start learning the stroke your natural swing can easily become a slow steering movement which guides the ball where you want but is completely lacking in the necessary racket head speed essential for an attacking forehand. This stiff stroke is common and is often the result of a limited take-back. Practice without a ball to check the features below.

Joining the take-back and the forward swing with a smooth looping action will increase racket head speed at the hit. This loop forms naturally if you momentarily relax the elbow of your playing arm at the end of the take-back. Under pressure many players fail to do this and keep the arm rigid.

Relaxing the elbow

At the end of the take-back relax your elbow so that your arm can straighten slightly. A stiff elbow at the end of the take-back will, at the very least, reduce racket head speed significantly.

A Preparation
A flowing looping movement unites the take-back and the forward swing so that the racket head reaches maximum speed just before impact. This loop encourages lift in the forward swing for controlling topspin. Keep reminding yourself to aim your front (left) shoulder towards the hitting point and only turn towards the net after the ball has been hit.

B **Hitting zone** The hitting zone begins opposite the rear hip and ends just after the hit. As you stroke through it keep your wrist firm. Present the racket face to the ball square to the line of flight.

C **Follow through**
Don't let the racket head drop after making contact with the ball. Follow the ball's flight with the racket, keeping the racket face steady and your arm extended to the finish.

Building the forehand into your game

Your opponents will vary the pace and direction of their shots, and in the normal course of a match you will have to deal with low, high, wide and short balls. For maximum control you should get to the ball as early as possible. Playing wide balls and short balls is shown below. When returning low balls make sure that you bend your knees well, keeping your back straight. Develop a feeling of "sitting" into the ball.

Whenever you are rallying from the back of the court and have to cope with a slow, high bouncing ball, move back during your preparation for the stroke and let the ball fall between shoulder and waist height before stroking upwards through the ball aiming deep towards your opponent's baseline. Lengthen your follow through for control.

Wide ball

1 Begin your run towards the hitting area.

2 Prepare with a shorter take-back than for the basic drive. Brake and pivot on your right foot planting it parallel to the flight of the ball.

3 Transfer your weight on to your front foot, stepping across further than for the shot not played on the run, and swing your racket.

4 After the follow through push off strongly with your right foot and return behind the centermark.

Short ball

1 Run forwards to the approaching ball with quick small steps. Start to take the racket back as you run.

2 Pivot on your right foot opposite where the ball would bounce a second time, keeping sideways to the flight.

3 Step in parallel to the flight of the ball and swing. You should feel as if you are running through the ball.

4 The rear foot continues through as you move forwards to volley the next return.

Practicing on your own

On court you will need as many balls as possible in any suitable container. Take one ball at a time in your non-playing hand and from the ready position behind the centermark on the baseline turn sideways taking the racket back. Drop the ball so that it bounces out to the side and a little in front of you and swing the racket head up to meet the falling ball opposite your leading hip. Repeat this and with each series of balls that you hit concentrate on a separate key element of the stroke. If you are unsure of any feature, practice your swing without a ball, stopping your racket so you can observe your error. Incorporate your improvements one at a time by hitting dozens of balls with the full stroke.

The best off-court practice is to hit stroke after stroke against a backboard. You can buy portable backboards (see p.276), or you might have access to one. Any sound wall with space in front of it will do. It is best to mark a line 90 cm (3 feet) high along the wall to show the height of the net, and another line 60 cm (2 feet) above this. Stand 15 to 20 feet from the wall and aim between the lines. Keep on your toes, returning to the ready position after each stroke before stepping in again for the next hit.

Practicing with a partner

If you have a practice partner you can feed balls to each other on court, first dropping balls for the strokemaker, then throwing balls underarm to simulate an opponent's shot. As you gain confidence go to your respective baselines and try to complete 10-, then 20-stroke rallies hitting forehand drives deep into each other's forehand corners as shown right. Good deep shots landing just inside the opposite baseline will keep your opponent away from the net. Keep on your toes and once you are hitting confidently make sure that you move back to your position behind the centermark of the baseline as you would in a game before moving to play the next stroke.

Off court, you can use a partner to play a practice game against a backboard. One of you must start by dropping a ball and hitting it against the wall between the 3 and 5 feet lines. Your partner then steps in and plays his stroke and so on alternatively until one of you

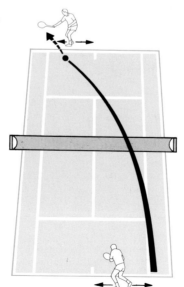

gives away a point by missing the target area or letting the ball bounce twice. Use the real game scoring system. If either of you feels that the technique of your stroke has deteriorated during this competitive practice, play rallies without scoring for a period paying attention to your strokes until you become confident again.

Using your forehand

The basic forehand is a point and match winner. It is likely that you will play it from the right-hand side of your baseline. From here you have three choices: to play a drive deep across the court to your opponent's forehand corner; to play a drive deep and parallel to the sideline to your opponent's backhand corner, or to play the ball a little earlier, further in front of your leading hip, in order to hit various angled drives again crosscourt, between the service and baselines.

Deep crosscourt and down-the-line forehand drives

Angled forehand drives

Vitas Gerulaitis holding the finish of a forehand. Notice how his racket arm is almost straight and the racket face is still under complete control. Hips and shoulders have swung around to face the net but the position of his feet shows that the shot was played sideways to the flight of the ball.

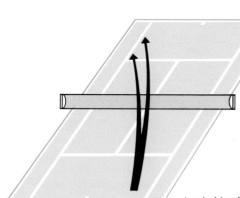

Topspin forehand drive

The topspin forehand is a variant of the basic stroke, the difference being the amount of topspin (see p.42) applied to the ball. For the basic stroke a minimal amount of topspin is applied, enough to control a hard-hit ball on a shallow trajectory. For a topspin forehand the more extreme effects of topspin (arcing trajectory and kicking bounce) are used to enhance aggressive forehand play.

Deep, effective topspin drives come from preparing for the forward swing early, sound positioning and weight transfer while hitting the ball. Racket face control and combined wrist and forearm action through the hitting zone are also vital for successful topspin driving. The stroke does not depend on a flicking action with the wrist but on a much steeper swing from low to high with the whole arm. As with the basic drive, build on a strong swing from the shoulder using the racket as an extension of your wrist and forearm. The same Eastern forehand grip used for the basic forehand is suitable for the topspin stroke. If you use the topspin stroke for most of your drives the slightly modified Eastern forehand grip will give more wrist freedom.

Compare the sequence below with that of the basic drive on pages 46 and 47 and you will see the change in the shape of the stroke required for topspin, the racket rising steeply to strike the ball and send it away on a steep, arcing trajectory as shown opposite. It is important to remember that when playing a topspin shot you can really attack the ball with great racket head speed in the safe knowledge that you are actually hitting control on to the ball. The extra spin applied allows for a greater margin for error than that afforded by the basic stroke as the ball can be sent 5 feet or more above the net and it will still land in court.

Playing the stroke

The racket must be taken back slightly below the height at which you will hit the ball with your wrist kept slightly freer than for the basic drive. You can then form a deeper loop shape as you step in parallel to or slightly across the line of flight and swing upwards at the ball. Wrist and forearm action will turn the racket face over a little in the follow through.

1 From the ready position take your racket back slightly below the intended hitting height.

2 Turn your shoulders, using your left arm for balance, until your left shoulder points at the point of impact.

3 With your weight fully over your rear foot, start a deep loop with the racket.

The shape of the shot

The comparison of a topspin forehand with the basic version, below, shows how the topspin applied to the ball creates an arcing trajectory, with the ball crossing the net at 5 feet or more. If you were to hit a basic drive to this height the ball would fly beyond your opponent's baseline, because the ball would lack the speed of rotation through the air. The more spin, the more exaggerated the arc can be. The steep angle of descent will make the ball bounce high and heavy spin makes it shoot forwards after the bounce at your opponent.

The topspinning ball does not float on an even arc. It approaches your opponent quickly, and will dip to the court sooner than originally seemed the case. The heavily topspun ball will then bound forwards after the bounce at a lesser angle than that at which it approached the court surface, but still steep enough to force the ball higher than it would reach with a basic stroke. The exact height and pace of the ball's second flight will depend on the court resistance and surface finish (see p.244).

Modified Eastern forehand grip

The "V" between thumb and forefinger has been moved towards the center of the top plane in the Eastern forehand grip shown right (see p.38). This modified grip affords a little more wrist freedom and will feel more natural if you use topspin a great deal.

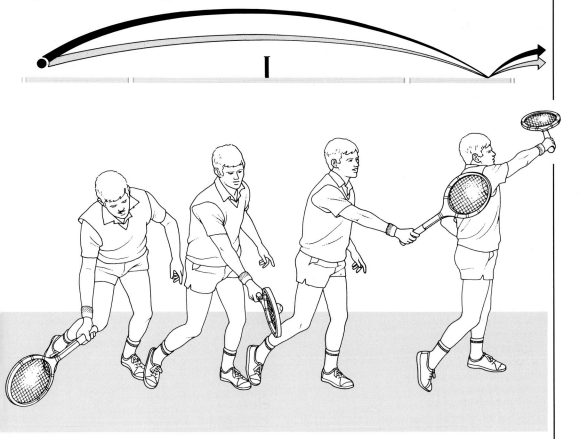

4 Step in parallel to the ball with your left foot, swinging up steeply towards the ball as your knees straighten.

5 Transfer your weight completely on to your front foot as you bring the middle of the racket strings up to the ball.

6 Combined wrist and arm action turn the racket face over slightly towards the horizontal.

7 Your body will straighten and turn to face the net as you follow through with your racket high across the body.

Improving your stroke

The steep forward swing of the racket from low to high for a topspin forehand drive starts with a much deeper loop shape at the end of the take-back than for the basic stroke. To accomplish this loop, turn your shoulders fully during the take-back. The racket face is not turned over at the hit as it sometimes appears to be, but remains in a vertical plane until a fraction of a second after the ball has left the racket. To perfect this swing you should be sideways to the ball position right into the follow through. It will help to change slightly the angle at which you step in with your front (left) foot. If a line between your front and back foot during a basic swing marked twelve o'clock on an imaginary clock face, then step in towards one o'clock for the topspin drive. This will discourage you from turning in to the net too early in the stroke. At the completion of the stroke your racket arm should finish nearly straight, high and across your body.

Brushing straight up the back of the ball with your racket strings may seem an easier option but will result in poor depth and pace.

A Preparation
B Hitting zone
C Follow through

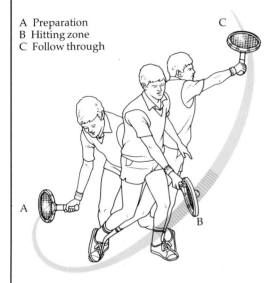

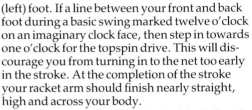

Correct   Incorrect

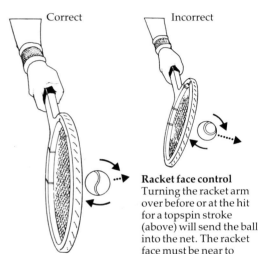

Racket face control
Turning the racket arm over before or at the hit for a topspin stroke (above) will send the ball into the net. The racket face must be near to vertical at the hit (left).

Practicing on your own

Go on court with as many balls as possible. From your ready position (see p. 37) behind the baseline drop balls with the non-playing hand as you did for the basic stroke (see p. 50), but this time let the ball drop from higher up so that you can hit the ball at waist level or above after the bounce. Get the feel of applying consistent spin to the ball, watching its trajectory over the net closely so that you can assess your results. To help your confidence, increase the net height to its maximum and then hit several dozen topspin forehands across the court and down the side-line. The topspin applied will still give plenty of margin above the net.

When using a backboard to perfect your top-spin shot, mark a line 5 feet above net height and aim for just above this line from about 15 to 20 feet. The action of topspin will tend to make the ball rise a little as it hits the backboard providing a high bouncing rebound.

Practicing with a partner

With a practice partner on court you can hit forehand drives crosscourt to each other as you did when practicing the basic forehand drive. This time, combine your basic and topspin shots, one player keeping to basic drives and the other to topspin. After five minutes switch roles. Your partner can also help you to build a sequence of forehand drives for future use in match play. Have your partner stand about 10 feet on the other side of the net and throw balls underarm to your forehand side. Play and repeat the following sequence: 1) topspin crosscourt drive, 2) basic forehand down the sideline, 3) topspin crosscourt angled forehand, 4) topspin forehand down the sideline.

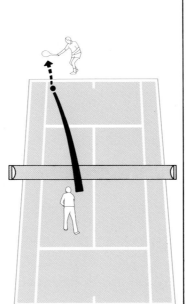

Using topspin drives

In match play the topspin forehand provides a considerable advantage. Use it to add variety to your baseline rallying. The greater margin for error and the higher bounce off your opponent's court will combine to apply consistent pressure. It is difficult and tiring to hit flat and powerful drives at shoulder height. Conversely, you will find high bouncing balls easier to attack with a topspin shot. The topspin forehand shot is also a good option for two types of passing shot, one dipping low, passing your approaching opponent at ankle level, and the other passing him high and wide at an angle. This is a difficult ball to reach and difficult to play with any success.

Natalia Zvereva topspin drives off her back foot. The alignment of her racket arm and her body position show that, from a semi-open stance, a low take-back combined with upper body rotation can apply attacking topspin from a defensive position. The ball will probably fall short, but nevertheless will create an awkward bounce.

Forehand slice

For the forehand slice the ball is hit in such a way as to achieve a mixture of underspin and sidespin (see p. 44). The slice was once used extensively in both the men's and women's game, particularly to attack an opponent's weak backhand. It remains a useful variation to add to your repertoire, but the stroke is now generally used more sparingly because of rising standards in the top class game. Kurt Nielson, who reached Wimbledon finals in 1953 and 1955, was probably the last top class player in the men's game to use the sliced forehand drive almost exclusively.

Study the differences between the sliced forehand and the basic and topspin forehand. For the slice, the shape of the forward swing of the stroke from high to low around the outside of the ball combines with the racket face angle at the hit to produce the desired underspin. Underspin will tend to make the ball float and stay airborne longer and so it must be sent low over the net. The ball also tends to slow considerably in flight allowing opponents more time to get set for their replies. This low trajectory and lack of pace can combine to make the ball stay low after the bounce despite its underspin.

Using these characteristics to your advantage requires perfect timing and the ability to choose the right ball to slice. Generally, you should slice a rising ball because hitting the ball from above net height enables you to put pace into the shot, slicing the ball down into your opponent's court. Hit below net height the sliced drive will rise to clear the net and probably your opponent's baseline too.

Playing the stroke

Start from the ready position and prepare for the forward swing as you did for the basic stroke but take the racket back above the intended hitting height, cocking the wrist of your racket arm vertically. From this point, the sequence below shows how you step in and transfer your weight from rear to front foot as for the basic stroke. There is virtually no loop with the racket – the wrist simply uncocks while keeping the racket angle (tilted back from vertical) down into the hit.

1 At the end of the take-back your racket head should be up with the face slightly open.

2 Step in parallel to the flight of the ball with your left foot as you swing the racket down.

3 Meet the outside edge of the back of the ball a little below center and opposite your left hip.

4 Complete the swing down through the ball before lifting slightly in the direction of the shot.

Improving your stroke

Pay particular attention to your hitting wrist during the take-back. The height of the racket head at the end of the take-back is achieved by cocking the wrist. There is virtually no loop before the forward swing is started, the racket head being brought forwards and down to meet the ball with the bottom edge of the racket head leading into the hitting zone.

Cocked wrist

Racket angle at the hit

Practicing

You can practice the forehand slice on your own, but it is better to get a practice partner to send you high bouncing balls, either hand fed from about 10 feet on the other side of the net, or by hitting topspin forehand drives to you. The high, kicking bounce of the topspin shot makes it an ideal stroke to practice in conjunction with the forehand slice.

Concentrate on hitting down, round and through the ball, and on preventing the racket head from dropping in the low finish.

The shape of the shot

The sliced forehand drive must be hit from above net height wherever possible so that the ball can be hit firmly on a flat trajectory low over the net to bounce deep in your opponent's court. This is in contrast to the arcing trajectories of the basic and topspin strokes.

When hit from a height similar to the basic stroke, as shown below, the sliced forehand drive is a much weaker shot. The underspin applied to the ball will tend to keep it hanging in the air so the ball must be played close to net height and with little pace so that gravity has time to pull the ball down into court. At the bounce, the low trajectory and lack of pace will combine to keep the ball lower than in a basic forehand despite the direction of the ball's spin. A heavily underspun ball hit on a flat trajectory with more pace can be made to bounce up more steeply, at a greater angle than that at which it approached the court surface, but still relatively low.

Using your sliced drive

Slicing the ball requires less energy than the other forehand drives and can be used to preserve stamina in a long match. Suddenly producing a slice during a baseline rally will introduce contrasted flight, pace and bounce. With its shortened take-back the slice is particularly useful for returning high, bouncing serves at the incoming server's feet. With slight modification the sliced drive can also be used from behind the center of your baseline to swerve drives wide to your opponent's backhand corner. To accomplish this the sidespin of the stroke is reversed by swinging the racket head from out to in across the back of the ball.

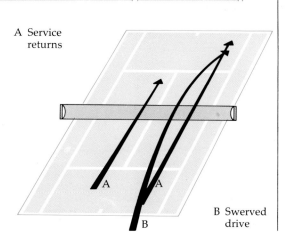

A Service returns

B Swerved drive

Forehand chop

Like the forehand slice, the chop is an under-spun stroke but the spin is more heavily applied by the strings biting much more steeply down the back of the ball. Although the ball can be chopped with good control, considerable speed is lost, with the ball tending to hang in the air making it easy prey for a volleying opponent. The underspin will also pose few problems for an aggressive and competent baseline player.

Technically the forehand chop can best be perfected by using a Continental grip (see p.39), although it can be effectively developed by the Eastern grip player.

Improving your stroke

The shape of the forehand chop, shown below, is similar to the slice shown on the previous pages. The difference lies in the shorter, higher take-back which starts the steeper high to low swing. The racket face should be similarly angled back from the vertical. This combination of racket path and racket-face angle will create heavy underspin. As you chop down the back of the ball, let the slight out to in nature of the swing apply some side-spin. As the strings meet the ball, make sure that your weight is transferred on to your front foot.

A **Preparation** Point at the oncoming ball with your non-playing hand as you turn on your back foot. As you take up the racket, lock your wrist.

B **Hitting zone** Keep the wrist firm as you chop down to meet the ball behind your leading hip at about waist height.

C **Follow through** Finish low and slightly across the body.

Using your forehand chop

The trajectory, loss of pace and the height of the ball after the bounce have reduced the use of the forehand chop to almost nil in top class play. It remains, however, a useful forehand variation at other levels of play where baseline rallying often predominates. The floating trajectory of the chop may upset the rhythm of a baseliner (see pp.212-213). Mixed with basic, topspin and slice shots, it can have an unnerving effect providing an extra change of pace, flight and bounce. You may find that slow-moving opponents and those who are not used to spin have much more difficulty in playing the chopped ball.

As with all baseline driving, chop the ball deep to your opponent's baseline as a general rule. Played short, the chop will provide your opponent with an ideal opportunity to play an approach shot.

Racket face angle at the hit
The forehand chop depends on the racket strings travelling down through the hitting zone in a steep line, almost as if you were chopping wood. In the picture above, the racket face is slightly angled back from vertical at the hit. This technique will put little pace into the shot.

Double-handed forehand drive

There have been very few players in the history of tennis who have reached world class using a double-handed forehand drive. Gene Mayer, a world ranking player today, is double-handed on both wings. His footwork and positioning, allied to good serving and excellent one-handed volleying, make-up for the severe restrictions in reach imposed by double-handed driving. The double-handed forehand stroke can be played with the same variety of spin shown for one-handed driving.

Improving your stroke

Whereas the two-handed backhand, is played with an unwinding action with both arms fully extended at the hit, the double-handed forehand is a cramped stroke played with a winding-up action, with the arms slightly bent. As with the one-handed stroke, full power depends on good weight transfer, stepping in with the front as you start the forward swing and getting your weight completely over your front knee at impact and in the follow through. The shape of the swing, as shown below, is similar to the one-handed version of the stroke.

Double-handed forehand grip

For best power place the supporting hand at the butt end of the grip midway between the Continental and Eastern backhand grips, and the playing hand nestled above it in an Eastern forehand grip (see p. 39).

A **Preparation** Turning on your right foot, you should take the racket back at about hitting height while you watch the approaching ball over your left shoulder. Step in close to the flight of the ball with your left foot.

B **Hitting zone** Meet the ball opposite your leading hip with your arms as extended as your firm wrists will allow.

C **Follow through** Finish about head height with playing arm extended.

Gene Mayer's well-placed rear foot and prepared racket allow him to step in parallel to the ball's flight as he turns in to hit the ball. He is thus perfectly positioned for this double-handed forehand drive.

Backhand drive

The backhand is essential to your game, firstly as the natural complement to your forehand and secondly because match players attack your backhand side. Any player is only as strong as his weakest stroke, and a poor backhand is particularly easy to spot by an alert and proficient opponent.

The backhand drive is played on the opposite side of the body to the forehand, and the ball is consequently hit with the reverse face of the racket. The key components of a good backhand are a firm wrist (as a result of the proper backhand grip) and correct footwork. Once these two major elements have been built into your stroke, it is surprisingly easy to master.

The stroke is played sideways to the ball, instead of from a more square-to-the-net stance which was used in the past and produced defensive, cut strokes. A sideways preparation, with your feet parallel to the flight of the ball and your shoulders turned around until your back is almost facing the net, allows you to hit the ball with a swinging, lifting movement as you unwind from the take-back. This uncoiling movement is the basis of the modern backhand. It is an action which generates considerable power, often greater than that in the forehand. This may seem surprising until you consider which part of the body a right-hander would use to break down a door; almost certainly the back of the right shoulder.

The backhand requires a change from the Eastern forehand grip to the Eastern backhand grip, as shown opposite. Once you have mastered the backhand grip it is vital to become familiar with changing from forehand to backhand grips, and vice-versa. The approach to perfecting the stroke is similar to that used for the forehand drive and depends on the ability to analyze your own stroke, as discussed on pages 62 and 64.

Playing the stroke

Make your changeover to the Eastern backhand grip. Then start the take-back smoothly, keeping the racket at about hitting height and turning your shoulders well around so that your back is almost facing the net. Move your weight on to your left foot and release your supporting hand from the racket throat to allow the head to make a shallow loop to start the forward swing. The unwinding action starts as you step in with your front foot, swinging the racket out and up at the ball as you transfer your weight on to your bent front knee. Meet the ball as it starts to fall in front of your leading hip. Follow through a good distance in the direction of the ball's flight.

1 Take up the ready position behind the centermark of the baseline.

2 Turning on the left foot, change to the Eastern backhand grip. Take the racket back.

3 Turn your shoulders well around moving your weight fully on to the left foot.

Eastern backhand grip

The Eastern backhand grip is more secure than any other grip in tennis and promotes a very firm wrist. You must make the change from forehand to backhand grip, shown below, by feel, not by sight, using your non-playing hand to support the racket.

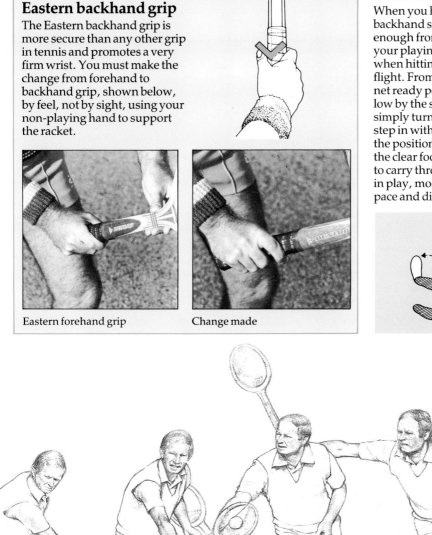

Eastern forehand grip

Change made

Footwork

When you hit the ball on the backhand side, you must be far enough from it to be able to keep your playing arm extended when hitting sideways into the flight. From your square-to-the-net ready position, shown below by the shaded footprints, simply turn on your left foot and step in with your right foot to the position shown below by the clear footprints. Always aim to carry through this footwork in play, modifying it to meet the pace and direction of each shot.

4 Make a shallow loop with the racket head and step in parallel to the flight of the ball.

5 Transfer your weight fully on to your front foot. Tighten your grip as you swing up.

6 Lift the racket head through the ball, following through in the direction of flight.

7 Finish with your playing arm extended and the racket above head height.

Improving your stroke

Whether you are a beginner simply trying to improve your backhand, or an experienced player who wants to correct a weak backhand, breaking the stroke down into its key components will help.

You will not improve your backhand unless you have previously perfected the Eastern backhand grip and the forehand to backhand changeover shown on the previous page. The correct grip encourages both the economical take-back characteristic of the stroke and the wrist firmness required for control. As important is turning your shoulders (during the preparation of the shot) beyond an imaginary line drawn at right angles to the line of flight.

Like the basic forehand drive (see p.48), the racket path for a basic backhand travels from low to high through the hitting zone, imparting a little topspin to the ball which controls the arc and depth of your shot. This shape is achieved by taking the racket back at about hitting height and making a shallow loop shape with the racket at the end of the take-back. The ball is usually hit a little further in front of your leading hip than for the forehand.

Using a full shoulder turn and then stepping in to transfer your weight into the hit should make you feel as though you are cocking and releasing a powerful spring.

Shoulder turn
The use of your shoulders is crucial for a powerful backhand. Make sure that your hitting shoulder is turned well away so that your back almost faces the net. You will have to look over your hitting shoulder at the ball.

C

A **Preparation** Before you step in and unwind, you should be poised with your weight on your rear foot, your shoulders turned away from the ball, and your grip level with your trailing hip.

B **Hitting zone** Meet the ball a little in front of your leading hip with your racket face slightly tilted back to encourage lift. Squeeze your grip and lock your wrist before and through the hitting zone.

C **Follow through** As your weight moves well forward over your front foot keep your wrist locked and your racket arm extended. Hold the finish with your racket well out in front at about head height.

A

B

Building the backhand drive into your game

When developing the forehand (see p.49) you will have learned how to deal particularly with wide and short balls in a baseline rally. The same advice applies for the backhand. Get to the hitting area quickly so that you can play a stroke as close to standard as possible. Below, you can see how to return a ball which has been hit at your body too fast for you to move into a position sideways to the ball, and how to hit a high bouncing ball.

Ball close to the body

1 Step well away from the line of flight with your front foot.

2 Transferring your weight, lean away from the ball so that you meet it with your playing arm extended.

3 Follow through along the original flight of the ball.

Modified footwork

The two diagrams, right, show the difference between the basic footwork required for the backhand, near right, and the modified footwork required to play a ball which is flying at, or close to, the body. Stepping away from the flight of the ball allows a fuller stroke.

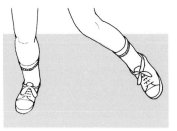
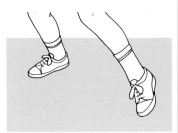

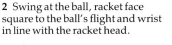

High ball

1 Prepare with a higher take-back than for a standard shot.

2 Swing at the ball, racket face square to the ball's flight and wrist in line with the racket head.

3 Follow through in the direction of the shot, keeping your hitting arm extended.

Practicing on your own

Now that you have mastered the basics of the backhand, you should concentrate in your practice sessions on refining each aspect of the stroke until it becomes second nature. Practice the stroke without a ball. Whenever you feel that you need to correct an error (see p.50). A practice wall will encourage consistency.

During your practice sessions on court, concentrate on improving your ability to alternate between down the sideline and crosscourt shots, as shown right, by simply meeting the ball earlier or later.

Down the sideline
To drive the ball straight down the sideline you must make contact with it fractionally ahead of your leading hip.

Crosscourt
To play a similar drive, but crosscourt, meet the ball some way in front of your leading hip to create the required angle.

Practicing with a partner

You will need more time for practicing as you now have to include both forehand and backhand drives in the session. Warm up by playing 10- and 20-stroke groundstroke rallies with your partner using both forehand and backhand drives. Then, allowing 10 minutes for each type of stroke, practice crosscourt forehand and backhand drives, and down the sideline forehand and backhand drives, each player returning behind the centermark between shots. Finally play competitive rallies with one player hitting crosscourt drives while the other puts all his shots down the line, both players hitting forehands and backhands alternately, as shown right. Reverse roles and repeat.

Once you start playing competitively most of your shots will have to be hit on the run. In your practice sessions make sure that you train realistically for match play situations by returning behind the centermark on the baseline between strokes.

When practicing strokes with a partner, get to the ball as quickly as possible, preparing your racket as you run. Then place your weight on to your rear foot so that all that remains for the stroke is the step in and swing. This will help to prevent rushing the stroke.

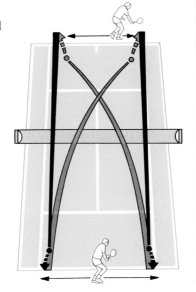

Practice aid

If you are finding it difficult to get your shoulders far enough around to put any real power into your drive, take up the ready position with your back actually facing the net. Get your partner to drop the ball to your side and behind you at racket arm's distance from you. Watch the ball over your shoulder as you turn, step in and make the stroke.

Using your backhand

The backhand side of the court is naturally the defensive one. But with practice, the backhand can be transformed into an offensive shot. As with the forehand, your usual tactics must be to drive deep to the corners of your opponent's court, as close to the baseline as possible, or to play crosscourt angled shots off your opponent's poorer shots to win the point outright or to force point-winning situations which leave your opponent out of position.

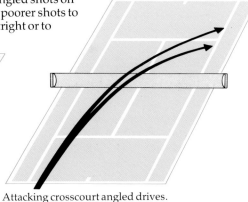

Attacking crosscourt angled drives.

Deep crosscourt and down-the-line drives.

John McEnroe prepares to play a basic lifted backhand drive. The support hand on the racket throat, the full body turn, and over-the-shoulder sighting of the ball highlight the ideal way to prepare and position yourself. Although McEnroe's grip is not a full Eastern backhand, he has perfect racket head and face control, leaving little doubt that this will be a very powerful stroke. He will step in with his front foot parallel to the line of flight as he swings his racket up to meet the ball in front of his body. This sideways on positioning gives a solid hitting platform for basic strokeplay.

Topspin backhand drive

The same difference exists between the basic backhand and the topspin backhand drive as there is between the basic and topspin forehand. The gentle topspin required to control the length of hard-hit basic shots is dramatically increased for the topspin version so that the characteristic flight and bounce of a ball hit with topspin (see p.42) are exaggerated. These characteristics (an arcing trajectory taking the ball between 3 and 6 feet above the net, and a bounce which shoots forwards and up at the receiver) make the topspin backhand an attacking shot.

The development of the topspin backhand occurred relatively late in the history of the game when the topspin forehand had been in use for some time. But since the Second World War the topspin backhand has been part of most world champions' repertoires from Budge Patty to the incomparable Swede, Bjorn Borg.

Some players practically always use top-spin as part of their strategy whereas others reserve it as an attacking alternative. Many develop a wristy, whiplike action to produce topspin but a stroke which requires the minimum of wrist action and complements the Eastern backhand grip is less difficult to master (see p. 61).

Topspin is best added to the basic stroke by simply steepening the angle of your forward swing at the ball. The angle of your racket face at the moment of impact should be the same as for the basic stroke, although wrist and forearm action will be in the process of turning the racket face forwards.

Because the higher trajectory of the ball in a topspin drive allows it to pass over the net with more room to spare than with a basic stroke, it gives you a greater margin for error. Failure to play the stroke correctly – to hit up and through the ball before closing the racket face over – will lead to shots which fall short or, worse still, land in the net.

Playing the stroke

The low to high swing which characterizes the topspin backhand depends on a deeper loop with the racket at the end of the take-back than for the basic stroke. Let your knees bend and take the racket back below your intended hitting height (normally at, or above, waist height). Then release your non-playing hand from the racket and make a lower loop than for the basic stroke. Your weight should then move forward as you step in with your right foot parallel to the ball's flight. Unwind by swinging the racket head up steeply to meet the ball. Let your extended racket arm turn forwards as you follow through.

1 From your ready position turn to the left changing to your Eastern backhand grip.

2 On your left foot, bending your knees. Take the racket back below waist height.

3 Release your non-playing hand and start to make a low loop with the racket.

Improving your stroke

If your topspin results are disappointing on the backhand side, the most likely features of the stroke needing improvement are shown, right. Get the feel of applying topspin off court as shown below. When playing the stroke on court let the steep upwards swing of the racket impart the topspin to the ball.

Getting the feel of topspin

Get the feel of applying topspin by brushing up the back of the ball with the racket face angled as shown below. The ball will dip and bounce just in front of you.

A **Preparation** Loop low with the racket head.

B **Hitting zone** Keep your wrist and grip firm and racket arm extended.

C **Follow through** Let your arm turn over as you finish strongly high and across to the right, with the hitting face of the racket downwards.

4 Step in parallel to the flight of the ball, moving your weight forwards. Swing the racket up.

5 With your weight over your bent front knee, hit the ball with racket face almost vertical.

6 Allow your wrist and arm to roll the racket over and your legs to straighten a little.

7 Finish with the racket high and across your body with the hitting face aiming downwards.

Practicing on your own

With the topspin backhand start, as with the other strokes, on court with as many balls as possible and drop them one by one with your non-playing hand, waiting for them to bounce, then step in to play the stroke. Bounce each ball so that you can attack it realistically above waist height. Practice without balls, stopping to check any of the key features of the stroke which you may suspect, but always work improvements into the complete stroke as soon as possible by hitting balls down the sideline and crosscourt. As with the other strokes, a backboard can be very helpful.

Practicing with a partner

Starting from the baseline rally position, with your partner supplying good-height balls to you by hand, run out and play your topspin backhand cross-court, returning behind the centermark between each shot. Switch roles with your partner and when you are both playing the stroke well, progress to rallying corner to corner. Then alternate strokes with your partner, first you hitting topspin strokes and your partner basic strokes, then vice-versa, for ten minutes each way.

You can then move on to the sequence shown right, with one of you hitting basic forehands and backhands crosscourt while the other plays topspin forehands and backhands down the sideline. Once you are both hitting well, introduce points scoring. The player who wins a rally by forcing an error from the other wins a point, and then starts the next rally. When one of you reaches 11 points, switch roles playing for one set of points and basic strokes for the next.

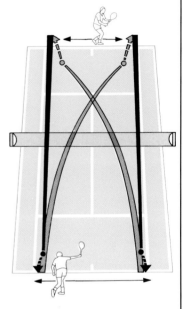

Using your topspin backhand

The inclusion of the topspin backhand in your choice of strokes will especially help you to counter-attack when your opponent comes in to the net, as you can produce dipping returns to the feet. It will also help you to return an approach shot which draws you wide to the backhand as you can now produce a topspin passing shot.

The topspin alternative will help you to keep your opponent guessing. However, beware of producing short balls. Make sure that your shots penetrate after the bounce by applying enough pace.

Boris Becker imparts heavy topspin to the ball as he comes off the ground to attack. He has played the ball a little too close but, by straightening his body and leaning away slightly, he uses muscle power and strength of arm to brush aggressively up through the ball in typical counter-attacking style. The full extension of his playing arm shows that perfect racket face and ball control have been maintained under pressure. The high finish and upright body position suggest that this topspin drive is aimed to dip at the feet of an advancing opponent.

A Down the line
B Dipping return
C Crosscourt

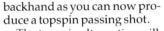

Sliced backhand

To become a complete tennis player, you need to include the backhand slice drive in your choice of strokes. Unless, however, you can develop it in the way Ken Rosewall did, you should look on the slice as a useful variation to your basic and topspin drives and certainly not as a replacement for either.

A ball hit with underspin (see p.42) tends to hang in the air, and if it is not hit on a flat trajectory, to bounce up without forward momentum. Such characteristics are clearly defensive and in keeping with the more naturally defensive backhand side. The backhand slice drive retains a respectability in top class tennis (especially in the women's game) that the forehand slice has lost. At their best, Britain's Wimbledon champions,

Ann Jones and Virginia Wade, were both very adept at the backhand slice, and German player Steffi Graf has an aggressive backhand slice drive.

As shown on the forehand slice (see pp.56–57), underspin is hit on to the ball by combining a high to low swing with a controlled open racket face (bottom edge leading) at the point of impact. So as to counteract the disadvantages of a long, floating flight and an easy bounce, it is best to slice high bouncing balls, especially ones which are still rising. This will allow you to hit the ball hard, on a flat trajectory, low over the net. Lower balls hit with the same strength may fly out of court unless hit with sidespin (see opposite).

Playing the stroke

Make the change to your backhand grip as you begin turning to your left. The preparation for the stroke must be above the height at which you will play the ball so that the forward swing will be from high to low. As with the forehand slice, cock your wrist as you take the racket back. Your

wrist must be firm and your racket arm extended as you bring the racket down to meet the ball ahead of your leading hip with the bottom edge of the face leading. Most of the swing should come from your hitting shoulder. The follow through will be low, the racket coming up slightly.

1 Turning on your left foot, take the racket back above hitting height with wrist locked.

2 Step in with your right foot as you release your non-playing hand and swing downwards.

3 With the top edge of the racket face still angled back, meet the ball in front of your hip.

4 Follow through maintaining the sideways position as the stroke finishes low.

Improving your stroke

The shape of the forehand slice (see p.56) will show you the high to low line of the forward swing for your backhand slice. The standard spin for a back-hand slice is shown on the ball below. To achieve this mixture of sidespin and underspin your racket face must hit down, through and around the ball in the direction of the arrow. It will help to take the racket back with the face more open (bottom edge leading) than in the basic shot preparation. Make sure that after the hit you do not let the racket head fall away but rather rise again after the des-cent through the ball.

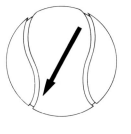

Using an alternative slice

The slight sidespin which the standard backhand slice carries as a result of hitting around the outside, as well as through and underneath, the ball, ensures at least a straight flight if not one that curves in towards the middle of the court. This is the shot which you should use as a regular variant to your basic and topspin strokes. There is, however, a way of sidespinning the ball in the direction shown, below, by preparing your racket further away from your body and then hitting inside the line of flight. Keeping the racket face open as for the standard shot, the out to in swing will draw the strings across the back of the ball.

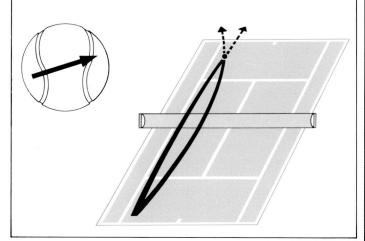

Practicing on your own

Practice the stoke on court by dropping balls with your non-playing hand. Smooth out any imperfections in your technique by stroking without a ball. Always go back to hitting batches of balls to test your re-sults. Watch the flight of your practice shots carefully, making sure that the balls travel lower over the net band than for a basic drive and deep towards the opposing baseline on a flat trajectory. Experiment with a batch of balls hit with the alternative outward swerving shot shown above right, and finish your session by playing your new stroke in sequences with the other backhand shots that you have learned.

Practicing with a partner

"Alley driving", or "tramline hitting", is a very useful practice for developing controlled power once you have mastered the basics of a groundstroke. Use the narrow band of court between the singles and doubles sidelines as your full court, and with your partner opposed to you at the other end, shown right, practice your back-hand slice while he or she im-proves their forehand shots. Balls must land in the alley area to count. Basic, topspin or slice strokes, or all three at once, can be practiced in this way. After 15 minutes, change ends or use the other alley, and switch roles. Try to keep 20-shot rallies going, or play for points.

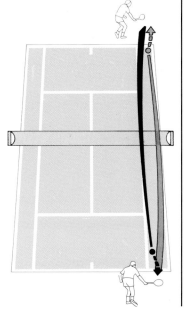

Using your backhand slice

The strategic value of the slice lies in the problems it creates for your opponent. It can be used to upset his settled hitting rhythm. The effectively sliced ball skids through low after the bounce. Aim for this result and use the stroke against rising topspin balls at waist height. Mix in the alternative out-to-in slice.

As with the forehand stroke, the backhand slice with a shortened preparation can be used as a controlled approach shot (see p.214). Its prolonged flight will give you more time to gain a good volleying position. Make sure that you choose shorter, poor length balls.

Avoid using the slice as a passing shot (see pp.208-209). because underspin will keep the ball in the air, making it easy for your opponent to volley.

Ken Rosewall *slices a backhand down the sideline. This finish shows that the ball has been struck on a flat trajectory. His wrist locked as the hitting arm straightened.*

Drive practice sequences

When you feel confident of your basic, topspin and slice shots, on both the forehand and the backhand sides, give them realistic match-play practice by undertaking the following sequences with your practice partner.

Player 1	Player 2
basic forehand	slice backhand
topspin backhand	basic forehand
slice forehand	topspin backhand
basic backhand	slice forehand
topspin forehand	basic backhand
slice backhand	topspin forehand

Sequence B
Player 1 hits down the sideline drives while player 2 hits crosscourt drives only, both following the order of strokes shown left, and creating the pattern of play below.

Player 1	Player 2
basic	slice
topspin	basic
slice	topspin

The pattern of down the line and crosscourt drives for sequence B

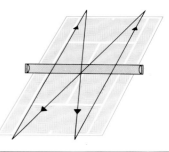

Sequence A
Hit either forehand or backhand strokes as play dictates, but follow the order of strokes shown in the table above.

Backhand chop

The backhand chop is a similar stroke to the backhand slice but is more compact and applies fiercer underspin to the ball. The path of the racket is steep from high to low in a chopping action, so that the angle between the racket face and ball through the hitting zone manufactures the heavy spin. The characteristics of a ball hit with underspin (see p.42) are even more accentuated in the chop making the ball sit up rather than shoot through low so its use is more limited than the slice in baseline rallies unless your opponent is particularly susceptible to a floating, slow bouncing ball.

Pick balls which bounce above net height so that you can chop them aggressively, deep into your opponent's court. If you chop balls which have fallen below net height you will have to hit them without pace to make them fall short of your opponent's baseline.

Improving your stroke

The preparation for the chop should be high, with the bottom edge of the racket face slightly leading, but make it shorter than for the backhand slice. Simply uncock your wrist as you bring the racket head down. Meet the ball ahead of your leading hip, hitting down and slightly across the back of the ball to apply some sidespin for extra control, shown below.

Hitting down and across the ball

A **Preparation** Cock your playing wrist so that the racket is high during the short take-back. Cut down strongly with racket face slightly back from vertical.

B **Hitting zone and follow through** Keep your wrist firm through the hitting zone and meet the ball fractionally ahead of your leading hip. Finish low across your body.

Using your backhand chop

As with the forehand stroke, the backhand chop is a stroke to be used sparingly during baseline rallies with a view to breaking an opponent's rhythm. You should only use it more frequently when your opponent shows himself inept at dealing with the chopped ball. The chopped return is sometimes an effective foil to high bouncing, topspin shots, and if used as such, should be chopped deep to your opponent's baseline. If you are tired during a match remember that the chop requires a minimum amount of energy and precise footwork is less vital than for other strokes. So for defensive purposes alone the backhand chop is a worthwhile stroke to include in your game.

The compactness of the backhand chop and its tolerance of imprecise footwork makes it useful for returning service (see pp.200-203), especially against topspin services when the receiver can chip the ball to the feet of the incoming volleyer.

Double-handed backhand drive

Playing the backhand with two hands on the racket grip strengthens the hitting and control of very young players and often seems quite natural. Other players find the extra hand on the grip allows them to play topspin backhand shots more easily.

Your two-handed grip will determine the development of your stroke (see p.39). Your dominant hand should hold the racket grip at the butt end and the supporting hand should nestle above it, using the grip below. Release your support hand for wide balls.

Improving your stroke

The shape of the basic double-handed backhand should be similar to the one-handed version. The double-handed stroke requires shoulder turn and body rotation, especially through the hitting zone. Change of grip, shown right, takes place during the first step of preparation as you turn from your ready position. Most double-handers stand in the ready position with the supporting hand not at the throat of the racket as usual but lower on the shaft and with the backhand grip lightly formed.

As you take the racket back past the left hip, point the racket head down slightly making a shallow loop before you swing upwards through the ball. Such a racket path will apply enough controlling topspin to limit the length of your strokes. Transfer your weight on to your front foot as you make the shot and make sure that you unwind through the forward swing. Extend your arms at the hit and finish about head height.

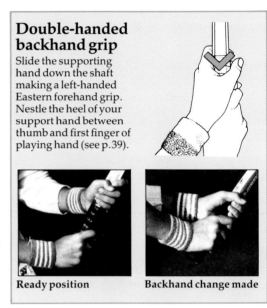

Double-handed backhand grip

Slide the supporting hand down the shaft making a left-handed Eastern forehand grip. Nestle the heel of your support hand between thumb and first finger of playing hand (see p.39).

Ready position   **Backhand change made**

A **Preparation** Get sideways to the ball as you take the racket back at the intended hitting height. Make a shallow loop and step in with your front foot as you swing your racket head up to meet the ball.

B **Hitting zone** With firm wrists and racket face almost vertical, meet the ball just in front of your leading hip.

C **Follow through** Drive through in the direction of the shot with your weight fully over your bent front knee to finish about head height.

Dropshots

The dropshot family of strokes encompasses the short-range shots played after the ball has bounced and designed to fall short of your opponent. The basic forehand and backhand dropshots, shown below, are played with underspin. Variations, shown overleaf, are the dink shot, which is usually played with topspin, and the dump shot, which is a simple push through the ball from the forecourt normally played against balls above net height. All dropshots can be played with your regular grips.

Forehand dropshot

1 From inside the baseline, take your racket back above hitting height, as for the forehand slice drive (see p.56). Step in.

2 Push the racket head down the back of, and underneath the ball.

3 Finish the stroke low in the direction of the shot.

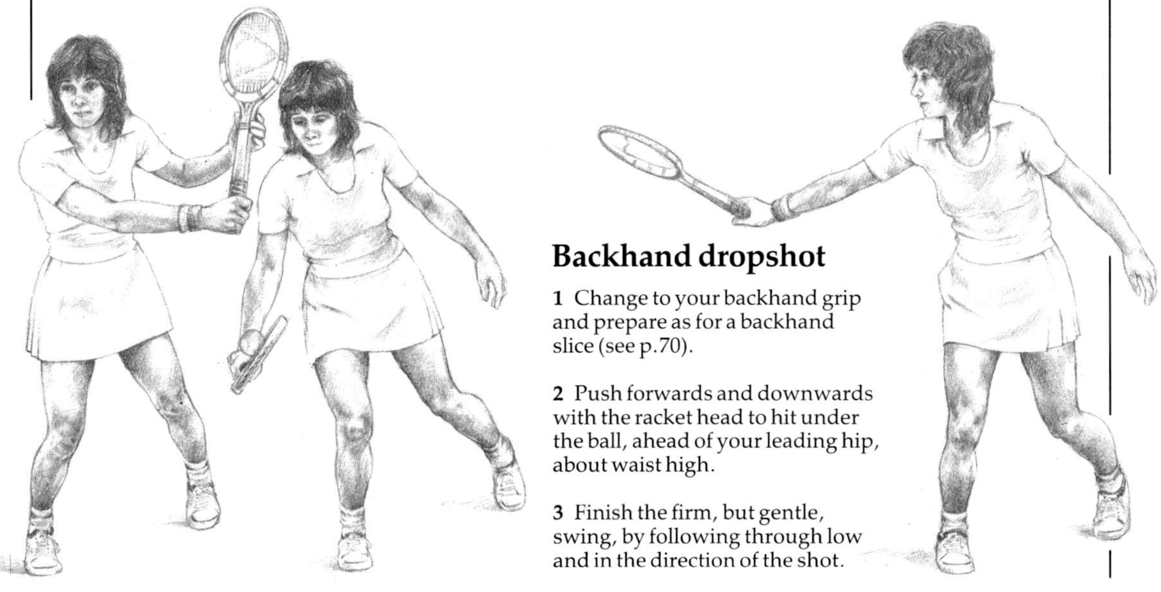

Backhand dropshot

1 Change to your backhand grip and prepare as for a backhand slice (see p.70).

2 Push forwards and downwards with the racket head to hit under the ball, ahead of your leading hip, about waist high.

3 Finish the firm, but gentle, swing, by following through low and in the direction of the shot.

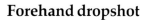

Building the dropshot into your game

Dropshot play is exciting and full of suspense, especially on grass courts where the ball dies quickly. Its success depends on surprising your opponent so that it is very difficult for him to recover and play the ball which you have placed only a yard or two over the net. You can often use the similarity between the dropshot and sliced drive preparations to disguise your intentions when hitting the basic dropshots. There are two varieties of the dropshot, shown below, the dink shot and the dump shot. Having previously learned the topspin drives (see pp.52 and 66), the soft topspin forehand and backhand dink shots should come easily enough to you. The dink shot is especially effective when played from near the service line but it can also be played with underspin or sidespin from no man's land (see p.195). The dump shot is played from quite near the net, with your bodyweight almost static, with higher balls which can be placed over the net.

Forehand dink shot

1 From near the service line, turn on to your right foot, taking the racket back level with, or slightly below, hitting height.

2 After forming a shallow loop, step in, swinging your racket forwards and up to meet the ball opposite your leading hip. Lift the racket through for topspin.

3 Finish with the racket across your body towards the left shoulder.

Backhand dump shot

1 Turn on to your left foot with your knees slightly bent. Take your racket back a short distance at hitting height, changing your grip. Step in early.

2 Release your non-playing hand and push the racket head forwards to meet the ball (racket face flat) in front of your leading hip.

3 Keep your follow through very short, dumping the ball over the net with minimum spin and with very little pace.

Practicing on your own

On one side of the net place targets opposite each other on the sidelines, one pair 3-5 feet from the net, and another pair 10 feet from the net. Firstly, take up a position just inside the service line on the other side of the net with your basket of balls. Drop balls for yourself practicing both forehand and backhand dropshots using the targets to assess your accuracy. Persevere until you get 75 per cent of your balls to bounce gently between the 3-5 feet targets and the net, and the remainder short of the 10 feet targets. You can then move back a yard for your next basket of balls, and finally to just inside your baseline.

If you have the use of a practice wall, mark a line on the ground 3-5 feet from it. Retire to your usual driving position 15-20 feet from the wall and play and repeat drive followed by dropshot, as shown right, aiming to make the ball fall between the 3-5 feet line and the wall with every dropshot.

Using your dropshots

In match play, adopt the mental rule that your dropshots will never fall on your own side of the net. Giving yourself this margin for error will mean that, at the outset, your dropshots will force weak returns from your opponent rather than outright winners. This is far better than being discouraged by the sight of an overambitious dropshot falling into the net. Generally, play dropshots against medium paced balls, aiming to the side of the court as far away as possible from your stranded opponent. If there is no advantage in playing to either side, aim for the middle of the court so that the ball travels over the lowest part of the net. Dink shots, and dump shots played from close to the net, should be similarly used. Remember that the dink shots can be usefully directed towards opponents' feet when they are approaching the net.

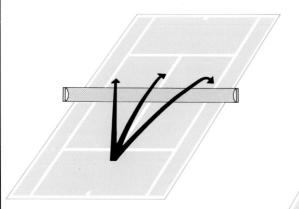

Dropshots played to the side and center of the court

A Dump shot

B Dink shot to opponent's feet

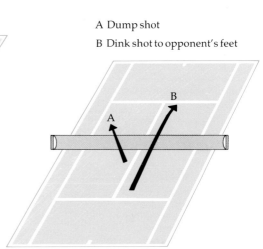

Half-volley

The perfectly timed half-volley is often a defensive, pick-up stroke and gives the impression that the ball meets the court surface and your racket face at the same time. In fact, the racket strings meet the ball just as it begins its upward flight after the bounce. The stroke is a shortened basic drive played from any part of the court, but because it is seldom selected by choice, most players half-volley in no man's land (see p.195) where there is often no alternative. Forehand and backhand versions of the half-volley are shown below. These highlight the importance of getting right down to the bounce, watching the ball and playing the stroke with a short, firm-wristed swing.

Although it is regarded as the most difficult shot to time well, and has even been labelled the lazy man's shot, it does play an important role in both the singles and doubles game. You should practice it on your own and with a partner on a regular basis or your attempts to half-volley in match play will be disastrous.

Forehand half-volley

Backhand half-volley

78

Improving the stroke

You should take your racket back only a short distance at low level, keeping your racket head up level with your wrist. On both forehand and backhand sides, let your knees bend as you turn on to your rear foot. There should be no loop in the forward swing so simply step in on to your front foot getting as low as possible. The racket face must meet the ball opposite your leading hip and open (tilted back from vertical) enough to give the angle of deflection to clear the net. Keep your wrist firm and follow through with a lifting motion, staying with the ball.

Just before the hit
Timing the half-volley requires practice. Your forward swing must bring the strings to the pitch of the ball just above court level.

Just after the hit
The ball has been deflected just as it begins to rise after the bounce.

Practicing on your own

Place two targets inside the baseline, one near each of the corners of the singles court, and also two targets inside the service line each about halfway between the centerline and the sidelines, as shown right. With your basket of balls, go to the other end of the court and start practicing both your forehand and backhand half-volleys aiming at the far baseline targets. Firstly on the forehand side of the baseline, then the backhand side, simply turn and drop balls for yourself as you bend and prepare low with a short take-back. Be sure to get down well to the ball and to transfer your weight as you swing the racket forward in a lifting motion. This will improve half-volleying deep down the sidelines and crosscourt with both strokes. With your next basket of balls take a few steps forward on each side before starting, so playing your half-volleys from no man's land, again aiming for the far baseline targets. When you feel confident of hitting the far targets, move forwards to your service line and aim your half-volleys at the targets that

you placed just inside the service line on the other side of the net. Play the ball from both forehand and backhand sides. As you half-volley from nearer the net, you will find that you must shorten your take-back and angle your racket face slightly further back at the hit.

Continuous half-volleying against a backboard is another very good way to develop your technique and timing.

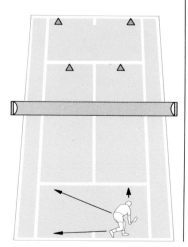

Practicing with a partner

On court, practice forehand half-volleying from the baseline against your partner who must volley the ball back to your forehand from the net position. Try to keep a 10-, then 20-shot rally going. After 10 minutes, practice your backhand half-volley for the same period of time, then ask your volleying partner to mix forehand and backhand balls for a further 10 minutes' practice. Switch roles and repeat the routine.

Progress to half-volleying to each other from your respective service lines. If you can keep a rally going in this manner you are on the way to mastering the half-volley. At this stage you can include the half-volley in realistic match-play practice. Adopt the serving position and get your partner to take up a receiving position. Serve to your partner and if he plays a successful return dipping to your feet, half-volley the return as you move into the net. Repeat this sequence for 10 minutes before switching roles with your partner.

Using your half-volleys

The half-volley has to be used when you are caught in no man's land as you approach the net. It is much better to hit a well-placed half-volley than to try and make a drive or a volley for which you are out of position. A good half-volley can regain the initiative which has been momentarily lost to your opponent's good return.

In singles play, half-volley down the nearest sideline when your opponent is on the baseline, as shown above right. This will give you the best chance to cover any possible return as you move forwards to the net position. If your opponent is approaching the net, however, aim your half-volley so that it lands at the net-rusher's feet.

In doubles play, you must be careful to avoid your opposing net man when playing the half-volley. Direct most of your half-volleys crosscourt.

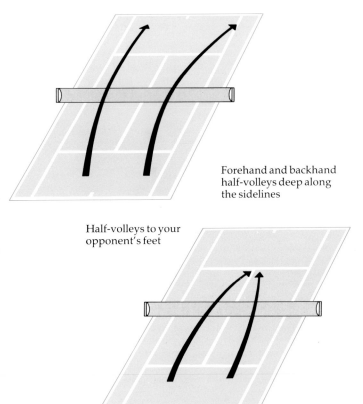

Forehand and backhand half-volleys deep along the sidelines

Half-volleys to your opponent's feet

Martina Navratilova picks the ball up using a delicate forehand half-volley to return a low shot from her opponent. The American's bent knees and low playing arm wrist are signs of full control. She has aimed the ball crosscourt, giving it room to clear the net near the lowest point. She watches the ball intently – if it stays low enough over the net she may maintain the initiative, or even win the point with this stroke.

Developing a style: groundstrokes

John McEnroe prepares for an attacking topspin backhand. He uses modified forms of two of the three styles of groundstroke play – Eastern and Continental – to produce a unique combination of firm and free-wristed play. Like McEnroe, some players develop forms of these styles, and the third, Western.

Forehand drive

Modern players use a mixture of power and control in their basic forehand driving. Each player's style depends on the original grips and techniques learned, and modified by individual physical and mental make-up.

The Eastern and Continental forms of forehand show in the styles of, for example, Evonne Cawley, Jimmy Connors, John McEnroe and Chris Evert Lloyd. The Western style is physically tiring and an advantage only on courts where the bounce is high. The flatter drive hit by Connors contrasts with the lifted drive of, say, Vitas Gerulaitis, but both combine power and control.

Contrasted styles

The Eastern and Western forehand grips, below, of Evonne Cawley and Sue Barker, respectively, show how much squarer to the net the Western player stands and how the ball is played higher, closer to the body and with wrist above racket head.

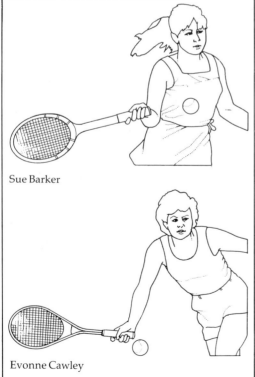

Sue Barker

Evonne Cawley

Martina Navratilova, using a modified Eastern grip, follows through after a solid crosscourt forehand. She remains well balanced as she watches the ball. She often uses considerable wrist movement to gain extra racket head speed when hitting the ball.

Sue Barker demonstrates the Western style of forehand drive, with the racket head swinging below wrist level. She spreads her index finger for control. She can hit with blinding speed as well as applying heavy topspin – the main feature of Western gripping.

Steffi Graf plays a powerful, if cramped, forehand drive. She has met the ball rather late and too close, and has become airborne. Her body straightens to provide sufficient room for maximum racket-head speed to develop and weight transfer to occur prior to meeting the ball ahead of her leading hip. Her Eastern forehand grip gives excellent control of racket and ball, and her left arm helps her to maintain her balance.

Evonne Cawley uses a spread first finger with her modified Eastern grip, which helps her to swing the racket through the hitting zone in perfect line with the ball. She has been forced to step across more than she would prefer, but her left arm aids her balance.

Topspin forehand drive

Most leading players make use of the topspin forehand drive, because it provides maximum control while allowing aggressive attack. Rod Laver and Bjorn Borg have used modified Continental and modified Western styles respectively, to produce punishing topspin, and women power players such as Virginia Wade and Martina Navratilova use it, aggressively in passing shots and with a more rolled effect in baseline play. Sound positioning is essential to achieve pace – without pace a topspin shot may land short and bounce high, leaving the ball open to exploitation. The topspin forehand is particularly effective in doubles, because it can create extra angles for crosscourt play, and make dipping returns to the feet of servers as they approach the net.

Guillermo Vilas shows the cramped, bent elbow style of the full Western topspin forehand. He produces a high, bounding ball with the stroke, which is a constant embarrassment to most of his opponents. He has had to play this shot closer to the body than he would have liked, but has made room.

Vitas Gerulaitis has run around his backhand to hit this topspin drive on the forehand. His use of the Eastern grip has produced a more extended arm and a higher finish for the racket head than with the Western-style shot as demonstrated by Vilas. He finishes the stroke in a more sideways position.

Contrasted styles

A comparison of Eastern and Western styles shows the marked difference of the follow-throughs. Gerulaitis, using an Eastern grip, finishes high and in front of the left shoulder, with only marginal closing of the racket face. Vilas, with the Western grip, has finished his shot much squarer to the net. The racket has followed through lower and much more across the body, with the hitting face of the racket closed over.

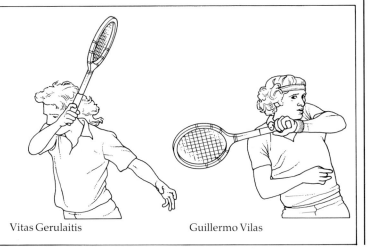

Vitas Gerulaitis

Guillermo Vilas

Forehand slice

As Evonne Cawley and other modern champions have shown, the forehand slice and chop remain effective groundstrokes and should be included in every match player's repertoire. They can be very useful as returns of service and, when defending, the easily performed slice often rescues players who have been put under extreme pressure.

Virginia Wade prepares to play an aggressive forehand slice with racket head well above wrist level. Her racket face is slightly angled so that sidespin and underspin can be applied. the stroke will be played in attack as bodyweight moves forward on to the front knee and the ball is met opposite the left hip.

Backhand drive

The basic, lifted backhand is an essential stroke in modern play. Its development has created a more balanced baseline game. The Eastern backhand grip suits a shorter swing and firm-wristed control needed to counter aggressive opponents. The stroke should be neat and powerfully hit with a swing from the shoulder. Its natural potential for defense allows a full range of chops, cuts and slices to be employed as variations.

Adriano Panatta, an Eastern stylist, has turned his hitting shoulder well away, and his racket begins its forward swing from below hitting height. This lifted stroke will control the falling ball perfectly.

Arthur Ashe's straight take-back is a prelude to a typically flat backhand, with only a modest amount of topspin for control. He is perfectly balanced on the rear foot, while his left hand is an excellent example of how to support the racket when preparing a backhand.

Jimmy Connors uses two forehand grips in his double-handed style of backhand. In this case he has had to release his right hand for his high follow through.

Bjorn Borg's playing hand holds the racket with an Eastern backhand grip, while his supporting hand adopts a left-handed Eastern forehand position on the handle – an ideal two-handed backhand grip.

Chris Evert Lloyd epitomizes the Eastern backhand style. Only her double-handed grip and extra body rotation are significantly different. She has a firm-wristed swing through the hitting zone from the shoulders.

Topspin backhand drive

Leading players use the topspin backhand to dip returns past or at the feet of incoming volleyers. The extra margin for error and increased angle for crosscourt play makes the stroke ideal for tactical use. The Eastern style topspin backhand can be used against a wider range of balls than the Western style topspin, which is mainly suitable for countering high-bouncing balls above waist height. Good positioning for maximum weight transference is essential, or the stroke will lack pace and be more open to attack from your opponents.

Guillermo Vilas again shows the high bent elbow finish of a Western style stroke, this time on the backhand. He has had to play this stroke off his rear foot, brushing up through the ball fast.

Thomas Muster plays an attacking topspin drive off a low ball. His full backhand drive grip is ideal for applying both spin and pace to the ball. The sideways-on position and bodyweight transfer highlight the control he has mustered.

John Lloyd plays an aggressive topspin backhand drive off his rear foot using a basic Eastern backhand grip. Lloyd's great strength lay in his backhand, and he was adept at playing passing shots when under pressure from positions that appear to be defensive.

Improvising attack

Although on the wrong foot and unable to transfer his weight forward, John Lloyd has compensated well by thrusting upward sharply with the racket, shown below, applying topspin and so turning defense to attack.

Alberto Mancini, under pressure, meets the ball in front of his body as he plays an aggressive topspin drive off his rear foot. His grip, turned beyond the full Eastern backhand, is typical of many of today's stars, who lash on topspin with a powerful wrist action.

Backhand slice

The backhand slice has been an essential stroke since tennis began. The stroke, and its many variations, are useful alternatives to basic lifted and topspin drives when attacking. However, the slice has a narrower margin for error, so the ball must almost skim the net to be effective; otherwise it will provide an easy kill for the volleyer. The world's top players rely on the sliced backhand for attacking from the baseline on the slower playing surfaces, and as the basic slice can be produced quickly it is vital for defensive play from the baseline. When the stroke is played with the firm-wristed Eastern style of Ken Rosewall, with his sound technique and perfect timing, topspin strokes seem unnecessary. However, it would put a top level player at a considerable disadvantage to rely solely upon a sliced drive on the backhand side today.

Evonne Cawley plays an aggressive backhand slice. Although the racket face is laid well back, the racket is approaching the ball on a flat trajectory as it makes contact. It will meet the ball just in front of her at about waist level. At this height her swing will not be impeded by her front leg.

Martina Navratilova has played an inside-slice variation of the backhand slice, from just inside her baseline and near her right-hand sideline. She has played the ball in front of the body at about knee height and has aimed her slice to go down the line, with the spin providing control.

Inside slice

Note the high-to-low and out-to-in swing of the racket head as it approaches the ball. Some underspin is added with this shot, but its main feature is the swerving sidespin that is applied as the strings are dragged across the back of the ball. This makes the ball move towards the middle of the court as it crosses the net, and then swerve back towards the sideline, away from the right-handed opponent's backhand. This inside backhand slice causes the ball to rotate clockwise, and this makes it curve and bounce off the court – from the receiver's point of view – from right to left.

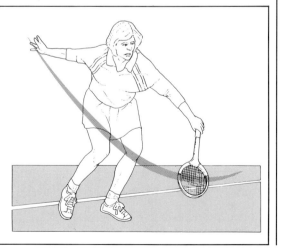

Dropshots

The dropshot is an essential shot in a skillful player's game. Its subtle use at strategic moments and economy of effort when employed as a contrast to powerful groundstrokes can tire opponents and win points outright with regularity. It can be perfected like any other stroke. It should be played from within the baseline against a medium-paced shot, allowing for a certain margin of error through controlled racket face angle. Jaroslav Drobny, Manuel Santana in 1966 and Billie Jean King throughout her reign as the world's leading woman player constantly used the dropshot to break up their opponents' rhythm and morale. Of today's players, Arantxa Sanchez-Vicario is an outstanding dropshot artist. Players often favor the backhand when playing this sensitive "touch" shot, however it can, of course, be equally well taken on the forehand in favorable circumstances with your opponent stranded at the back of the court.

Vitas Gerulaitis has just executed a delicate but firm-wristed dropshot on the backhand, and displays superb balance in the follow through. Although he is positioned only just inside the baseline of the court, Gerulaitis has the speed to reach any counter dropshot which his opponent might play.

Ilie Nastase plays a superb dropshot off a low ball from behind his service line. He has stepped well across, bending his knees as he would for a volley to angle his shot across the court.

Surprise return

Nastase is caught in no man's land by a low shot down the sideline, as shown below. Many players would panic in such a situation, but Nastase plays a surprise crosscourt angled dropshot. It lands just over the net near the sideline, totally deceiving his opponent who is still in the back court. His grip provides exact racket face control.

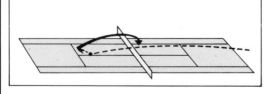

Anne Hobbs plays this dropshot against a ball that has bounced high and towards her. Instead of going down like Nastase she has come off the ground as she plays forwards and under the ball to apply the controlling backspin. She uses her left hand for balance.

Half-volley

The half-volley is thought of as an emergency stroke, but with improved service returns players are meeting more situations that call for this shot. By practicing the half-volley you will also be schooling yourself in playing the ball early. However, it is not generally wise to play a half-volley when volleying the ball is possible. The shot is often used as an abbreviated pick-up in doubles, when perfect timing is vital.

Bob Hewitt, above, has been caught out of position with the ball at his feet and has played a pick-up half-volley, taking the initiative from his opponent.

Arthur Ashe, left, plays a stroked half-volley, and will follow through in the direction of the shot. He has used the shot to maintain his initiative in the rally.

Contrasted recoveries

Ashe has advanced the leg nearer the ball so that he can maintain balance and control over this shot. Body weight is being transferred, and his wrist is well down and almost level with the racket head. In contrast, Hewitt has his weight leaning back and his racket face extremely angled. He has turned the shot into a half-volley lob, catching his opponent in turn by surprise. Pace is not an important factor from this position.

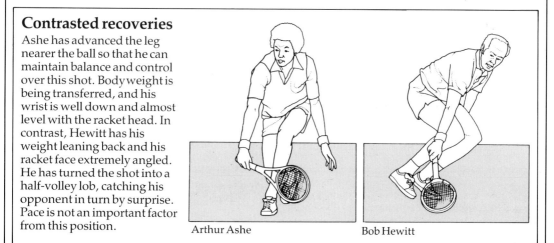

Arthur Ashe

Bob Hewitt

Vitas Gerulaitis was confronted with a service return to the feet as he advanced towards the net. With wrist and racket head practically level, Gerulaitis has picked the ball up opposite his back foot – again, the foot nearer to the ball. He must aim short or deep to the baseline, because Connors is waiting to pounce on any short or mid-court reply. Note that the score is 6-6, 30-30 – a vital point for both players.

THE SERVE

An effective serve is a crucial aspect of one's game. Without a powerful and accurate serve, it is impossible for any player to reach a reasonable level of competence.

There are three types of service, all based on the elementary throwing action (see p.33): the basic or flat serve, the topspin or American twist serve and the slice serve. As their names imply the difference between these serves lies in the degree of spin applied. The basic serve is hit on a flat trajectory with minimal spin. It is the easiest for beginners but also the fastest when developed and hit with power by top players. The topspin serve, like all topspin strokes, has a high arcing trajectory and a high, kicking bounce. The slice serve is hit with sidespin (see p.44) and some topspin, making the ball swerve in the air and after the bounce. The service you

choose will depend on your physique and the requirements of your game. Generally, the basic service is used for first serving and the topspin serve for second serving, with the slice serve reserved as a variation.

The service stance is vital to the direction, rhythm and timing of the serve. The ideal grip for serving is the Continental grip which will allow you maximum snap in your wrist for power and spin when you hit the ball, but the Eastern forehand grip may give you easier control to begin with for the basic service. Holding the ball correctly before releasing it is an important factor in the control of the place-up. Most adult players find it easy to hold two balls in the placing-up hand, but children under 10 and double-handed players may prefer to pocket one ball.

Service stance

However you modify your stance for each type of service there are common essentials. Your feet should be shoulder-width apart, your front foot a ball's width from the baseline and within 2 feet of the centermark, and knees bent.

Serving grips

The Continental grip (see p.39, near right, is the perfect grip for serving because of the relative freedom of wrist movement it allows. As a beginner you may find that the Eastern forehand grip (see p.38) gives you more control.

Holding the ball

Holding one ball
Grasp the ball which you are about to serve between your thumb and all four fingers.

Holding two balls
Hold the first ball with your thumb and first two fingers and the second ball with third and fourth fingers.

Basic serve

A fast first serve is the most intimidating stroke in modern tennis. The power and combination of rhythm, pace and accuracy in the Boris Becker service in today's game are the epitome of first serving.

The accuracy that comes from intense practice is critical to good quality first serving. A powerful basic serve hit as flat as possible by a 6-foot player, the ball just clearing the net, will only have about a one foot band of the service court in which to land. As it is impossible to hit the ball without any spin at all, your basic serve action should impart mild topspin so that the ball arcs downward slightly. This will have the additional effect of enlarging the target area.

It is only an advantage to be tall if you use your full height and reach. A tall player serving ineffectively with a bent hitting arm and low place-up, will always be beaten by an opponent who is serving well even if he is 5 inches shorter and 25 pounds lighter.

The stroke

Settle into the service stance, and let the stroke begin slowly. Part your arms just ahead of your front leg, letting your racket swing down past your body as your tossing arm swings up and you transfer your weight from your back foot forwards over your bent front knee. Release the ball when your tossing arm is at full stretch and your racket, hitting face downwards, is at the end of its take-back. Bend the elbow of your racket arm while lifting with your wrist to bring

1 Take up the service stance from the right court holding the racket with the Continental serving grip.

2 Push your weight forwards as you part racket arm and tossing arm. Turn the hitting shoulder so the racket and tossing arms align.

3 Toss the ball up in front and slightly to the right. Bend the racket arm elbow to bring the racket up leaving the left arm pointing at the ball.

4 Drop your racket into the throwing position keeping your elbow high. As the ball begins to fall the left arm begins to drop away to the side.

Positioning your feet

Align your feet so that an imaginary line, joining the toes of your shoes, points towards your target area. The toe of your front foot should point towards the facing net post.

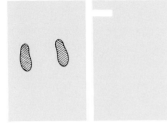

The toss

The ball should be tossed in front, slightly to the right of your leading shoulder, and at least a little higher than you could reach with your racket so that the ball is hit after it has fallen 4 inches or so. Release the ball when your tossing arm is at full stretch, when a diagonal line could be drawn from the wrist of the tossing arm, across the shoulders and down the racket arm to the tip of the racket head (see step 2). When the ball is at its peak the racket head points upwards.

the racket head up. At the peak of the toss drop the racket head into the throwing position behind your back. Straighten your legs pushing your weight upwards and forwards behind the racket arm as you throw the racket head up.

5 Straighten your legs as you snap your wrist throwing the racket head up to meet the ball when it has fallen 4-6 in.

6 Strike the ball with the racket arm at full stretch and weight well over the front foot.

7 As forward momentum continues and rear foot passes front foot, keep the racket swinging in the direction of your selected target area.

8 Follow through, the racket swinging down past the left side of your body and your right foot coming down firmly for a balanced finish.

Improving your stroke

It is essential to join each of the key features of the service stroke into a fluent, powerful movement. Preparation for the swing at the ball includes taking the racket back and lifting it into the throwing position between your shoulder blades as you toss the ball. Keep your hitting elbow high and your arm and racket away from your body. This is the trigger for the hitting thrust at the ball, shown right. As the racket head approaches the ball it must gather maximum speed with legs, shoulders, hitting arm and wrist all playing their parts.

Take-back
The inside of your hitting wrist and the hitting face of your racket should point towards the court surface at the end of the take-back.

A **Hitting platform** Push your front hip forwards as you move your weight over your bent front knee, stabilizing your front foot.

B **Hitting shoulder** The back shoulder must turn in to add its power to the hit as the racket head is thrown up to meet the ball. Turning the hitting shoulder too early or too late will waste this power.

C **Hitting zone** Keep your head up with your eyes on the ball. At the hit the wrist should snap forwards to present the strings to the back of the ball, with an up, through and over action.

D **Follow through** Let the racket arc past your left leg as your momentum carries you forwards onto your right foot which has swung through across the baseline.

Rhythm and timing

The rhythm of your service directly affects your timing and the effectiveness of your serving. Find out your own natural serving rhythm following the general principle of beginning slowly and finishing with maximum racket head speed just before impact.

Although a continuous rhythm is vital, there should be a feeling of pause after the racket has been taken up and prior to dropping it into the throwing position. If your racket is brought into the throwing position too soon in the course of the stroke it will stay there too long and all the momentum built up will be lost. If you feel that

you do not have enough time to drop the racket head low enough, place your ball a little higher.

I encourage rhythmical serving by repeating various set commands to my pupils throughout their services in the rhythm that suits them best. "Down, up and hit" is most useful, with emphasis on "UP" and "HIT". You can say this to yourself: "Down" as you begin the movement; "UP" to coincide with the toss and taking the racket back and up; "and" should coincide with the feeling of pause when the ball is up and the racket is dropping into the throwing position, and "HIT" when the racket springs up.

Practicing on your own

Off court, you can usefully develop your basic serving technique with a backboard. Stand 15 to 20 feet from the wall and use a line at net height to gauge your aim. Concentrate on each key feature of the stroke individually as you serve ball after ball. Practice timing the hit so that you hit the ball on the sweet spot (see p.272).

On court, place a target such as a ball box, racket head cover or tin, in the forehand and backhand corners of both the right and left service courts, and one in the middle of each service court just inside the service line. Take a bucket of balls to the opposite end of the court and take up your service stance to the right of the centermark. Serve half of your balls into the right service court, aiming a pair of balls at each of the three targets in turn, starting with the target in the backhand corner for an imaginary right-handed receiver. Repeat this until you run out of balls then serve the other half of your balls in the same sequence from the left of the centermark to the left service court.

Practice wall
When using a backboard to improve your service stroke use wall markings to make the practice as realistic as possible. As well as a line at net height, mark a net band so that you can judge service courts.

Serving at targets
Serving at targets, as shown right, is a good way of improving your stroke and measuring your progress. Keep a notebook for recording your target hits and concentrate on the targets that you most often miss.

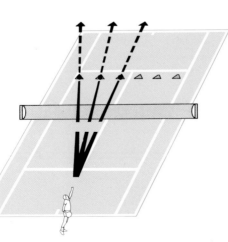

Practicing the toss

Take up your serving stance on court with a racket head cover placed 12 to 14 in inside the baseline, exactly where the ball would land if you did not hit it. Perform the first half of your stroke, really stretching as you toss the ball in front and just to the right of your tossing shoulder for the basic service. Reach as far as you can with your racket held in your tossing hand. Try to release the ball with little or no rotation. Let the ball fall to the ground and persevere until one after another lands on the target in front of you.

As soon as you feel proficient combine the toss with the whole stroke again. Whenever you isolate any part of a stroke for practice, it is best to unite it with the complete stroke as soon as you are able.

Footfaulting

The most common footfault occurs when you step on the baseline with your front foot before hitting the ball. This usually happens when your feet are too close together in your service stance or you are moving your weight too late in the stroke. If, on the contrary, you transfer your weight too soon in the stroke you are likely to footfault with your rear foot as it swings through too early, coming down on, or over, the baseline before you strike the ball. Try keeping your rear foot on the ground for several practice serves, tossing the ball up only fractionally in front. A similar mistiming of weight transfer in the service stroke causes some players to land over the baseline with both feet just before hitting the ball.

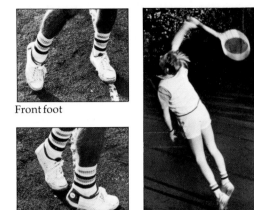

Front foot

Rear foot

Both feet

Using your basic serve

The player with the most consistent first service has a definite advantage in a match provided that his serve possesses speed and accuracy. If you have to rely on too many second serves you will take pressure off your opponent and put it on yourself. Aim at getting 70 per cent of your first serves into play. As the first serves of many top players illustrate, this can best be done by serving with three-quarters power so that both speed and accuracy can be maintained. This type of first server is more feared than the type who serves with full power on his first delivery achieving accurate placement with only one in every five or six balls and all the time wasting precious physical and mental energy.

The speed of your first serve is essential because the flight of the ball is easily read by the receiver if it is not travelling fast enough. This speed requirement makes fast surfaces, like grass, ideal for first serving.

You should be able to place your first serve into the forehand or backhand corner of either service court or straight at your opponent in order to expose a weakness in either a right- or left-handed receiver, or to exert pressure by varying your attack. Being able to choose the direction and length of your first serve with confidence is vital for your success against right-, left- and double-handed players.

Left service court,
right-handed receiver

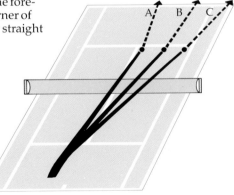

A Forehand
B Body
C Backhand

Right service court,
right-handed receiver

A Forehand
B Body
C Backhand

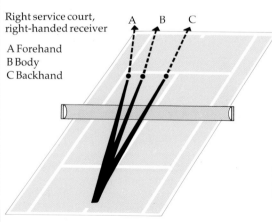

Roscoe Tanner *places the ball characteristically low for his very fast first service. His racket has still to fall into the throwing position before he attacks the ball with a straight racket arm. Notice how Tanner leans well in over his bent front knee and how his hitting shoulder is turned away just enough to unleash its full power at the right moment.*

103

Topspin service

Once mastered, the topspin (see p.42), or American twist, serve is extremely reliable because the spin applied to the ball creates a dipping flight allowing high net clearance. The degrees of speed and spin applied can be varied, making the stroke suitable both for aggressive first serving and especially for consistent second serving. If the spin is not applied strongly enough a topspin serve will simply bounce to an easy height.

Although you can employ the Eastern forehand grip when starting to master the basic serve, you should use the Continental serving grip for the topspin service from the start. The foot positions that you established for the basic service stance have to be slightly altered, so does the toss, the way you arch your back and rotate your body so that the racket face can be brushed sharply up and across the ball at the hit.

Altering your preparation

Stand sideways to the baseline for the topspin service. However, whereas for the basic service a line connecting your toes would project straight at your target, for the topspin service you should withdraw your rear foot a little from this imaginary line. Toss the ball up a little higher than for the basic service and directly above your front shoulder.

◌ Topspin

◌ Basic

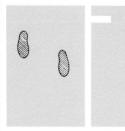

Contrasted tossing techniques
The offset stance and toss of the topspin service make it necessary for you to flex your knees and arch your back more than for the basic service stroke, as shown above and in the diagram, left.

Shape of the shot

The mixture of severe topspin and some sidespin applied to the ball by the topspin service action will make an arcing trajectory, the ball spinning up from the racket and clearing the net by up to 6 feet before dipping into the service court. On bouncing, a good topspin serve will bound forwards as well as breaking to the receiver's left, if you are right-handed, because of the sidespin added to the topspin.

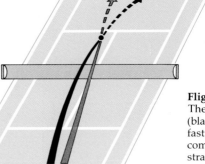

Flight and bounce
The topspin serve (black) breaks high and fast to the receiver's left, compared with the straight flight of the basic service (grey).

Playing the stroke

Begin slowly tossing, letting both racket and place-up arm move down a little together before they part to start the take-up. While your weight is moving forwards over your bent front knee and you are tossing the ball up, let your racket swing down past your body and turn your hitting shoulder away more than you would for a flat service. As you lean in, keep your racket wrist relaxed and let the elbow of your racket arm bend, lifting the racket head up before dropping it into the throwing position as the ball starts to fall. Keep the tossing arm up as long as you can, using it to track the ball. Now straighten your legs, and, at the same time your racket arm, elbow and wrist, sending the racket up almost edge-on so that the strings bite the ball, brushing up and across it.

Your rear foot comes off the ground and will swing forwards as the racket arcs up and out to your right side.

1 Swing the racket down past your body and turn your hitting shoulder well away as you release the ball.

2 Cushion your weight over your bent front knee. Bend the racket arm elbow bringing the racket up.

3 Drop the racket into the throwing position as the ball begins to fall.

4 Straighten your knees powerfully and throw the racket head up almost edge-on to meet the ball.

5 Snap the wrist forwards so that the racket face strikes the ball a glancing blow from below.

6 Completing its up and across action, the racket leaves the ball and arcs up and out to the right as the rear foot begins to swing across the baseline.

Follow through
Follow through with the racket down past the right side. Your back foot will come down inside the court but not so far over the baseline as for the first service.

105

Improving your stroke

Keep sideways to the baseline and tossing shoulder up as you begin to attack the ball. As the racket head approaches the ball, turn your hitting shoulder in sufficiently to add power to the wrist snap which produces most of the spin. If your front shoulder drops early the hitting shoulder will turn in too far bringing your racket face to the top of the ball first and probably dragging it down into the net.

Basic

Topspin

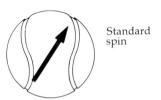

Standard spin

Hitting for topspin

The diagram, left, shows how your racket should be angled at the hit for the topspin serve as compared with the basic, flat serve. Think of the back of the ball as if it were a clock face and hit up and across it from seven o'clock to one o'clock, as shown above, to produce severe topspin and a little sidespin.

Increasing sidespin

To vary your attack you can increase the amount of sidespin that you apply to your topspin serve by hitting from eight o'clock to two o'clock making the ball break more to the side after bouncing.

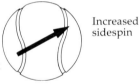

Increased sidespin

Practicing with a partner

Once confident of your topspin serving technique, mark off with tape the half furthest from your serving position of both service courts and, using 40 balls, serve half into each court. Aim into the limited area while your practice partner marks off the landing positions of each of your attempts on a map of the court. When you can serve all of the balls into half-court targets, divide the service courts into progressively smaller areas down to the corner eighths.

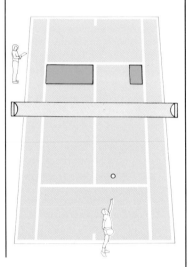

Practicing on your own

You will need to devote a lot of time at the beginning to developing the brushing action of the strings up the back of the ball. Once you have the feeling that the more you sweep up and across the ball the more consistent your serve is, raise the net above its correct height to its full height, and then thread some rackets with their head covers on through the net to provide an even higher barrier, as shown right. You will find it very encouraging to discover that you can serve over this barrier and still get the ball to dip down into the service court.

Using your topspin service

The topspin serve is the most consistent one that a player can use. Practically all of today's top men players use it as their main second serve in the singles game and as their major serve for both first and second serving in the doubles game where reliable first serving for serve and volley strategy (see p.204) is essential. An effective spin second serve in singles play will allow you to go for more winners with your first ball, safe in the knowledge that your opponent will not hit winning shots, or at least returns which will force errors, off your second delivery. Vary the amount of sidespin you apply and aim towards any weakness, as for your first service.

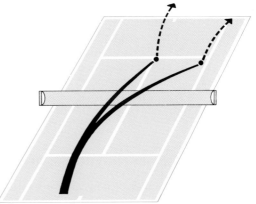

Right court topspin services

Left court topspin serves

Gabriela Sabatini finishes an aggressive topspin service, as her right foot swings through across the baseline for the first step of her forward run. She has left the ground in delivering this serve, but has maintained a sideways on position throughout the hitting zone, and even in the follow through her left shoulder is controlling the degree of upper body turn towards the net.

Slice serve

The slice serve is hit with sidespin (making the ball swerve) and only a little topspin added by virtue of the basic upwards hitting action which is part of all serving. It is principally a second service in which role it is reliable and often used as a very necessary variant to the topspin service. The slice serve is favored by many women players and quite a few men because it continues to swerve and stays low after the bounce. Like the topspin serve, the slice serve can be used as a first service if you find that you are not getting enough balls in to make flat first serving worthwhile. By hitting the ball aggressively with slightly more speed and less spin than you would if you were making a second delivery, the slice serve can be consistently effective with a higher percentage of first balls finding the service court, as John McEnroe and Martina Navratilova have shown at the highest level of play.

Concentrate on placing the ball up accurately so that the racket strings can travel on a curving line through the hitting zone. As with the topspin service, you should use the Continental grip (see p.39).

The stroke

Alter your serving stance from the basic serving stance only slightly, as shown opposite, by moving your rear foot a fraction back from your line of aim. The ball must be tossed to the right of your front shoulder and not as far in front as for the basic first serving.

The line of the racket path through the hitting zone should be from right to left. As you attack from the throwing position snap your wrist forwards sending the racket head away almost edge-on, hitting the ball just below center on its right side. After contact let your racket continue outwards around the ball before it follows through down past your left leg.

1 Toss the ball forwards and a little to the right.

2 Turn your hitting shoulder away and cushion your weight over your front knee.

3 Keep your racket elbow high as the racket head falls deep into the throwing position.

4 Weight transferred forwards and upwards as your knees straighten and you throw the racket head edge-on to the ball.

Follow through
The slice serve stroke finishes with the racket past your left side similar to the basic first service.

Altering your preparation

The preparation for a slice serve, shown in the picture below, is only slightly different from that for a basic, flat serve. The diagram, right, clarifies the differences. Look at the foot positions diagram, below right, and you will see how for a slice service you should move your rear foot back a little from the basic service stance, then place the ball up about 6 in to the right of your front shoulder.

basic   slice

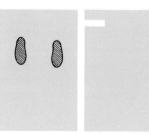

Improving your stroke

To achieve the correct alignment prior to hitting the ball for a slice serve, you must turn your shoulders more than for a basic, flat serve when getting into the throwing position, but not so much as for the topspin serve.

Get the feeling of brushing the strings strongly up, across and around the right-hand side of the ball. At the hit you must turn the racket face slightly away from edge-on to the ball or you will hit the ball with the racket frame. The diagram, right, shows the angle of the racket at the hit for a slice service compared with the angle for a basic, flat service.

slice   basic

Hitting for slice
To apply sidespin and a little topspin to the ball for a slice service you must hit up and around the outside of the ball.

Practicing

Follow the same practice method as for the other services, first trying the whole stroke, then concentrating on components of the stroke. Remember that each part which you separate for conscious practice must be worked back in as part of the whole stroke again before going on to the next.

To develop effective match-play accuracy, go on court with a basket of balls and try the practice shown below. When a ball is slice served into the right service court to a right-handed opponent's forehand the swerve and break will take him well outside his doubles sideline to make the return, and that by slice serving down the center of the court the ball can be made to swerve viciously into the receiver's body. Mark a box in the forehand and backhand corners of the service courts and place targets at the four points shown below, where the ball should bounce for the second time. Serve into each court, to both sides, aiming to hit first and second targets with each service.

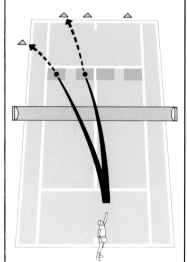

Using your slice serve

The court diagrams below show slice serves to the forehand and backhand in both right and left service courts. For a right-handed opponent the slice serve can be swerved very wide to the forehand side in the right service court, as shown. If your match strategy is to win by testing your opponent's mobility and stamina then this tactic is useful, as the receiver will have to move very quickly to recover an effective court position after playing a difficult return. Aimed at the backhand in the same court, the ball will swerve into your opponent's body. This tactic is useful for forcing errors, especially when mixed with flat or topspin serves to the same flank.

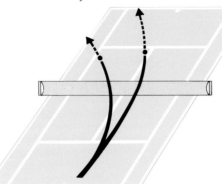

Right court

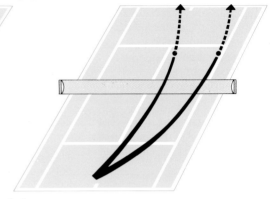

Left court

John McEnroe straightens his legs powerfully as he starts to hurl his racket head up to hit out and round the ball. His attack will apply the powerful, swerving slice for which he is renowned. McEnroe's concentration on the ball will not falter as his racket travels through the hitting zone. The sideways position is characteristic of all spin serving at the delivery stage.

Reverse services

Reverse serves are now only occasionally introduced by top players in exhibition matches. The reverse topspin service carries a combination of topspin and sidespin opposite to that of the topspin service (see p. 104). The reverse slice service carries opposite sidespin compared with the orthodox slice service (see p.108) so that the ball leaves the right-handed server's racket rotating counterclockwise. Use the Western forehand and backhand grips respectively.

Western forehand grip

The unorthodox Western forehand grip (see p. 39) presents the racket face at the correct angle for reverse topspin serving. For the reverse slice serve you will find the Western backhand grip ("V" on the rear plane) more suitable.

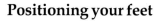

Reverse topspin service

The awkward looking shape of the reverse topspin serve stroke, shown right, produces topspin and the opposite sidespin than that applied to the normal topspin serve. From the square-to-the-net stance, shown far right, toss the ball in front, and slightly to your right, to just above head height. At the same time swing your racket down past your right side with the hitting face of the strings facing downwards. Rotating your hitting wrist, brush the racket head sharply up and across the back of the ball. Finish with the hitting face aiming forwards.

Positioning your feet

The reverse topspin serve breaks after the bounce in the opposite direction to the normal topspin service (see p. 104). As a right-hander you can use it to reproduce the left-handed topspin service from the left court. Start the preparation by adopting the stance, below.

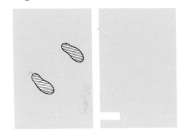

Reverse slice service

The reverse slice service stroke, shown right, has a conventional throwing service shape. As you toss the ball, take the racket up into the service throwing position using the abbreviated action employed for the smash (see p. 161), and shift your weight on to the left foot. Throw the racket head up almost edge on to slice round the inside edge of the ball rather than the outside edge of it. Meet the ball in front of the body, and follow through to finish past your right side again as your rear foot swings through.

Positioning your feet

The best use of the reverse slice serve for a right-handed player is from the left court to a right-handed receiver's backhand. Start by standing as shown below, with both toes pointing towards the baseline.

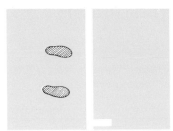

Underarm serve

Underarm serving has no place in the higher levels of tennis, but at lower levels there are a surprising number of underarm services delivered for a variety of reasons. Underarm serving is an effective method for beginners who want to start playing and enjoying the game while they are still learning an overhead serve. For a player with an injured shoulder, or some other disability, serving underarm may be the only way of participating. When undercut, shown below right, the ball can be made to swerve sharply to the receiver's left and stay low after the bounce. Use the basic forehand drive preparation (see p. 46) and a similar sideways stance, as shown below.

Basic underarm service

Toss the ball to your right, to about head height, as you take your racket back at waist height with your weight over your rear foot. Transfer your weight on to your front foot as you swing the racket slightly up through the ball, meeting it at waist level opposite your leading hip. Follow through as you would for a basic forehand stroke, keeping your wrist firm.

Underarm cut service

If you are serious about the use of the underarm serve in your game, the cut variation, shown below, will have more effect on your opponent's timing. The ball will swerve sharply from left to right through sidespin applied by cutting the racket face across and inside the back of the ball. Take the racket back higher than for the basic underarm serve, with the racket face angled back slightly (bottom edge leading). Swing down sharply across and under the ball's flight and follow through across the body, keeping your wrist action and racket face under complete control as you apply underspin and sidespin.

Placing the ball

When you place the ball for an underarm service, make sure that you do not let the ball bounce before you hit it as this would be a foul under rule seven (see p. 276). Simply let the ball drop from your non-playing hand to meet the racket.

Positioning your feet

For the basic underarm service, simply position yourself a ball's width behind the baseline in a sideways forehand driving position. For the undercut version, move your front foot back a little, as shown right, so that you are slightly more square.

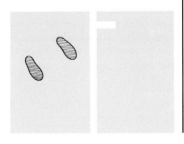

VOLLEY

The volley is a short, punched stroke, played against the ball before it bounces on your side of the net and usually before it falls below net height. The basic punching action of the volley is shown on page 33. This short, sharp, uncomplicated movement forms the foundation of all volleying, both forehand and backhand. The function of the volley is to give your opponent as little time as possible to play his next shot, and with this in mind many players make the mistake of trying to hit the ball as hard as possible. As you move up the court to volley there is certainly not enough time to make an unwieldy attempt to hit the ball hard.

Your choice of grip will depend on the stage you are at. If you are a beginner, use your normal groundstroke grips. The Eastern forehand and backhand grips will be particularly useful for racket control because of the wrist firmness they naturally produce. However, the speed of exchanges in the net area can be so fast in top class tennis that you must change to one-grip volleying as you improve your standard. There will simply be no time for grip changing. The grip to use is the Continental, shown right, the same grip required for serving. Using the same grip for serving and volleying will simplify your serve and volley strategy (see pp. 204-207).

An essential part of volleying is the shoulder turn, shown right. Where possible, combine this with stepping forwards and across with the front foot, to get all your weight behind your volley. When there is no time for footwork, pivot from your hip so that your shoulders are turned, getting the top half of your body sideways to the net.

Other volleys, such as the drive, stop, drop and soft volleys, are described on the following pages.

Continental grip

The Continental grip (see p. 39) is particularly suitable for volleying. The fingers are spread up and behind the handle, forming a sensitive grip which will give you flexible control of your racket face, and feel for the ball.

Keeping your side to the ball

Forehand preparation

Volley ready position

Backhand preparation

Pivot your hips so that your shoulders are aligned to the ball. The backhand position involves a greater shoulder turning movement, so make sure that you allow enough time to prepare for this stroke.

Forehand volley

The basic forehand volley is played with the racket presented almost flat to the ball with only a little controlling underspin. As with all volleys, its basic action consists of punching the racket head at the ball, the punching action being slightly down but very much through the back of the ball. The sequence of the basic forehand volley is shown below, from preparation to the follow through. At the outset use the Eastern forehand grip (see p.38). Although this will involve a grip-change when volleying on the backhand side, it will give you the advantage of using a familiar grip while learning a new stroke. As you gain confidence and experience, however, you should use the Continental grip as described on the previous page. The finger spread of the Continental grip will give you increased "feel" for the ball which is most suitable for controlled forehand volleying.

Having mastered your grip and shoulder turn techniques, there are other points you will have to concentrate on, such as foot-work, the take-back and the hitting zone. Once you have learned the basic forehand volley, you can then adapt it to suit different situations as in the high, low and angled volleys, described on page 117.

Playing the stroke

Prepare for the stroke by turning on your right foot until your racket is brought back level with, or a little behind, your playing shoulder and your weight placed over your bent rear knee. When punching the racket head forwards, meet the ball with the full face of the strings and hit right through the back of the ball. The slightly downward path of the forward stroke will give a little underspin to your volley, providing extra control. Keep your playing elbow away from your body as you punch; keep your racket head up. Your rear foot should come forwards when you complete the stroke.

1 Move your weight fully on to your rear foot and complete a short take-back.

2 Step in with your left foot, transferring your weight. Keeping your wrist firm, punch the ball with the racket head.

3 Follow through a short distance in the direction of the ball's flight.

Footwork

Footwork is all-important for aiding racket and ball control. The three examples shown below illustrate how the basic principle of stepping in can be adapted to suit different situations. However extreme your footwork must be to reach a ball, always try to transfer your weight forwards as you make your volley.

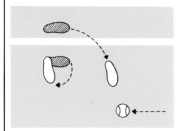

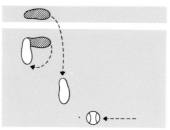

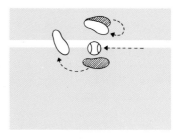

Ideal ball
Turn on your right foot and step forwards with your left foot parallel to the line of flight of the ball.

Wide ball
Anticipate the ball by stepping right across with your left foot as soon as you realize the ball is wide.

Ball straight at you
Pivot on your left foot, stepping back with your right foot to get sideways before leaning into the stroke to play the ball.

Improving your stroke

The effectiveness of your forehand volley will be improved by concentrating on certain factors shown right. The take-back is a vital part of preparing the racket for volleying. You should not take your racket much further back than level with your playing shoulder. By carrying the racket in the ready position and thinking of the preparation as simply turning to the side you will be able to play forwards to the ball consistently. Use the tips in the practice section (p.117) to make best use of the little time you have preparing to volley. When playing the stroke present the full face of the string to the ball and punch the racket head forwards and slightly down through the back of the ball between hip and shoulder height. Keep your wrist really firm and always aim to keep your racket head up above the level of your wrist. Your racket head should stay with the ball for a short distance after impact. Although the follow through is very short, it is necessary for control.

A **Take-back** There is no loop. The volley take-back should be as short as possible so that you have maximum time to position yourself and play the stroke.

B **Hitting zone** This should begin in front of your rear hip and end just ahead of your leading hip. Squeeze your grip for maximum control of the racket face.

Building the forehand volley into your game

Once you have mastered the forehand volley, learn how to adapt it to suit the different types of volley which you may have to make. The three most important – high, low and angled – are described below. When playing high volleys it is vital to have your side towards the ball; otherwise you may pull the ball down into the net or hit it out over the sidelines. Angled volleys should be hit well in front of your body with the bottom edge of the racket slightly leading, applying sidespin and underspin for extra control. When returning angled volleys down the sideline, play the ball later with the wrist locked back as you punch down, through and across the back of the ball.

High volley

1 Turn well to the right as soon as you can. Take the racket a little further back and higher than for the basic volley.

2 Step in with your left foot, punching the racket head down and through the ball. Keep your wrist firm, and racket head up.

3 Follow through with the racket head in the direction of the shot.

Low volley

1 Turn right, bending your knees to get down to the low ball.

2 Step in with the left foot. Punch under and through the ball, using underspin to make the ball rise more sharply off the strings.

3 Follow through upwards in the direction of the shot. Keep your head down and your knees bent so that the ball stays low.

Angled volley

1 Turn right, taking the racket back a short way between waist and shoulder height. Keep your wrist firm and your racket head up.

2 With the bottom edge of the racket leading slightly, punch the racket head well forwards and around the outside of the ball, applying sidespin and underspin.

3 Allow the racket to follow through in the direction of the shot, which should be crosscourt.

Practicing on your own

Regular volleying against a backboard is an ideal way to develop your forehand volley punching action. Stand about 6 feet from the wall and practice turning, stepping forwards and punching the ball against the wall with your racket. (At first practice the shot by standing sideways between shots.) Stay close to the wall to limit your take-back and try to volley the rebounds quickly, aiming for a 20-shot rally. Use a target circle as shown in the picture below.

Using a target circle
Volleying into a target circle will strengthen your wrist and develop control and accuracy.

Practicing with a partner

Take up the ready position with your back against a backboard. Have your partner stand about 10 feet away and throw balls underarm to your forehand volley. Your take-back will automatically be restricted by the wall, which will encourage you to play forwards in good time. Then practice on court from your respective volley positions on either side of the net. Take turns feeding balls to each other at increasing speeds, progressing to a volley rally. Keep the emphasis on quick reaction, fast footwork when turning and stepping in, and minimum take-back. Let your non-playing hand come away from the racket as you turn and really step in as you punch the racket head down and through the ball.

Restricting your take-back
Take turns feeding balls. A barrier close behind the stroke-maker will encourage a limited take-back.

Using your forehand volley

The main objective in a tennis rally is to put your opponent at a disadvantage by hitting the ball as far out of reach as possible. The easiest way to do this is from the net position, so gain this whenever possible. At net, you have two main choices on the forehand side: to play your volley down the sideline – as deep as you can – or to play a low crosscourt shot deep to the baseline, or angled sharply to land short of your opponent's service line. As much as possible do not attempt to play low volleys down the line – you will find it more difficult to get net clearance and depth. Whichever alternative you choose, use your attacking forehand volley behind an approach shot or a spin service for maximum effect (see pp.204-207).

Maximum control must be your priority for successful match-play volleying (see p. 204). Whereas the volleyer who uses his Eastern forehand grip is able to hit volleys more severely on the forehand than the Continental gripper, the advanced one-grip volleyer has the advantage of having more time for control on the forehand, especially during a volley rally when there may be no time to change grips at all.

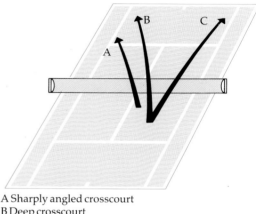

A Sharply angled crosscourt
B Deep crosscourt
C Down the line

Chris Evert Lloyd intercepts a low crosscourt passing shot attempt with a superbly executed forehand volley from below the net. She is at full stretch; her front foot is well across and her extended playing arm controls the racket head perfectly at wrist level as she meets the ball in the middle of the angled racket face.

Forehand drive volley

The forehand drive volley, shown below, is a powerful shot and is at its most effective when played aggressively from mid-court. As its name implies, it is a cross between the forehand drive and the forehand volley, and contains elements of both strokes. The main features the drive volley shares with the normal volley is that it is a shorter stroke than a groundstroke, and the ball is hit before bouncing on the volleyer's side of the net. In other respects, however, it is more similar to the forehand drive: the ball is hit between waist and shoulder height with a swinging action rather than the punching action normally associated with volleying, the racket take-back being wider and more looped. Also, unlike the basic volley, it has added controlling topspin (see p.42). Although the drive volley can be very effective it should be used sparingly because there is always some risk involved in using groundstroke techniques when volleying.

Improving the stroke

The key elements of the stroke are the looped take-back and upward swing of the racket. Position yourself sideways-on to the ball, and, from a shallow looped preparation, swing through the back of the ball as you transfer your bodyweight on to your front foot for increased power. If you lean back or stop your forward movement, the ball will fly out over the baseline or beyond the sideline, so play forwards confidently. The ball is hit between waist and shoulder height with the full face of the racket strings meeting the back of the ball. The forward swing up and through the ball will apply topspin and your stroke will finish above head height.

A Preparation
B Hitting zone
C Follow through

Using your forehand drive volley

The drive volley requires a lot of practice – and skill. It should be used sparingly in match play, and then only on the right sort of ball. Your best alternatives, shown right, are to play this stroke deep to the center and corners of the baseline, or angled crosscourt. Choose slow-moving, high balls to drive volley from the mid-court area, playing them from about shoulder height. When the shot is timed perfectly, its power will have a demoralizing effect. If your opponent can attempt a volley return, he will have to cope with a dipping ball and awkward spin off the racket face as he hits the ball.

A Deep drive volleys

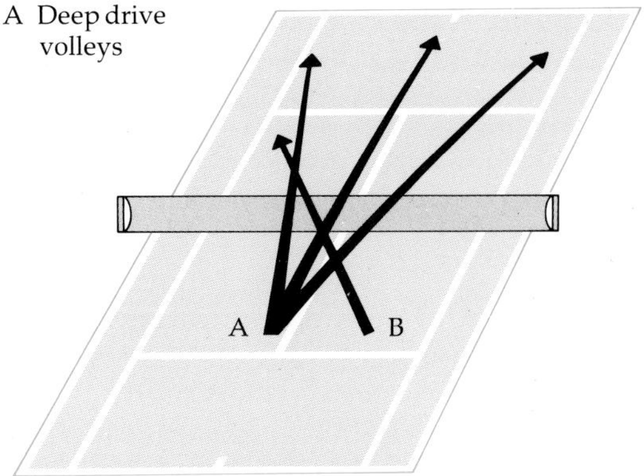

B Angled crosscourt drive volley

Forehand stop and drop volleys

The forehand stop and drop volleys are both essentially touch strokes, designed to drop the ball gently over the net and leave your opponent stranded on the baseline. The main differences between them are that the stop volley is played off a fast ball and the drop volley off a slow ball, and that the stop volley has slightly more underspin. In the stop volley, the racket is withdrawn a little at impact and the racket head comes down under the ball with the bottom edge leading, so that severe underspin is applied to the ball

before it is released. The ball then rebounds enough to land just over the net and then, because of the spin applied, bounces like a lead weight. There is virtually no follow through of the racket.

When playing the drop volley, however, the racket need not be withdrawn on contact the strings are slid down the back of and underneath the ball. Because the drop volley is played off a slow-moving ball, the follow through of the racket has to be longer than for the stop volley to guide the ball.

Improving the stroke

There is no racket take-back when preparing for the shot; your racket head should be up and in line with the ball. Step forwards and across with your front foot, transferring your weight as early as you can, and blocking the ball's path ahead of your leading shoulder with your racket face. Hit the ball with the bottom edge of your racket leading, so that the strings come down the back of, and slightly under, the ball. If you hit the ball too high, so that it takes too long to reach its destination, then you are probably tilting your racket face back too much; if the ball repeatedly lands in the net, try opening the racket face more.

A **Hitting zone** Slide the racket face under the ball. To stop a fast ball, do not follow through. Slightly withdraw the strings, turning the racket face further under the ball for increased controlling underspin.

B **Follow through** When playing a slow-moving ball, end the stroke with a very short follow through for more control.

Using the strokes

The stop and drop volleys can be exciting winning shots. Play them from your normal volleying positions in the net area, when your opponent is either stranded behind his baseline or out beyond one of his sidelines, and in no position to reach your touch shots. Hit them at a slight angle to right or left, making sure that they do not land too far into your opponent's court; otherwise he may be able to reply with a passing shot. Use the stop volley to return fiercely hit drives which you can only just reach. Played at the right time, when you are a point or two in the lead, stop and drop volleys can have a demoralizing effect on a tiring opponent.

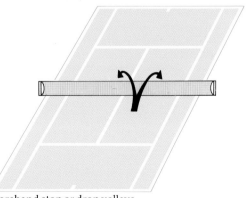

Forehand stop or drop volleys

Forehand soft volley

The forehand soft volley is a touch shot which is played as a shortened version of the basic forehand (see pp.46-51). It has a shorter racket take-back than the groundstroke, but is played with a similar low to high swing applying a gentle topspin to the ball which will help it to dip over the net. It is usually played off a low ball which, in turn, must be kept low over the net to your opponent's feet, forcing him to play a high return which is easily dealt with, or angled wide.

Get down low with a short racket take-back as you turn your side to the ball. Step in, swinging the racket up gently underneath the ball. You must angle the racket face with the bottom edge leading to get the ball over the net, and allow the lift in your forward swing to apply the topspin.

Double-handed forehand volley

The double-handed forehand volley is a cramped stroke. The lack of reach which the grip imposes can make defending difficult. The disadvantages of the stroke are most easily negated in doubles play, as has been exemplified by the South African, Frew McMillan. The double-handed technique comes into its own when playing short, high balls, especially when punching aggressive volleys from mid-court, against balls which would force single-handed players to defend.

Double-handed forehand grip

Your dominant hand should be placed on top using the Eastern forehand grip. The supporting hand, at the butt end of the racket, should be between the Continental and backhand grips (see p.39).

Frew McMillan drive volleys a ball hard between his opponents off his forehand side during a net exchange. The speed of shot will win the point.

Backhand volley

The backhand volley must have all the attacking qualities of the forehand volley. The backhand volley is a simpler stroke than the forehand volley because with your side to the net your playing arm is already well in front. Your grip will depend on your ability. If you are a beginner two grips, one for forehand, and the Eastern backhand grip (see p.38) for your backhand volleying. If you have progressed to one-grip volleying, use the Continental grip (see p.113).

The sequence of the backhand volley is shown below, from preparation to follow through. To develop an effective backhand volleying technique concentrate on a short preparation from an alert volley ready position, on shoulder turn so that at least from the waist up, your side is to the ball, on good weight transfer through stepping forwards and across with the front foot and on meeting the ball ahead of the playing shoulder. Finish off your backhand volley with a short follow through in the direction of the shot, keeping the racket head above wrist level. You can adapt this technique to play high, low and angled volleys, as well as drive, stop and drop volleys.

Playing the stroke

From the ready position, with your knees more bent than when playing groundstrokes, and your racket held well up and forwards, start turning to the left as soon as you see the ball is approaching your backhand. Take your racket back slightly above hitting height. Step in with your right foot, punching your racket head forwards so that the full face of the strings meets the ball. Squeeze your grip and lock your wrist as your racket punches through the ball. Your arm should be extended when the shot is completed. The racket face should be slightly angled with the bottom edge leading.

1 Get sideway to the ball and take your racket back level with your left shoulder. Keep your wrist firm.

2 Step in and across with your right foot and punch the racket at the ball so that the full face of the strings meets the ball.

3 Follow through a short distance in the direction of the shot, keeping your racket head steady.

Improving your stroke

As with the forehand volley, the most important elements of the backhand volley are the preparation for the stroke and the hitting zone. Your racket should be taken no further back than your trailing shoulder when preparing for the shot; your elbow should be flexed and your racket head well above wrist level. When playing the stroke, punch crisply down and through the back of the ball. Squeeze your grip, keeping your wrist firm and the racket face steady as you move through the ball starting ahead of the left shoulder and finishing in front of your playing shoulder just after impact.

A **Preparation**
B **Hitting zone**
C **Follow through**

Building the backhand volley into your game

You will have to be just as flexible in your approach to backhand volley play as you are to forehand volleying, being ready to play high, low and angled volleys on this side too. Your success depends on effective footwork. Always step in with the right foot if you have time. For balls coming straight at you, step away with the right foot, pivot on it and bring your left foot back.

High backhand volley

When preparing to play a high volley, take your racket back further and a little higher than for the basic volley. Keeping your non-playing hand at the racket throat will help you to steady the racket and limit its take-back. The line of the stroke will be from high to low. Keep your racket head up in the follow through, to ensure that the ball does not hit the net.

1 Get sideway to the ball and take your racket back further and higher than for the basic volley.

2 Release your non-playing hand and punch the racket head down through the back of the ball.

3 Follow through a short distance in the direction of the shot, finishing at about waist height.

Low backhand volley

Prepare well for the low backhand volley by bending your knees so that your eyes are almost level with the ball's flight. Your racket head should be at wrist level, or slightly above, with the bottom edge leading to allow enough rise off the strings for net clearance. As you release your supporting hand, step forwards and punch through and under the ball. Your rear knee should be almost touching the ground at the hit and follow through.

1 Turn left, bending your knees as you take the racket back.

2 Bottom edge of the racket face leading, step in and punch the racket head under and through the ball, applying underspin.

3 Follow through upwards in the direction of the volley. Keep your knees bent so that the ball stays low after the hit.

Angled backhand volley

Prepare for an angled volley in the same way as for the basic volley, with your non-playing hand at your racket throat. On playing the stroke, the racket head is punched forwards, with the bottom edge leading, around the outside of the ball, applying sidespin as well as underspin to get the angle required. Your wrist should be kept steady as you follow through a short way in the direction of your volley, which will be over the net in a crosscourt direction.

1 Take your racket back a short way with your non-playing hand supporting the racket throat.

2 Punch the racket head forwards, bottom edge leading, around the outside of the ball.

3 Follow through in the direction of the shot, which will be crosscourt. Keep your wrist firm.

Practicing on your own

As with the forehand volley, you can practice the short, crisp, punching action of the backhand volley against a backboard into a target circle. Stand about 6 feet from the wall and practice stepping forwards and punching the ball against the wall with your racket. Keep your wrist firm and your racket head up, and try to volley every rebound from the wall. Start by practicing with your side toward the wall. When you feel confident of your technique, change back to the ready position between strokes. Try to make the ball rebound between waist and shoulder height so that you can keep the ball under control. Hitting the ball with your side to the net will help you to prevent the ball bouncing off the wall at an angle. Practice your forehand and backhand volleys alternately, progressing to a volley rally when you feel confident enough to do so.

Practicing with a partner

Follow the practice exercises for the forehand volley (see p.117), concentrating on the parts of your stroke which may need attention, such as making sure your wrist is firm at impact. You can also practice different types of volley using your partner to feed the right sort of ball to you. A mat may be useful when practicing low volleys: you can let your back knee come down on it when playing the stroke. Take turns driving from the base- line while the other one volleys, then play forehand to forehand before alternating forehand and backhand. Volleying for goals, as shown below, is a good way to end your volleying practice. Take up volleying positions on one side of the court and, using the service lines as goal lines and the corners of opposing service courts as goal posts, try to score goals by volleying the ball past your partner over his goal line but within his baseline.

Volleying for goals
Score goals by volleying the ball past your partner over his goal line, but within his baseline. Do not score with the first shot.

Using your backhand volley

The general strategy of playing shots which will be out of your opponent's reach applies for all volleys, and the backhand volley is no exception. Basically, you should aim to volley deep into your opponent's court, especially when playing your volley from mid-court. If you are nearer the net, angled volleys may well be effective – aim for half- or three-quarter-court angles. Whenever possible, play your volley straight and reserve crosscourt volleying for particularly good shots, as returns are more difficult to make. Low volleys, on the other hand, may have to be played crosscourt to gain sufficient height for net clearance and depth. When playing high volleys, aim to hit them deep. They should be punched confidently with a flat racket face and a firm wrist. The backhand volley will be particularly useful when returning a ball which is unexpectedly coming straight at you and you have no time for footwork – simply pivot from your hips leaning to the side and getting your weight forwards on to your right foot as you play the stroke. As with all other volleys, the backhand volley is more effective from close

range and against balls above net height which can be punched down into the court. Whichever type of volley you choose to play, use it behind an approach shot or behind a spin service in matches (see pp.204-207).

A Angled backhand volley

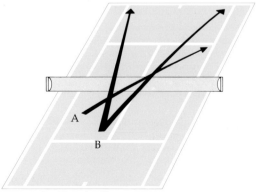

B Deep backhand volleys

125

Backhand drive volley

The backhand drive volley, shown below, is, like the forehand drive volley (see p.119), a shortened version of the backhand ground-stroke. The ball is played above net height, is hit between waist and shoulder height with a swinging action rather than the normal pun-ching action of the volley, and has added controlling topspin. Although forehand drive volleying comes naturally to many players, very few players employ the drive volleying technique on their backhand, un-less they use a double-handed stroke on that side. The same risks of using groundstroke techniques when volleying apply in the backhand as in the forehand, and the back-hand drive volley is therefore rarely used, although it is a useful way of dealing with slow-moving, high balls around the mid-court area. Always play this stroke positively for maximum effect.

Improving your stroke

As in the forehand drive volley, the main elements of the stroke are the loop at the end of the take-back and the upward swing of the racket. Release your non-playing hand and swing the racket forwards and slightly up through the ball, meeting the back of the ball with the full face of the racket strings. The shallow loop formed after the racket take-back will give added power to the stroke, and the forward swing up and through the ball will apply lift and controlling topspin. The stroke should end at about head height, with your wrist firm and your racket head up. Your body should be more sideways to the ball at the completion of the stroke than in the forehand drive volley.

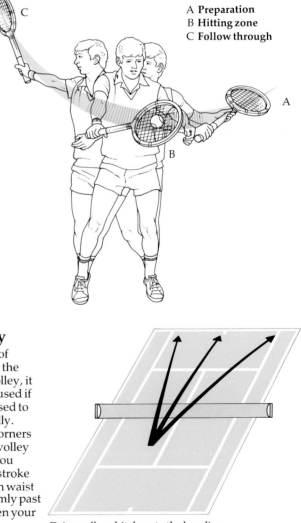

A **Preparation**
B **Hitting zone**
C **Follow through**

Using the backhand drive volley

The backhand drive volley is a useful way of returning slow-moving, high balls around the mid-court area. Like the forehand drive volley, it should be practiced thoroughly, and only used if you really have a flair for it. The stroke is used to its maximum effect when played powerfully. Aim deep to the baseline, or towards the corners of the court, using a more basic backhand volley action when going for angles. Make sure you have adequate time to play the ball as this stroke must not be hurried. Meet the ball between waist and shoulder height, and drive the ball firmly past your singles opponent, or perhaps between your doubles opponents.

Drive volleys hit deep to the baseline

Backhand stop and drop volleys

The backhand stop and drop volleys are, like their equivalents on the forehand (see p.120), touch strokes which are designed to drop the ball gently over the net. The main difference between them is that the stop volley is played off a fast ball and has severe underspin, while the drop volley is played off a slow ball. When playing the stop volley, the racket face is withdrawn slightly at impact with the ball and controlled wrist action slides the bottom edge of the racket head under the ball to apply underspin. This withdrawal, together with arresting your forward movement before impact with the ball, will take the speed off the ball.

Because the ball being returned in the drop volley is a slower moving one, the racket does not need to be withdrawn: the strings are slid down the back of, and underneath, the ball and there is a longer follow through.

Stop volley under pressure

The backhand stop volley can be particularly effective when returning wide, fast balls. Having hit a forehand approach shot down the sideline and moved up court to the right of center covering the down the line pass, you may find your opponent has gone for a half-court angled crosscourt pass which he knows he must hit hard if it is to get past you before you can intercept it. Deal with this situation by stepping quickly to the left, pivoting with your left foot as you prepare to step well across with your right foot and stretch your racket arm to its full extent to get your racket face behind the line of the speeding ball. As the ball meets the racket strings, withdraw the racket slightly and, with a controlled wrist, turn the racket face sharply under the ball to apply underspin (right), which will stop the ball progressing after it has dropped just on your opponent's side of the net in his right-hand service court.

Peter Fleming

Using your backhand stop and drop volleys

Use your backhand stop and drop volleys sparingly, unless you are following a deliberate tactic of tiring your opponent by getting him to run for almost impossible balls. Try to use these types of volley when your opponent is behind the baseline or wide of the opposite sideline, and therefore out of reach of the ball. Whenever possible, play them from well up in the forecourt. They are mainly for use in singles play, although they can be used in doubles if you are sure that neither opponent can reach your shot in time. The stop volley can be a particularly devastating shot when it is used to return fiercely hit drives from your opponent.

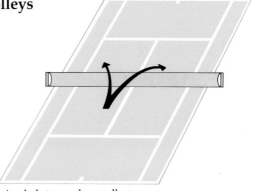

Angled stop or drop volleys

Double-handed backhand volley

Unlike the forehand, the backhand in general lends itself to double-handed play. In volleying, the extra hand on the grip will help you to limit your racket take-back. The extra strength and control provided by using two hands can be particularly useful when playing aggressive strokes, such as the backhand drive volley.

Double-handed backhand grip

Place your playing hand at the butt end of the grip, midway between the Eastern backhand and the Continental grip (see p.39). Position your other hand above the playing hand, with an Eastern forehand grip. Use this grip for all of your two-handed backhand groundstrokes.

Frew McMillan shows how a double-hander can punish balls above net height in the forecourt. The high finish shows that he has stroked aggressively upwards through the back of the ball applying topspin. The stroke has been played positively despite McMillan's position which suggests that he has been drawn wide towards the sideline.

Developing a style: service

The basic or flat service can begin each point and can also end it at the same moment. It is a key weapon in singles. Big servers often rely too heavily on this stroke, and when their timing is off the rest of their game becomes vulnerable. Pancho Gonzales was an outstanding first server who served at three-quarter speed to ensure that most of his first serves found the court. Good first serving is built around taking your time, developing a deep throwing action, and a high-hitting elbow so that maximum racket arm extension and racket head speed can be combined in timing the ball perfectly. Individual characteristics often develop in serving style due to the pressure of match play. The low place-up in Roscoe Tanner's super fast serve stroke is an example.

Boris Becker in full knee-bend position, just before launching himself upwards to meet the falling ball with the full force of his bodyweight for his first service. Becker shows an ideal hitting platform, with feet shoulder-width apart and weight perfectly balanced. The straight place-up arm, drawn-back racket-arm elbow, and skyward pointing racket head typify the technically sound Becker service.

Kathy Jordan times this first serve perfectly. She meets the ball at full stretch, leaning in to attack it with all her body weight behind the hit.

Roscoe Tanner about to launch himself at the ball with all his celebrated power. Note the height of his hitting elbow. Like many top players, Tanner becomes airborne as he thrusts at the ball.

Maria Bueno, opposite, on tip-toe as she times a first serve with grace and power. She is leaning well in, and, at full stretch, her modified Continental grip aids racket head speed.

Throwing position

As Tanner drops his racket head deeper into the throwing position the elbow of the racket arm rises to provide maximum leverage as the upwards thrust begins. This produces tremendous racket head speed.

Bjorn Borg shows model serving technique: his weight has moved forwards so that he can combine an upwards thrust of the legs with the racket head throw.

Topspin service

The second serve must be deep and accurately placed, and allow the server to gain the initiative. The topspin service is best suited to this task. It can also be easily speeded up to play the role of first serve in the modern doubles game of serve and volley play. With correct use of legs, knees, shoulders and wrist, you can spare your back from extreme use. A technically sound topspin service, therefore, can and should be developed by an athletically strong woman – it is not a male prerogative. Alice Marble, Althea Gibson and Billie Jean King have all used this service and, in today's top class game, Jennifer Capriati heads a number of young and top-ranking women who use topspin service.

Vitas Gerulaitis displays perfect topspin serving technique. Well balanced on the balls of both feet, he attacks upwards, with his back not over-arched. From this sideways position the racket strings will brush up and across the back of the ball from lower left to top right, to combine topspin and sidespin.

John Lloyd executing a typical finish to a topspin serve. His back foot is swinging forward as his racket follows through by his right side. Lloyd uses an almost Continental backhand grip for serving. He has stayed sideways as he finishes the stroke to avoid pulling the ball down into the net.

Peter Fleming, right, is preparing for a topspin service in similar style to the Gerulaitis delivery. His height and reach are supported by sound technique. With the ball falling ahead of the left shoulder, this will be a particularly aggressive topspin service.

Sideways to ball

Gerulaitis and Lloyd both show how important it is to maintain the line of the shoulders with the direction of the ball's proposed flight in topspin serving. The arrows show the direction the ball will take, so you can more easily appreciate position relative to ball and court. Lloyd's follow through to the right highlights how the sideway position is maintained in the early follow through, so that the desired angle of deflection is maintained.

Vitas Gerulaitis   John Lloyd

Ilie Nastase completes a topspin serve, and is beginning his run towards the net in true serve and volley style. His racket moves out well to his right as his back foot swings across the baseline. The Continental grip and its wrist-snapping style provide kick and twist to make an advance well worthwhile.

Slice service

John McEnroe has re-established the slice serve as a major threat. It has particular appeal in the modern game, because it can force the opponent outside the court when receiving in the right court (or in the left court by a left-handed server). This opens up the backhand corner of the court for an attacking shot can be made to that area. At the same time the recovering player is under constant danger of being wrong-footed. The topspin serve must kick to be effective, and women who find this difficult would be wise to perfect the lower-bouncing slice.

John McEnroe launches himself into the air to deliver his powerful slice serve. Observe the deep throwing position away from the body and the high-hitting elbow. The extra momentum he gains from his rotational build-up provides an explosive action through the hitting zone.

SLICE SERVE

Martina Navratilova, right, delivering her famous slice serve. She maintains a sideways-on position, and her racket arm will be at full stretch at impact. The racket face is angled to hit the ball at the three o'clock position, giving a slice that will take her opponent out of court. Navratilova's Continental grip allows free wrist action for greater racket-head speed.

Evonne Cawley delivers a slice serve from the right-hand court. Her left foot stays in contact with the ground, and her back foot is swinging through. She will be able to recover quickly behind the baseline, or use this as the first step in a run forwards.

Orthodox style

Conventional slice serving off the front foot, which stays on the ground throughout the delivery, is highlighted by Evonne Cawley.

A The ball is met in the "sweet spot", just below the center of the strings. Mrs Cawley's racket arm is at full stretch.

B The player is now looking ahead, although she has obviously been watching the ball up to the moment of impact.

C The left hand has dropped away to balance as the right shoulder and hip come through to add power to the service.

D The back foot swings through above the base-line, and will come down inside the court before the racket finishes past the left side.

Developing a style: volley

The basic punched volley and its variations epitomize the speed at which the modern game is played. By moving up-court at every opportunity, players such as McEnroe put opponents under constant pressure. Players who favor the Eastern grip for volleying tend to have a more powerful forehand volley, with which they try to dominate the net position when advancing behind their spin serve. One-grip volleyers are in the majority, and the grip which they favor is the modified Continental – close to their backhand grip. This leads to controlled forehand volleying and facilitates angled and stop volleys. It also leaves a greater degree of power for backhand volleying, except when drive volleys are used. Lew Hoad and Rod Laver exemplified this latter volleying style.

Stan Smith plays a low punched first volley from just behind his service line. He has gotten down to the ball so that he can meet it in front of his body. By stepping forwards with his left foot he has given himself an excellent hitting platform, from which he is able to keep his racket head at wrist level.

Ilie Nastase has just played a tantalizing drop volley from immediately behind his service line. His racket face control and balance are perfect, as he watches the outcome of this attempt to catch his opponent unawares. The audacity of Nastase's game is unique.

Hana Mandlikova strides forward to get low for this forehand volley. She is perfectly balanced. Note how her back knee is almost touching the court. Her back is straight and her racket head, held at wrist level, shows the excellent control she is exercising.

Virginia Wade steps across with her front foot to reach and cut off a wide return at full stretch. She will angle her shot for a crosscourt winner. Her Continental one-grip serve and volley style allows her to play around the outside edge of the ball with absolute control. Her power and agility are well shown here.

Rod Laver is here playing an almost identical angled volley to that of Virginia Wade, opposite, but Laver intercepts the ball slightly more in front of his body. In this way he gets more angle for crosscourt placement. The Continental style again allows the racket head to lead round the outside edge of the ball.

Jimmy Connors, using the Eastern grip, dispatches a high ball on the forehand. He goes for his shots at full stretch, with an aggressive approach. Notice how the front foot is well established across the body – vital when volleying balls which have to be reached for.

Frew McMillan plays a deft two-handed volley in reply to a drive aimed towards his body. He has played inside the ball, deflecting it up and over the lowest part of the net with both underspin and sidespin.

Billie Jean King, reacting to a fast reply from her opponent, leaps off the ground to thrust her upper body forwards, punching a forehand volley from above net height. Her balance, although she is air-borne, is flawless – see how her left hand is steadying her through the stroke.

Balance

Close inspection of Tanner's forehand volley shows how well he has distributed his weight. His center of gravity runs over his front foot and up through his shoulders. This allows him to play the ball well in front of his body with perfect control. His head remains steady as he watches the ball's flight over the net.

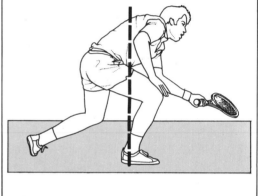

Roscoe Tanner plays a perfect forehand volley from below net level, just inside the service line. He has met the ball well in front of his body. His spread legs and bent knees highlight the extra racket and ball control which comes from lowering the waist to the height of the ball at the moment of impact.

Backhand volley

The one-grip serve and volley player always produces more power with his backhand volley. The minimum of racket preparation is needed before a crisp punch or forwards block with the racket head meets the ball well in front of the body. Many players prefer the backhand volley's naturally short action, especially when they are involved in fast volley rallies at the net. The backhand volleying style of today is markedly similar to that of Bunny Austin in the 1930s. Volleying may develop more slowly among women players than men, but many women today are great volleyers.

Ken Rosewall finishes a basic backhand volley after playing the ball well ahead of his hitting shoulder from a sideways-on position. His rear leg braced him against the impact of the ball. His left hand provides balance. This is a feature of all top-class volleyers – the spare hand plays an important role.

Margaret Court leans on to her back foot, left hand out for balance, to play this difficult low volley. She shows how a tall player can adapt body position and still produce an effective shot with sound racket work, providing balance is maintained through the stroke.

Sandy Mayer, below, completes a superb low volley at full stretch, thanks to a sound Continental grip and use of the correct angle of racket face. The lunge with the front foot has allowed Mayer to meet the ball in front of his body.

Mobility

Mobility is the keynote of Mayer's stretch to intercept an attempted passing shot. Note the angle (almost 45°) of Mayer's step. A lunge sideways would have failed.

Chris Lloyd, right, plays a well-controlled drop volley near the sideline. Her two-handed grip helps her to compensate for being too close to the ball. She has had to stay rather straight-legged, with her racket head lowered below wrist level.

Tracy Austin adapts her backhand drive to play an attacking drive volley in the forecourt. Double-handers like her often prefer to stroke their volleys on this side. whereas very few single-handed players drive volley on the backhand side.

Evonne Cawley, below, reaches almost to the sideline by stepping and extending her racket arm fully. Covering the net in match play requires players to step well across with the front foot if they are to intercept wide balls like this.

Kathy Jordan, above, gets well down for this low backhand volley, but her use of an Eastern-Western forehand grip will create spin rather than pace. Her balance suggests she will successfully return the ball, albeit defensively.

Martina Navratilova moves in to meet the ball above net height. She will be using her Continental volley technique to play around the outside edge of the ball, and angle it sharply across the court, creating a difficult shot for her opponent.

Billie Jean King plays a basic backhand volley shot just ahead of her hitting shoulder. This is sound technique with a good Continental volleying grip, although she could have stepped further towards the ball and met it further in front of her body. Her left hand aids the balance of her weight.

LOB

The lob is the instinctive reply to a hard overhead smash from your opponent. When defending, the ball is hit, or sometimes just deflected, high in the air over the net to land deep into your opponent's court within 6 feet of the baseline. Used mainly in defence, the lob will give you time to recover when you have been caught out of position or are under attack from a net-rushing opponent. The lob can be used offensively to break up a baseline or volley attack (see pp.216-217), and very occasionally in a game the lob can be played as an outright point winner. Learn to lob high and deep when you are defending, and just out of your opponent's reach when you are attacking.

The lob is very much a part of doubles play where passing shots are not so easily made, but it is still only sparingly used in the singles game where it generally receives little attention and where any player who consistently employs it is labelled a "moon-baller". As soon as any player, however, is exposed to extreme pressure he should resort to the lob. You must perfect your lobbing if only for these occasions. Your lobbing should be good enough to utilize opportunities other than emergencies.

Basic, topspin and underspin lobs, and the lobbed half-volley and lob volley, are shown on the following pages. Be sure to master the basic lob before passing on to the variations, using the Eastern forehand and Eastern backhand grips for the groundstroke lobs, as shown below.

Contrasted flight paths

The difference in the trajectories of basic, topspin and underspin lobs is highlighted below. The basic lob, with its minimal topspin, should be varied, but generally travels some 25 feet over the net in an even arc. The back-spinning ball in the defensive underspin lob is hit higher, perhaps reaching 30 feet, and floats before falling to the court. The topspun ball arcs lower – 15 to 20 feet over the net – and travels faster.

Choosing your grips

Except for the lob volley, the lobs are groundstrokes and should therefore be played using your groundstroking grips – the Eastern forehand and backhand grips shown right (see p.38). The firm-wristed control promoted by the Eastern grips is particularly effective for basic lobbing techniques.

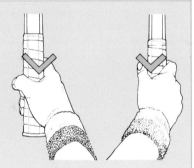

A Underspin
B Basic
C Topspin

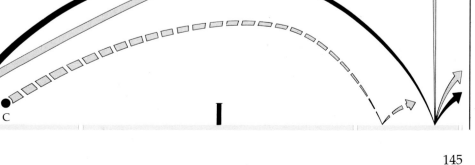

Basic forehand lob

The basic forehand lob is normally played from the baseline area and, in terms of grip and stroke preparation, is similar to the basic forehand drive (see p. 46). There is a similar stroking action for both but, as the ball has a greater distance to travel in the lob than in the normal groundstroke, a fuller stroke is used, with emphasis on a low preparation and a high follow through.

The basic forehand lob is played with a small degree of topspin which is applied mainly by the steep upwards path of the racket in the forwards swing. Slow forwards rotation of the ball will aid control and help you to limit the depth of your lob. The ball is hit with the bottom edge of the racket face leading, to apply lift and make it travel high in the air. The racket should stay with the ball, finishing with a high follow through which should, ideally, drop the ball within 6 feet of your opponent's baseline.

The basic forehand lob is used mainly as a defensive stroke, and in particular as a reply to the overhead smash, but can also be used offensively, to break up a combined baseline and volley rally.

The sequence of the basic lob is shown below. Perfect the stroke by regularly following the practice exercises described. Once you have mastered the basic forehand lob, you can then progress to the topspin, underspin and other variations.

Playing the stroke

Prepare for the stroke in the same way as for the forehand drive (see p. 48), using your Eastern forehand grip. At the end of the racket take-back relax the elbow of your playing arm and allow a low loop to form for extra lift. Step in with your left foot and swing your racket head, bottom edge leading, out and up through the ball, meeting it opposite your leading hip. Your racket should finish well above head height, with your rear foot acting as a stabilizer.

1 Turn on your right foot as you take the racket back, getting sideways-on.

2 Relax your playing elbow and form a low loop with the racket as you step in.

3 Swing the racket head up through the ball with your left hand still held out slightly for balance.

4 Complete your follow through with the racket well above head height and rear foot balancing.

Improving your stroke

The key elements of the basic forehand lob are the hitting zone and the follow through. As you play the ball let your knees straighten and make sure that your weight is well forwards: if you lean back and play off your rear foot your lob will probably fall short. Your right foot should act as a stabilizer throughout the hitting zone and follow through. Steadying yourself in this way will keep you on balance throughout the stroke.

As you make the forward swing, hold the left hand out for balance and hit the ball with the bottom edge of your racket head leading to aid the lifting action. Do not, however, open (tilt back) the racket face too far or again your lobs will most likely fall short. Squeeze your grip at impact, keeping your wrist steady for complete control as you swing from very low to high and time your forwards and upwards swing to meet the ball at about waist height as it falls. The lob follow through is very distinctive, with the legs straightening as you transfer your weight forwards and upwards in the direction of the ball, and racket head high.

A **Hitting zone** Make sure that you meet the ball with your weight mainly over your front foot while you use your rear foot to steady yourself. Squeeze your grip as the racket head travels steeply through the hitting zone. Remember that you need only tilt the racket face back slightly as you require some controlling topspin to be applied to the ball for a basic lob.

B **Follow through** As your racket swings through, keep the racket head up and let it follow in the direction of the soaring ball. Your racket will finish above head height, as shown above.

Lobbing under pressure

It will be difficult to use the full forehand lob stroke when countering a hard, fast smash. In this situation there is no time for a full preparation nor a lengthy follow through. Modify your preparation, as shown right, shortening it so that you have time to play the forwards swing without snatching at the ball. As the approaching smashed ball will have a great deal of pace already, simply play forwards and underneath the ball with a slightly tilted racket face, deflecting the ball sharply into the air.

Typical forehand lob preparation

Shortened preparation

147

Basic backhand lob

Since the lob is generally used as a defensive stroke it lends itself naturally to the backhand. The preparation for the stroke is the same as for the backhand groundstroke with the racket forming a similar deep loop after the low take-back. The stroke is played with a slight degree of topspin which is mainly applied by the steep upward swing of the racket, ending with a long follow through and high finish. The ball is hit with the bottom edge of the racket face leading to provide lift and control. Use your Eastern backhand grip, changing from your forehand by feel as you begin your stroke preparation, just as you would during an ordinary groundstroke rally. The sequence of the backhand lob is shown below, from the takeback to the follow through. Follow the practice exercises described on page 150 to perfect the stroke.

Playing the stroke

Take up your normal ready position behind the baseline. Turning to your left change to your backhand grip and take your racket back at or below hitting height with your non-playing hand still supporting the racket at the throat after the grip change. With your weight moving on to your rear (left) foot get your shoulders well round to the ball, preparing your racket back past your rear hip before releasing your spare hand and relaxing your elbow to produce a low loop for added lift. As your racket arm starts to unwind, transfer your bodyweight on to your front foot by stepping in parallel to the ball's flight. Swing the racket head out and up through the ball, with its bottom edge leading, and meet the ball just ahead of your right hip.

1 Using your backhand grip, take your racket back at or below the hitting height turning your shoulders.

2 Form a low loop with your racket. Step in with your right foot and swing your racket steeply up towards the ball.

3 Having made contact at waist height, swing your racket head up through the ball, straightening your legs.

4 With your weight over your front foot, finish with your racket above head height as the follow through is completed.

Improving your stroke

The key elements of the back-hand lob are the preparation, hitting zone and follow through. Make the change from your forehand grip to your backhand grip as you begin to prepare for the stroke, taking your racket back at or below hitting height as you begin to turn to your left. Get your shoulders well around to the ball as you take your racket back still further and your bodyweight moves on to your rear (left) foot. Release your non-playing hand as you form a deep loop with the racket head so that it can be brought steeply up towards the ball to apply a little topspin. The ball is hit with the bottom edge of the racket face leading to provide extra lift and control. The racket should meet the ball at about waist height and just ahead of the leading hip, and the front knee should begin to straighten to add to the lifting effect as the racket swings up and through the ball finishing above head height as the follow through is completed. The rear foot should keep contact with the court and act as a stabilizer throughout the hitting zone and the follow through before the ready position is regained.

A **Preparation** Change from your forehand to your backhand grip as you begin to prepare for the stroke. Your shoulders should be turned well around to the ball as your playing elbow relaxes to allow the racket to form a loop.

B **Hitting zone** The racket head is swung steeply up and through the ball to apply the required topspin. The bottom edge of the racket face

should be slightly leading as it meets the ball at about waist height and just ahead of the right hip.

C **Follow through** The racket should finish above head height as the follow through is completed. The rear foot acts as a stabilizer throughout the hitting zone and the follow through.

Lobbing under pressure

As when playing the forehand lob, you may sometimes find yourself under pressure, with no time to make a full racket preparation for the basic backhand lob, and so you may have to shorten your normal take-back. The modified, short take-back for a pressure situation is compared with a normal take-back, right. In the modified version of the stroke, there is only limited shoulder turn. The racket head simply intercepts and deflects the smashed ball, staying with it for a shorter time after the hit.

Typical backhand lob preparation

Shortened preparation

Practicing on your own

Go to one end of the court and mark a line 6 feet within the baseline, as shown right. Take up your ready position behind the baseline at the other end of the court and systematically lob balls on the forehand high and deep into the court so that they land within the area you have marked out. Drop a ball out to your side and practice swinging your slightly tilted racket head up from a low take-back to meet the ball and aim to hit it a good 15 feet or more, above net height. Practice your backhand lob similarly. Changing grips while you drop the ball will only create extra difficulties, so make sure you start with the correct

Eastern backhand grip. Both strokes should have only mild topspin, so watch the flight of your practice lobs to see that you are achieving the correct even trajectory. If you tilt the racket face back too far, the underspin applied will keep the ball in the air longer, possibly landing it out of court. If you tilt the face forwards, the extra topspin will make the ball dip earlier, falling short of its intended depth. When you can regularly lob a whole basketful of balls off both forehand and backhand strokes into your target area, progress to workouts with your practice partner smashing your lobs.

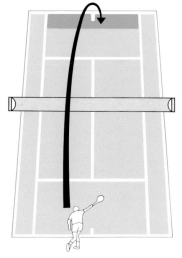

Practicing with a partner

Have your partner practice his overhead smash against your lobs, as shown below, for realistic match-play practice. Starting from behind your centermark,

with your partner in his basic volleying position, begin a lob and smash rally by playing a basic forehand lob. Lob on either side as necessary. Try to

lengthen your lob and smash rallies remembering to return to your basic positions after each stroke. Change after 15 minutes.

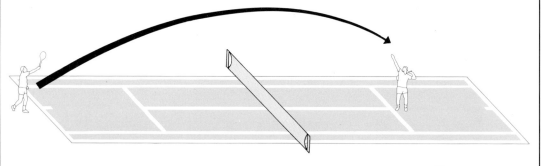

Using your lobs

Do not omit the lob from your tactical plans. The basic lob can be used to disrupt both baseline and volley attacks (see pp. 208 and 212). As a general rule, lob deep, as shown right, to your opponent's backhand making a smash return as difficult as possible. If you are under pressure, lob higher than usual to gain time for recovery. High, deep lobs can also be played to take advantage of wind and sun, as shown on page 242.

A Backhand
B Forehand

When using your basic lobs to attack a volleyer, play the ball lower, just out of your opponent's reach. If your opponent is a strong overhead player, alternate high and low lobs.

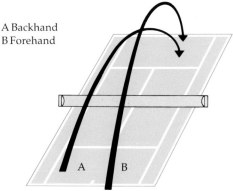

150

Evonne Cawley *has stepped well across with her front foot, straightened her body and lifted high with her racket to produce a basic lob off the backhand. Her outspread arms counter-balance her precise footwork and highlight her grace and the artistry of her game.*

Topspin lob

The topspin lob is essentially an attacking stroke which can produce winners when played unexpectedly. It can be played with the Eastern forehand and backhand grips and is used to its best advantage when disguised as a topspin drive. Your net-rushing opponent will anticipate a dipping return which he will then have to volley as early as possible. You will take him completely by surprise when you follow your deep looping preparation with a fiercely rising swing and high follow through as you flick the ball just high enough to clear his outstretched racket arm before dipping sharply towards the court. The ball will continue to shoot forwards after the bounce.

The sharp topspin (see p.145) which must be applied to create the desired dipping flight requires perfect timing and a controlled wrist and forearm action plus maximum racket head speed just before impact.

Improving your stroke

Compare the shape of the stroke for a topspin forehand lob, shown right, with the basic forehand lob on page 147, and you will see how different are the positions of your body and racket during the preparation, at the hit and in the follow through. The take-back is low, as for the basic lob, but the loop formed as you relax your playing elbow, deeper. This deeper loop is further encouraged by cocking the wrist at the end of the take-back in preparation for snapping the wrist upwards when you attack the ball. The racket face angle at the hit will be only just tilted back from the vertical line.

A **Preparation** The racket is taken back to form a deep loop, which will bring the racket head up from below wrist level. At the end of the take-back the wrist should be cocked so that maximum racket head speed can be developed through the hitting zone with wrist snap.

B **Hitting zone** The racket approaches almost vertically from beneath the ball, meeting it opposite the middle of the body at waist height.

C **Follow through** The racket has a very high finish across towards the left shoulder.

Topspin finishes
The two pictures, right, show the characteristic positions of the racket at completion of both the forehand and backhand topspin lobs. You will notice how, in both cases, the hitting face of the racket ends up almost pointing downwards at the court. This results from wrist and forearm action in the hitting zone, and is a sign of the severe topspin applied at the hit.

Forehand

Backhand

Practicing on your own

When practicing the topspin lob on your own, follow the same procedure outlined in the basic lob section but instead of turning to the side and dropping the ball, turn and throw the ball up high enough for it to rebound off the court to at least waist height. Remember to get sideways to the net as you prepare. Cock your wrist and loop really low before snapping your wrist forwards to bring the racket against the ball almost vertically and at great speed. Try to stay with the ball for extra control and do not snatch the racket away. Follow through high and across your body after stepping in with your front foot as you start the forwards swing. Remember the importance of establishing the right arc – the ball should clear the net by about 13 feet and then dip down behind an imaginary opponent in the forecourt before bounding on again. If you have a ball machine, set it to feed slow or medium-paced balls which bounce halfway into your no man's land area (see p. 195) and bound up so that you can easily swing up from underneath the flight and play the ball at waist height.

Practicing with a partner

In turns, feed each other medium-paced three-quarter-length drives which bounce high enough for you to practice the topspin lob. Concentrate particularly on footwork and positioning – you may well be running when the opportunity to play a topspin lob occurs, in which case you will have to steady yourself to establish a sound base to hit off. Stepping forwards and across as you swing at the ball will give added momentum to your stroke. You may find that it is not so easy to cock the wrist and snap it forwards on the backhand, and so rely more on forehand topspin lobbing as most players do.

Have your partner play a series of net attacks – either serve and volley or approach shot and volley (see pp. 204 and 214) and see if you can surprise him with a topspin lob. You can do this by disguising it as a topspin drive until the last moment and then looping extra low and snapping the racket head sharply up to apply severe topspin and so dipping the ball over his head, as shown above.

Using your topspin lob

The main features of successful topspin lobbing are disguise and surprise. It is one of the most effective ways of breaking up a strong net attack and can be a point-winner if it is disguised as a passing shot until your opponent commits himself to playing a volley. Avoid playing the topspin lob against your opponent's hardest shots or when you are well behind the baseline. You will need time to play the stroke and if you are too far from the net your main advantage of surprise will be lost. Generally, try to lob crosscourt and, ideally, over your opponent's backhand shoulder.

A   Backhand
B   Forehand

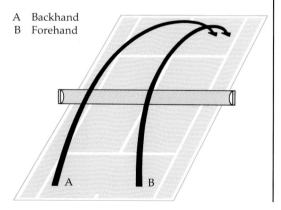

Underspin lob

The underspin lob is normally the last line of defense against extreme pressure. The stroke itself is played in a similar way to the volley, but you use your groundstroke grips and put the emphasis on deflecting the ball high into the air. Normally played from behind the baseline, it should be aimed about 30 feet above the net and deep towards the opponent's baseline, where it should fall and rebound almost vertically. The underspin will help keep the ball airborne longer, and provide you with a breathing space to regain your position if you have been drawn out of court. As it is marginally more common to defend on your backhand, the main features of the backhand underspin lob are described below, but the key elements are similar on the forehand side.

Improving your stroke

The most important features of the backhand underspin lob are the shortened racket preparation, the angle of the racket face at the hitting zone, and the follow through. Holding the racket with the Eastern backhand grip, take your racket back slightly above your intended hitting height with your non-playing hand at the racket throat. The bottom edge of the racket face should be slightly leading as you release your support hand and step in and punch forwards so that the strings bite down and under the ball. The angled racket face will impart massive underspin, sending the ball up 30 feet or more. The wrist should be firm and the racket face controlled at impact. Follow through upwards in the direction of your lob for maximum control, finishing at about head height.

A **Preparation** Take the racket back a short distance as for the volley. Keep your wrist firm.

B **Hitting zone** Meet the ball in front of your leading shoulder as

you block forwards and under the ball with the bottom edge of the racket slightly leading.

C **Follow through** Keep your racket head up as you follow through.

Shortening the stroke

When under extreme pressure use your underspin lob simply to deflect the ball, pushing the racket at the oncoming smash with the racket face held slightly open. The picture on the right shows the finish of a backhand underspin lob used in this way. The racket head has been pushed forwards and under the ball without a noticeable take-back to the stroke.

Practicing on your own

Because of the need to return fast balls continuously, you will best be able to practice the underspin lob on your own with the aid of a ball machine. Set the machine at maximum speed so that the balls will bounce just within your baseline towards your forehand or backhand corners. Start from behind your centermark, run the ball down, hoist up a defensive underspin lob, and then try to return to your centermark before the machine fires the next ball.

Practicing with a partner

Try the following advanced lob and smash exercise. Start from your normal lob and smash positions and play one set in each role using tennis scoring and with the lobber starting every point. The net player must smash or volley any ball but may only let deep defensive lobs bounce – those which fall within a line marked across the court 6 feet in and parallel to the baseline. The lobber must lob every ball smashed from the forecourt, but may drive any smash played from no man's land or after the bounce.

Using your underspin lob

The underspin or defensive lob will come into its own when you are under extreme pressure. Use it as a natural foil to the overhead smash, aiming for height and depth every time, and occasionally combine it with the basic lob to unsettle the rhythm of your opponent during baseline play. The diagram, below, shows underspin lobs played on the backhand and the forehand deep to a right-handed opponent's backhand.

A Backhand

B Forehand

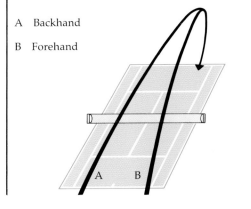

Ken Rosewall, under severe pressure from his opponent, covers the full width of his baseline to play this controlled defensive lob. His non-playing hand is used to counter his extreme racket arm movement out and under the ball, helping him maintain perfect balance. Note the precise angle of his racket face.

Lobbed half-volley

Although the basic, topspin and underspin lobs form the nucleus of any player's lobbing skills, variations like the lobbed half-volley will still require your attention if you wish to become a complete all-around player.

The lobbed half-volley is played immediately after the bounce and is, therefore, technically a groundstroke, but is included in this section because its function is that of a lob, not a drive. It is often a defensive stroke, sometimes played from choice, but usually used when there are few other options. The stroke is easily played with the Eastern forehand or backhand grips and has a similar short racket take-back to the basic half-volley. The ball is hit with the bottom edge of the racket leading to add lift, and the stroke ends with a high follow through.

Improving your stroke

Preparation, hitting zone and follow through are the most important points to concentrate on when playing the lobbed half-volley on either forehand or backhand side. Get sideways to the net, releasing your non-playing hand from the racket throat, and prepare your racket with a short, low take-back, just as for a normal half-volley from around mid-court. Your racket should be kept level with your wrist as you bend your knees well to get down to the ball, and your weight should be poised over your rear foot. Step in or across to the ball with your front foot, with your weight over your bent front knee as you play forwards with a short, firm-wristed swing to meet the ball opposite your leading hip on the forehand, just in front on the backhand. Hit the ball just after the bounce, with the bottom edge of your racket leading to provide extra lift. As you lift up and through the ball, straighten your knees for sharper elevation to carry the ball over your opponent's head. Your knees should begin to straighten at impact and should continue to do so as the racket moves up to complete a higher follow through than when basic half-volleying.

Forehand

Backhand

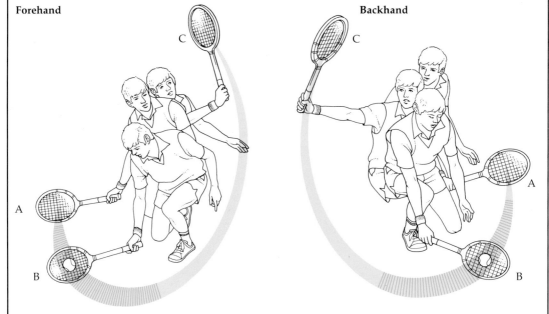

A **Preparation** Take your racket back short and low and bend your knees to get down to the ball, keeping your racket head level with your wrist.

B **Hitting zone** Hit steeply up and through the ball, bottom edge of the racket leading. Straighten your knees through the hitting zone for control of height and depth.

C **Follow through** The follow through is up and through the ball in the direction of the shot. The finish should be noticeably higher than in the basic half-volley.

Practicing on your own

Position a ball machine on the service line at one end of the court and set it to feed medium-paced balls which will land just beyond your service line at the other end of the court. Get into position and practice the lobbed half-volley, at first having the balls fed to you at 12-second intervals, and reduce this as you improve the stroke. By adjusting the machine and your own position you will be able to practice crosscourt and down the line half-volleys, both forehand and backhand.

Practice without a ball machine by turning, dropping a ball as you take your racket back, and playing the forward stroke in the normal way.

Using the court fence
Use a backboard or fence to help you imagine the height of an opponent's outstretched racket arm when you practice your lobbed half-volley. Stand inside your baseline, facing the fence, and play a lobbed half-volley over it. Repeat until you just skim the netting.

Practicing with a partner

You can practice your lobbed half-volley with a partner by getting him to volley balls from his net position and returning lobbed half-volleys from around the mid-court area. As you hit the ball, the racket should be tilted at a greater angle than for the basic half-volley. Begin to straighten your knees at impact with the ball. Both these features will help you control the height and depth of your shot. When you have worked on both strokes take over the volleying role while your partner practices his lobbed half-volley. Follow this practice with a general volleyer-to-baseliner rally with the baseliner playing a lobbed half-volley whenever the opportunity arises. The volleyer must try to retrieve or smash this ball and then return to his volleying position at the net to continue the rally. Alternatively, the volleyer may omit the smash but after retrieving the lob from the back of the court he stays there to take over the baseline role while his partner who played the lob moves up court to take over the volleying until he in turn is lobbed and the process is repeated.

Using your lobbed half-volleys

The main strategic value of the lobbed half-volley is to surprise and repulse an opponent or opponents who are at the net. It can be a very effective way of getting the ball back when you are under great pressure. A successful lobbed half-volley will drive an attacker away from the net and will also provide the player under attack with a time for recovery and an opportunity of taking the offensive himself. Disguise your intention to play a lobbed half-volley as much as you can by staying down with the stroke until the last moment as if you were going to play a basic half-volley. As shown right, try to play both your forehand and backhand strokes to the backhand side of your opponent.

A Backhand
B Forehand

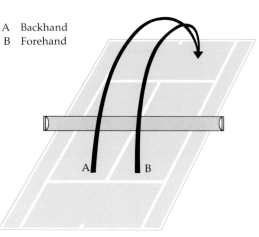

Lob volley

A lob volley winner can be as spectacular to watch as a beautifully executed overhead smash. It must be played with surprise and audacity because the player risks all in attempting it, knowing he will lose the point if the shot is anticipated.

The stroke itself is basically a low volley which is suddenly lobbed with sharp topspin, usually from inside the service line, over the head of a well-positioned net player or players who, expecting a defensive volley, are moving in to finish the job.

Surprise and deft wrist and forearm action are the prerequisites of this stroke. It should not be used too often, and practice is essential before it can be played confidently. It can be played with any sound grip but best lends itself to the modified Eastern grip (see p.53).

Improving your strokes

Preparation, hitting zone and follow through are the most important elements to concentrate on when playing both the forehand and backhand lobbed volleys. The preparation for the stroke should be similar to that for the low volley. Holding your racket with the Continental or modified Eastern grip, with your side to the net prepare your racket with a short take-back, about hitting height. The bottom edge of your racket should be leading, and your knees bent with your weight poised over your rear foot. Step in with your front foot and using a combined wrist and forearm action, swing the racket deftly up and over the ball, applying sharp topspin to it. The ball should be hit opposite the front leg at about knee height, and the body should gradually begin to straighten at the moment of impact. The racket should finish above shoulder height, with the top edge of the racket head leading at completion of the strokes.

Forehand   ## Backhand

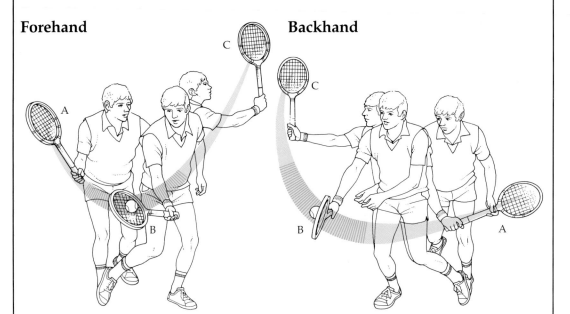

A **Preparation** Prepare your racket as for a low volley, with a short take-back at about hitting height. The bottom edge of the racket should be leading, and your knees bent as you turn to right or left.

B **Hitting zone** The combined wrist and forearm action flicks the racket head up and over the ball applying considerable topspin. The ball should be met opposite the front leg at about knee height.

C **Follow through** The racket should finish high across towards the left shoulder for the forehand stroke, or the right of the body for the backhand. The top edge of the racket head will lead at the completion of the stroke.

The shape of the shot

The combined wrist and fore-arm action as the racket face meets the ball will apply sharp topspin, causing the ball to rise steeply off the racket strings. The ball will rise into the air with an arcing trajectory, clearing the net by about 10 feet before dipping into your opponent's court, and penetrating after the bounce (shown below) as the topspin makes the ball bound forwards off the court.

Underspin version

If the approaching ball is very low and fast, leaving you no time to use the correct wrist and forearm action to play the topspin lob volley, simply tilt your racket face back a little more as you play forwards to the ball. The open racket face will apply underspin to the ball, de-flecting it upwards.

Practicing on your own

Stand inside your service line with a basket of balls and pre-pare your racket with a low take-back as if you were going to punch underneath the ball, ap-plying underspin. Throw one ball at a time to the side and playing short swings forwards, use your wrist and forearm to hit the ball up to about 10 feet above net height, over the imaginary head of your opponent. Your racket face should be open as it hits the ball, closing over as you complete the follow through of the stroke.

Another practice exercise is to mark a line on a backboard ab-out 10 feet above the net line and, standing back, to perform the same exercise to see if you can hit the ball above that line by using your wrist and forearm flicking action at the last mo-ment before impact.

Practicing with a partner

Have your partner stand at the opposite side of the net and hit low volleys to you which you will have to play at between knee and ankle height from in-side your own service line. Carry out the same exercise as when practicing on your own, concentrating on disguising your intention to play the stroke before using your wrist and forearm to flick the ball over your partner's outstretched racket arm, as shown right. This exercise will provide a good realistic situation for you to practice in and will provide good practice for lobbed volleys played off both the forehand and backhand sides. After prac-ticing 10 of each, hit the same number of low volleys for your partner to lob volley over your head. Progress to rallying, with one partner playing a serve and volley game, and the other, af-ter returning service, getting into position to play the lob vol-ley. Occasionally you should in-troduce an underspin lob volley into your practice rallies.

Using your lob volleys

The lob volley's main function in match play, whether forehand or backhand, is to subtly and skilfully turn defence into attack. If possible, try to disguise your intentions to use the stroke till the last possible moment, as surprise will be one of your main advantages.

Try to play your lob volley where your opponent will play his most defensive shot if he reaches your lob with his racket. As he will be in the net area you should invariably aim diagonally over his backhand shoulder (right), forcing him to twist and leap at the same time. In doubles, play a straight lob volley through the middle.

A   Backhand
B   Forehand

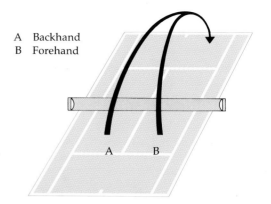

Tom Gullikson *is seeking to outwit his opponent by playing a surprise backhand lob volley. He might well be punching a deep volley, but his upright stance and arrested forward momentum, together with his racket face angle and the sharp rise of the ball off the strings, show that he has played an excellent underspin backhand lob volley.*

Smash

Smashes are exciting strokes and are an effective counter to lobbing. They are similar in power and effect to service strokes. Both are based on striking the ball above and in front of the body with a throwing action of the racket. The main difference between them is that when playing the smash you have to move about the court and position yourself according to where the ball is falling, rather than tossing the ball for yourself, as in the service.

Although both strokes can have an equally devastating effect, the emphasis in the smash is on timing rather than power: the approaching ball already has plenty of pace, and there is not the same need for it as there is in the service.

Always use your service grip when smashing. If you are still using your Eastern forehand grip for serving, use it for smashing too. If you have progressed to the Continen-

tal grip, this will enable you to develop an attacking game of serve, volley and smash without having to change grips.

There are several types of smash in addition to the basic smash, including the bounce smash, the jump smash, the angled smash and the backhand smash, all of which are described on the following pages.

Continental grip

As soon as you have progressed to the Continental grip for serving, use it for your overhead strokes too. The flexible racket control provided by the Continental grip will give you "feel" for the ball and help you to apply more power to your basic smash through wrist snap.

Preparing to smash

A short racket take-back and correct timing of the ball are vital in overhead play. Bring the racket up across your shoulders before lowering it down your back into the basic throwing position. If you continue to watch the ball, pointing your left hand towards it will aid positioning and help you time your hit to meet the ball in the middle of the strings with your racket arm fully stretched.

Path of racket wind-up

Turning sideways
As you see your opponent lob, turn sideways to the ball with your feet shoulder-width apart and your weight evenly distributed.

Sighting the ball
Lift the racket up, bending the elbow of your right arm. Straighten your left arm and look up along it as you point towards the ball.

Basic smash

The basic overhead smash is a powerful stroke, hit before the ball bounces on your side of the net. It is played with the racket face flat to the ball so that very little spin is applied, to enable the ball to travel fast and deep towards your opponent's baseline and bounce forwards low and with maximum penetration. This makes it particularly useful for returning most lobs. Used decisively, and with the proper timing, the basic smash can be a real point winner. All smashes are basically shortened versions of the service stroke, but the basic smash is the one which most closely resembles the basic, flat service. The ball is hit with both feet firmly on the ground, although your weight must be well over your front foot at the point of impact. There is less forward momentum in the basic smash than in the flat service stroke as control is a priority. Use only 80 per cent power.

Whichever smash you use, it is important to watch and time the ball so that it is hit with the center of the racket strings. If you play the stroke too early you will probably catch the ball high up on the strings and cause it to hit the net. If you play late and catch the ball below the center of the strings, you will probably send the ball out of court.

When playing smashes you should use your service grip. Ideally, this should be the Continental grip (see p.39). The extra wrist control it provides will help you to add spin and power to your overhead play.

Follow the practice tips on pages 165 and 166 to help you perfect the stroke.

Playing the stroke

As soon as you know a lob is coming, get sideways to the ball and prepare yourself for the shot in a similar way as for the first service (see p.100), except that in this case you must position yourself behind and below where you think the ball will fall. You may have to adjust your positioning with short skipping steps before you actually hit the ball, but maintain your sideways positioning throughout. Keep your left hand up for as long as possible, but let it fall away as you throw at the racket head. Snap your wrist forwards and straighten your racket arm to strike the back of the ball about a racket's length above your outstretched arm. Let your racket head follow up and over the ball and in an arc and your rear leg swing through to the front.

1 Hold the racket with your serving grip and support it at the throat with the fingers of your non-playing hand.

2 Turn right, placing your right foot behind and about a shoulder's width apart from your left foot.

3 Lift the racket into the throwing position, pointing at the ball with your left hand.

The shape of the shot

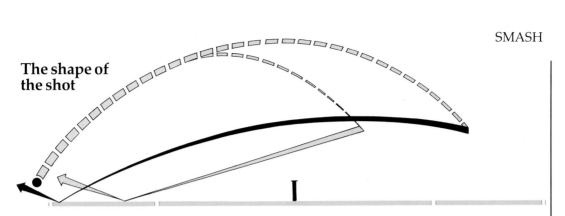

The most frequent use of the smash is to return the lob, so the approaching ball will be high with an arcing trajectory. The basic smash is played as a flat service stroke; the racket face is presented to the ball as flat as possible. Very little spin is applied and the ball travels deep to no man's land, and then penetrates deep after the bounce.

The flight of the ball when playing a smash will depend on your own position. If you are near the net you can smash the ball deep, angle the ball away from your opponent, or smash it short to bounce over your opponent's head. If you are quite far from the net you may have to apply some controlling topspin to the ball.

4 Keep pointing up at the ball as the racket drops into the throwing position and the right side arches slightly.

5 Let your left hand drop. Straighten your racket arm and hit the back of the ball with the full face of the strings.

6 Follow through with the racket head up and over the ball, while the rear leg swings through.

7 Finish with the racket down past the left side of your body.

Improving your stroke

The most important elements of the basic smash are the preparation, the hitting zone, and the cross-over footwork (illustrated below). The racket has an abbreviated wind-up – it should be simply lifted from the ready position by bending the elbow of your playing arm. The left arm should be straightened and pointed up at the ball as you continue to turn in, bringing the racket in across your shoulders before lowering it down your back into the basic throwing position for serving. At this stage your feet should be shoulder-width apart and your weight evenly distributed. Remember to turn early, pointing and preparing as you position yourself so that you have plenty of time to ensure that your racket meets the ball at just the right moment. You should strike the ball approximately a racket's length above your outstretched pointing arm. If you are late getting ready and allow the ball to fall too low before hitting it you will probably meet it below the center of your strings, which will result in your smashing out over your opponent's baseline. Conversely, if you are over-anxious and play the ball too early you will smash it down into the net.

Preparation
Turning sideways, lift the racket up from the ready position by bending the elbow of your playing arm. Straighten your left arm and point it up at the ball as you continue to turn. Look up along your left arm as you point towards the ball, getting yourself positioned as for a first service. Providing you continue to watch the ball, the pointing of your left hand will aid your positioning and will help you to judge exactly when to throw the racket head.

Hitting zone
You should strike the ball approximately a racket's length above your outstretched pointing arm. The ball should be in front of you and a little to the right.

Footwork

To hit a basic smash successfully you must be correctly positioned, behind and below where you think the ball is likely to fall. This may often require you to move back rapidly after turning sideways to the ball. Two types of footwork will enable you to do this while holding your sideways positioning. These are side-stepping and cross-over footwork, illustrated right. Cross-over footwork, far right, provides more continuous movement.

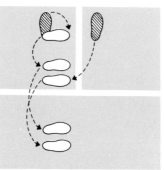

Side-stepping footwork
Use the side-stepping action shown above to help you keep your sideways positioning.

Cross-over footwork
Cross the foot nearest the net in front of your rear foot before stepping back with your rear foot.

Practicing on your own

Although it is more realistic to have a partner to lob the ball up for you, you can still do some worthwhile practicing on your own. Place ball boxes or racket head covers just inside the baseline and in the corners of the court; then, with a basket of balls handy, position yourself around mid-court on the other side of the net. Take a ball at a time and simply hit it up in the air with your racket. Put it up in front of you and high enough to allow you time to get ready. Practice hitting these easy balls first, aiming deep to the center and the corners of the far baseline. By noting how many

smashes bounce between the service and the baseline, and how many are accurate enough to hit your previously positioned boxes, you can monitor your own progress. Follow this by putting balls up to the left and the right, but still in front of you, so that moving to the ball becomes an essential part of your preparation.

Because of the difficulties in supplying yourself with balls behind you for smashing, it is best to have a partner to assist you with this more difficult type of smash. Alternatively, however, you can use a ball machine, as shown right.

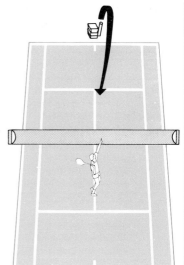

Ball machines

Ball-machines are ideal for practicing all-round stroke-making without a practice partner since they can be adjusted to feed balls from different heights and speeds to simulate match-play conditions. The model shown right is capable of propelling 135 balls up to c.33yd per second. A hopper is attached to the main body of the machine, which comprises an electric motor and a compression chamber and is in turn attached to a long narrow barrel. The hopper feeds balls into the main body of the machine, where compressed air is released and pushes the ball up the barrel. The barrel can be adjusted to several different positions according to the desired height of the ball. In the diagram, above right, it is adjusted to provide drives; below right, to provide lobs. The speed at which the ball is propelled out of the machine can be adjusted by turning a dial on the body, which opens and closes the air vents in the machine. Closing off the air vents will cause the compressed air to act more efficiently, applying more power to the ball and causing it to travel faster. Conversely, the more open the vents are, the slower the ball will travel. The ball can also be fed out at regular or random intervals as required. It is important to always use new balls when operating a ball machine, as worn napless balls will not be propelled consistently.

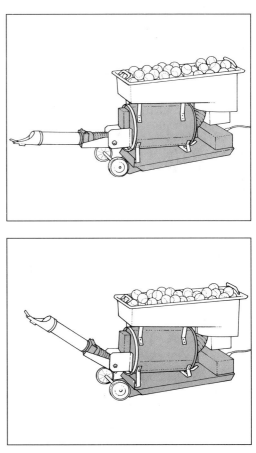

Practicing with a partner

It is much easier and more useful to practice the smash with a partner than to practice on your own. Get your partner to stand at the other end of the court and lob balls up for you to smash. As your partner lobs the ball get into the routine of turning, moving and preparing the racket before smashing the ball.

After turning sideways to the ball, run back if necessary, using a skipping, or side-stepping action, with your weight poised on the balls of your feet. Maintain your sideways position throughout your preparation. Some players move back from the net by bringing the foot nearest the net in front of the rear foot before stepping back with the rear foot and repeating the process. This is particularly good for maintaining the sideways position (see p.164). Have your partner follow his deep lob up with a short drive over the net which you must move forwards quickly to volley. Practice this combination until you can play six accurate smashes (use targets placed just inside your opponent's baseline) each followed by an accurate volley.

If you are concerned with improving your general stamina and match fitness, there is a pressure training sequence (see p.255) associated with the basic smash. Get your partner to lob ball after ball from the baseline for you to smash continuously. After each smash, run to the net and touch the net band with your racket, shown right. This is a very strenuous exercise designed to improve speed and agility as well as stamina, and should be part of a fitness program.

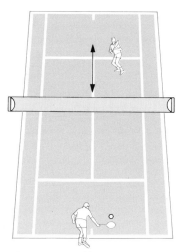

Non-stop smashing
After each smash, run to touch the net band with your racket head. Your practice partner must time each lob to coincide with the speed of your retreating run from the net. To start with, limit yourself to a series of five smashes.

Using your basic smash

Although the smash is an extremely effective stroke its use is somewhat limited by the fact that it can only be used to return a lob. Whenever possible, therefore, employ aggressive tactical play designed to force lobbed returns.

Where you aim your smashes will largely depend on your own position on court. If you are in the mid-court area or no man's land (see p.195), and are under pressure, your best option is to aim deep towards your opponent's baseline, using the longest distance to give you the greatest margin for error. If you are near the net you can hit the ball out of your opponent's reach more easily by angling your smashes to the sidelines and corners of the court.

Make sure that you are always sideways to the ball; otherwise you may pull the ball wide of the sideline or down into the net.

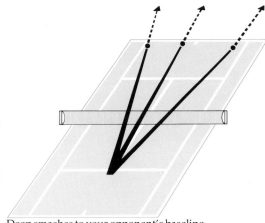

Deep smashes to your opponent's baseline

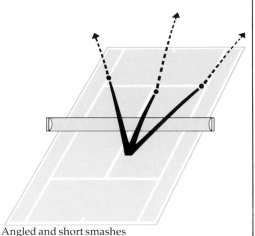

Angled and short smashes

Ivan Lendl *brakes on his back foot to prepare for a basic overhead smash. He has to move back from a sound volleying position to keep behind a lobbed ball* *from his opponent, and will now lift his racket into the throwing position as he points up at the falling ball with his left hand.*

Bounce smash

As a general rule, it is not usually advisable to let a lob bounce before hitting it: by running further back to play it you give your opponent more time to position himself. However, you will be faced with situations where it will make much more sense to let the ball bounce first. Examples are very high lobs which descend almost vertically and which may therefore require careful positioning and extra careful timing, and lobs played in windy conditions which are difficult to line up as they fall.

When playing this type of smash, position yourself very early, getting behind the bounce so that any adjustment you have to make is a forward one.

Playing the stroke

As soon as you know a high lob is coming, turn and run back quickly to get behind the ball before it bounces, with your side to the net. Point up with your left hand and prepare your racket with a short wind-up as the ball bounces.

Using your upwards-pointing left hand to aid judgment and balance, drop the racket head into the throwing position. Hit the ball so that the full face of the strings meets the back of the ball at full racket arm's length.

1 As the high lob goes up, run back quickly and get behind the ball before it bounces. Position yourself with your side to the net.

2 Prepare for the shot in the same way as for the basic smash and throw your racket head up to meet the back of the ball.

3 Follow through after the ball with your racket as your right foot swings through. The racket should finish past your left leg.

The shape of the shot

The flight of the ball will vary according to the type of lob which you are returning, and the type of smash which you use. When smashing the ball after the bounce from a deep position, you will probably hit it at a lower height than when smashing in the forecourt and your basic objective will be to get the ball to clear the net. To achieve this you will have to apply some controlling topspin to the ball (see topspin service, p.106) for an arced trajectory.

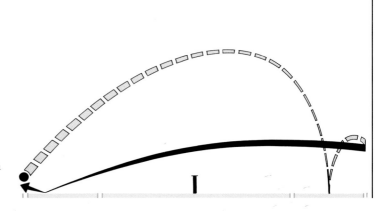

Smashing a very short lob

Sometimes your opponent may hit a very short lob which you are in no position to reach before it bounces. In these cases it is always best to let the ball bounce before smashing it, to give your-self more time for positioning. Smash the ball down hard and without spin to make it bounce very high, making it difficult for your opponent to return as shown below.

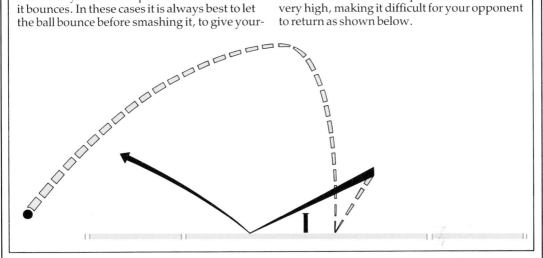

Practicing with partners

Practicing any smash on your own will not be very satisfactory unless you have a ball machine which can constantly feed balls for you to smash. It is much better to practice the bounce smash with a partner.

Place targets at the corners and centermark on the baseline at one end of the court. Have your partner stand at the end of the court, with a basket of balls. It may be easier for him to start by throwing the ball, as lobs are sometimes difficult to place correctly, and to progress to underspin lobs later. Smash the ball, aiming at the targets you have placed on court, and try to return to your volleying ready position (about 6-10 feet from the net) between strokes.

The lob and smash sequence of play lends itself to many game situation practices. Team up with your regular practice partner against two other players of similar ability to play the following competitive sequence. One pair starts at the net, with the other pair on the baseline. A baseliner drives a ball to the netmen, one of whom plays a deep volley. The play is now for points with the baseliners trying to lob over the netmen. If the netmen have to run back to play bounce smash-es or lobs, they must stay back and take over the lobbing role while the baseliners move up to take over the smashing role. Play to a fixed number of points before the opposing team starts a new "set" by driving once again.

Using your bounce smash

As when playing other smashes, it is important, when hitting the bounce smash, to hit deci-sively. The bounce smash will be put to its best use when returning very high lobs which fall vertically, as these are the most difficult to time correctly. After playing the bounce smash deep move quickly forwards to gain the net position. You must make every effort not to lose the initiative, which could occur if you smash gently and stay back. If the lob lands well in your forecourt it is tactically sounder to put it away fast with a deep smash down the middle or to the corners than to risk an acute angle or a soft smash.

A Forecourt angled winner

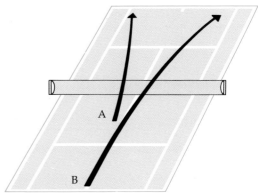

B Deep smashed return

169

Jump smash

Apart from enabling shorter players to overcome their lack of reach, the jump smash can be particularly effective against surprise or deep lobs which would otherwise fall behind you and not come up after the bounce. Its main tactical advantage is the difficulty the receiver has in judging your intentions.

A key element of this stroke is the scissors-like movement of the legs as the player leaps into the air to smash the ball. Hitting the ball from well above your normal reach will increase your power and hitting angle. Use the stroke decisively, aiming it where it will be easiest to win the point.

Alertness, speed and gymnastic ability are the prerequisites of the jump smash so, if you want this stroke to become an essential part of your overhead play, practice running back fast, sideways, and leaping high off your rear foot to hit imaginary smashes.

Improving your stroke

The main elements of the jump smash are the footwork and the racket action. Move back quickly to position yourself behind the ball, using skip-step or crossover footwork to help you maintain your sideways position, and begin to point and prepare your racket with the shortened wind up. Time your jump off the back leg, thrusting powerfully up as your knee straightens. As you throw the racket head up to meet the ball your back leg should cross over your front leg in a scissor action. Gain sufficient height to be able to hit up and over the ball. After impact, your racket should follow through as it would for a basic smash as you land on your left leg.

Making the jump
Jump into the air off your right foot, straightening your right knee as your weight is catapulted into the air. Bring your right foot in front of your left foot in a scissor-like action as you throw the racket head up to meet the ball. After hitting the ball, come down on your left foot.

A **Preparation** As for the basic smash, brake on your right foot as you put your racket into the throwing position.

B **Hitting zone** Jump as you throw the racket head up to meet the ball above and just in front of you, with racket arm out-stretched.

C **Follow through** Follow through as you land on your left foot. Your right foot will come forwards again.

Practicing with a partner

You can practice the jump smash with a partner, by getting him to hit deep lobs which are not too high, and which will force you to run back before leaping high off the ground to reach the ball before it can drop behind you. Practice smashing deep by aiming at targets placed near the baseline, moving quickly up court again and regaining your normal volleying position between each stroke. You may also find the vertical jump exercise helpful (see p. 256).

Jimmy Connors *has to leap high in order to smash a ball lobbed deep towards his baseline. Although moving back from the net quickly, the athletic Connors realized that, without jumping, the ball would beat him. After leaping upwards and backwards to prepare for the hit, the forwards action of his racket and upper body now counterbalances his legs.*

Angled smash

Although the angled smash technique is similar to that of the basic smash in the preparation and follow through, when hitting the angled smash, sidespin is applied to the ball in very much the same way as when the slice serve is played. It is perfectly possible to hit an angled smash by simply using the basic smash technique, but you will achieve a far greater degree of angle by using the slice serve technique. Whether you are smashing before or after the bounce, position yourself so that the falling ball is slightly to your right as well as in front of you. Hit round the outside edge of the ball. Although you will probably sacrifice some pace by using this technique, the sidespin will provide greater control, and the ball will penetrate and stay low after bouncing. The sidespin will make the ball swerve right to left, amplifying the angle of the shot.

Playing the stroke

Holding the racket with your normal serving grip, get sideways-on to the net, position yourself as for a slice serve place-up and let your racket drop into the throwing position. Let your right side arch slightly as your weight moves forwards over your front foot and throw your racket almost edge-on to meet the ball in front and a little to the right of your body. The racket strings will bite round the outside edge of the ball as slice is applied, angling the ball deep across court. Let your racket finish down past your left leg.

1 Get sideways-on to the ball and position yourself as for the slice service, with your feet well apart and knees slightly bent.

2 Point up at the ball with your left hand as you make your final foot adjustments. Racket into throwing position.

3 Let your left hand fall away as you throw your racket head up so that the strings hit the outside edge of the ball.

4 Let your racket follow round the ball as your right foot swings forwards. Racket finishes down past your left leg.

Improving your stroke

Correct body positioning is always important if a stroke is to be played accurately. When playing the angled smash, your side should be facing the net, positioned as for the slice service. The ball should be falling in front and slightly to the right of your body.

Probably the most important aspect of the angled smash, however, and the one which needs the most practicing, is the angle of the racket face on impact with the ball. Presenting the racket face around the outside edge of the ball at the right time and at the desired angle is crucial. The racket strings should be moving around the outside edge of the ball in the same way as for the slice service. The resulting sidespin will angle the ball crosscourt.

Practicing with partners

Take up the volleying position in the center of your court and have your partner stand at the opposite end of the court and hit lobs to your right, so that you can practice hitting angled smashes back towards his right-hand sideline. Angle your smash deep, between his service and baseline, making sure that you become proficient in this before attempting to practice hitting more acutely angled smashes into your partner's forecourt.

This type of angled smash, hit from right court to right court, can also be practiced off higher and deeper lobs as a bounce smash. Always aim towards strategically placed targets when practicing the angled smash. Practice 10 consecutive smashes for depth and accuracy and then play 10 lobs for your partner to practice his smash.

With four players on court practice basic and angled smashes from the forecourt by arranging yourselves, as shown right. Each baseliner must lob the opposing netman who must put the smash away. If he is beaten, his baseline partner must lob the opposing netman, and so on.

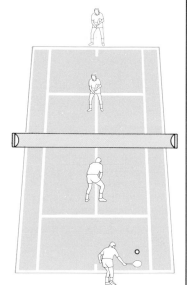

Using your angled smash

Use the angled smash against lobs which are falling or bouncing near the right-hand sideline: the slicing action will take an opponent well out of court to his right, forcing a weaker lobbed reply which can be easily dealt with. You can also use it on easy high balls at the net as long as you do not try to angle your smash too acutely. If your opponent returns your flat, deep smash, with a short lob, play an angled smash.

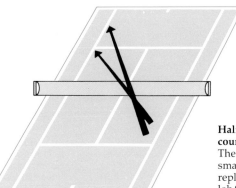

Half and three-quarter court angled smashes
The more acutely angled smash can be a useful reply to a poor defensive lob from your opponent.

Backhand smash

The backhand smash is more difficult and less decisive than the forehand smash. It is avoided by most players, when possible, because of the technical difficulties involved in producing the required amount of racket head speed with what amounts to a wrist flick. Controlling the racket face angle and timing the backhanded flick in order to generate power demands a degree of wrist and arm strength which few players possess. You should always try to hit the overhead from the forehand side. You may, however, find yourself in a situation where you are forced to play a ball that is not low enough to hit a high, firm-wristed backhand volley off, nor high enough to allow quick movement so that the more lethal forehand overhead action can be used.

If you do play the stroke, use your Continental grip, keeping a flexible wrist, and make sure that your right shoulder is turned well around to the ball (see below) to make enough room to swing the racket.

Improving your stroke

As the ball is lobbed over your left shoulder, pivot well over to your left, pointing your racket head down and your playing elbow up at the ball. At this stage your left knee should be slightly bent, and your weight poised over it, ready to be launched upwards just before hitting the ball. Whether or not you jump before hitting the ball, your back should be practically facing the net. Straighten your racket arm, snapping your wrist forwards to gain maximum racket head speed, and meet the ball above and slightly in front of your hitting shoulder. Let your forwards wrist snap continue into the follow through, with your racket head pointing down in front of you as your front foot aids recovery.

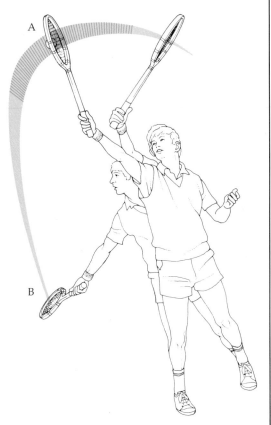

Preparation
If you are forced to play the difficult backhand smash, make sure that your right shoulder is turned well around to the ball. This will give you the room you need to swing the racket up and over the ball. Your racket head should be pointing down, and your playing elbow pointing up at the ball.

A **Hitting zone** The ball is met above and slightly in front of the hitting shoulder. Straighten your racket arm and snap your wrist forwards to give extra pace.

B **Follow through** The racket follows through downwards and should end pointing down towards the court as your right foot comes through for balance.

174

Practicing with a partner

You can most realistically practice the backhand smash with a partner. Get him to stand at the other end of the court and feed balls for you to smash. Initially, it might be easier for him to throw balls underarm over your left shoulder, until you get a reasonable feel for the stroke. Your partner can then hit your lobs. Concentrate particularly on turning your shoulder well around to the ball, so that your back is almost facing the net. You may find it easier to jump in the air to hit the ball, in which case practice leaping and smashing at the same time, aiming for rhythm and timing. Remember to keep your wrist and elbow relaxed and flexible so that you can really flick your forearm strongly, bringing the racket up and over the ball.

Using your backhand smash

Avoid the backhand smash whenever possible. If you do have to use it in match play, follow the same principles as for normal overhead play. If you are around the mid-court area but over towards your backhand sideline, aim for depth when smashing. If you are closer in to the net, try to hit your backhand smash at an angle. With practice, you will be able to achieve surprisingly good results by combining your wrist and elbow action to produce an accurate smash. The amount of power you can produce will be completely determined by the strength of your wrist and forearm. Since it is so difficult to generate power on a backhand smash it may be better to concentrate on accuracy rather than anything else. In general, aim your backhand smash towards a weakness in your opponent's game, forcing a weak return which you can then easily deal with.

A Angled smash
B Deep smash

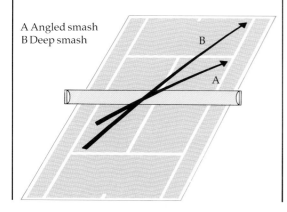

Stan Smith *leaps to smash a ball which has been lobbed over his left shoulder. He has pivoted to his left, completely turning his side to the net and has prepared the racket in classic style with bent elbow and relaxed wrist. He has used his playing elbow to aid his positioning and it is now helping to gauge the ball's descent as he leaves the ground to attack the ball aggressively. This quality of preparation will create maximum power.*

Windmill smash

Like the backhand smash, this stroke is rarely played from choice. You are most likely to play it if you have been caught out by a surprise lob against which you are too late to play a jump smash, because the ball has got behind you, and will have no time to run back and play it after the bounce.

The preparation for the stroke is more like that of a service than of a smash, but with the racket arm straightening at the end of the take-back. The ball is virtually caught behind the player and hurled over the net.

It is difficult to generate power with this stroke, because of the stiff arm movement involved, but there may be occasions when you will either have to try the stroke or lose the point, so it is still worth practicing.

A great exponent of the stroke was Jaroslav Drobny, 1954 Wimbledon Champion.

Improving your stroke

The key elements of the windmill smash are the preparation and the hitting zone. You probably have run back to smash the ball in a sideways position to find that you are too late to hit it with either a jump smash or a bounce smash. You must allow your racket to swing out and back, with your playing arm straight, below the falling ball. Jump off your rear leg as you virtually catch the ball on the strings just above your shoulder and hit it with a straight arm, over your head and back into your opponent's court. Then come down on your left foot, letting your racket continue down past the left-hand side of your body.

The jump
After the wide racket take-back, gain impetus by jumping off your right leg, executing a scissor-like movement in the air, and come down on your left foot.

A **Preparation** Let your racket swing back with your playing arm straight, getting it below the falling ball.

B **Hitting zone** As you jump off your back leg catch the ball on your strings just above your playing shoulder.

C **Follow through** Your racket should continue down past your left leg as you come down on your front foot.

Using your windmill smash

This stroke can have a tactical element of surprise because with the ball falling beyond your reach your opponent will not, theoretically, be prepared for any sort of effective return. This will take him unawares and probably catch him out of position, so place your windmill smash for maximum effect. Timing and placement are the main points to bear in mind: always aim deep for your opponent's baseline moving forwards to gain the initiative whenever you can.

Developing a style: lob

Evonne Cawley shows the tactical use of the basic lob when a player has been drawn wide of the playing area during baseline play. She has stepped across, well balanced, to place a basic lob deep across court. This gives her a maximum margin for error, and also time to regain her baseline position before her opponent can reply. Women players tend to use the basic lob, with a small degree of topspin, to discourage net advances and to break up baseline rallies. Men could perhaps make more use of this effective stroke.

Basic lob

As long as players seek to employ an attacking serve and volley game against their opponents, the lob will continue to flourish in match play as the ultimate defense. But as the modern tennis player has grown stronger and taller than his earlier counterpart so the lob can no longer form the basis of any player's game. How, where and when to employ the lob for the best effect has therefore become an important aspect of match play. Today's top players use the lob to surprise their opponents by lobbing on occasions when other and more likely shots are open to them. Knowing when to lob is an art which you will learn principally from match-play experience.

Sue Barker hoists a high basic forehand lob from behind her baseline. Taken wide under pressure, she counters her opponent's attack with a defensive, but excellently controlled lob which will give her time to regain a sound court position. Although airborne, her racket control and balance are maintained.

Mary Jo Fernandez in defense plays a firm-wristed backhand lob against a high-bouncing ball. Fernandez's two-fisted grip provides excellent control of the racket head, and her racket face is perfectly angled to lob the ball high and deep into her opponent's court, giving her ample time to recover.

Topspin lob

Although free-wristed players tend to top-spin their lobs rather more frequently than firmer-wristed stylists, topspin lobbing is by no means confined to exponents of the modified Eastern and Continental styles of play.

Western gripper Manuel Santana possessed one of the most effective topspin forehand lobs. The shot's deceptive flight and difficult bounce create problems for any attacking opponent in the net position.

Rod Laver plays a topspin forehand lob from the baseline, making a surprise return of service against an attacking serve and volley player. He straightens his legs as he finishes high and above the right shoulder with the racket face closing slightly.

Jimmy Connors, drawn wide and deep on his forehand, steps well across to produce a firmer-wristed topspin lob than Laver's. Connors's is more of a brushing than a whip-like action. As the racket finishes the face remains open. Some bodyweight has been transferred into the stroke.

Underspin lob

Underspin and sliced lobs can form an almost impenetrable barrier against the persistent serve and volley player. They are easily executed and use up little energy, relying mainly on your opponent's pace of shot for power. Racket face angle and good racket head control from a sensitive grip are all vital when controlling your underspin lobs. Top players sometimes introduce these lobs for variety as well as in defense.

Natalia Zvereva plays a beautifully controlled underspin lob. She has stepped across slightly as she cuts under the ball, with her racket face angled back to impart the spin. Her outstretched left arm balances her perfectly as she hits the ball. The underspin lob is a natural defense against an all-out net attack.

Billie Jean King plays an underspin lob with inside slice to aid control of height and direction. She is still looking at the point of contact in front of her right leg as her racket moves into the follow through position after hitting the ball.

Improvised style

The diagram, below, shows the curved racket path of Billie Jean King's modified underspin lob. From a high preparation the racket has been brought down so that the strings draw under and across the back of the ball.

Guillermo Vilas stretches wide beyond his left-hand sideline to play a defensive underspin lob reply. Caught by surprise, he plays off the foot nearest the ball using his other leg to retain his balance. The ball is almost past him but he will just have time to play slightly forwards and under the ball.

Lobbed half-volley

Lobbed half-volleys are played by adventurous, imaginative and, sometimes, desperate players. Perfect timing and well-disguised intentions are vital if the stroke is to be carried out successfully and to produce a good tactical result. Like the half-volley itself, it is usually not a stroke you would choose to play. Once committed to it, play it with delibera-tion and purpose. It is used to outwit a well-positioned net player – or players – when passing shots are difficult. If you do not gauge height and depth accurately, the result is easy prey for a volleying opponent. But when there is little chance of success with other strokes, top class players show why the lobbed half-volley is worth a try.

Ilie Nastase plays a lobbed half-volley off the foot nearer the ball – not a shot for a beginner to try. As his racket follows upwards, his right leg will come through for him to continue his advance towards the net if he has successfully lobbed the ball over his opponent. He keeps his head low and watches closely.

Lob volley

The effectiveness of the lobbed volley depends on surprise, height and depth. The topspin lob volley is invariably a winner if it clears the opponent's outstretched racket, for it shoots away quickly after bouncing. The underspin lob volley is less risky, and some players find it easier to judge correct height and depth with it. It is best used to drive an opponent from the net position rather than to win the point outright, for the ball tends to come up after the bounce, where it can be readily retrieved by an agile player.

Steffi Graf, right, in a strong forecourt position, plays a surprise lob volley to outwit an opponent who has moved in too close to the net. She shows perfect volley techniques, stepping forward and across to meet the ball with her wrist firm and racket head up. Only the late impact point and racket face angle indicate that she has lobbed the ball rather than punched it.

Maria Bueno completes a difficult lobbed volley on the backhand with the poise and grace of a ballerina. Her Continental volleying grip provides absolute control over the racket head and the angle of the racket face. Although her feet are close together, the extension of her arms balances her perfectly.

Developing a style: smash

Arthur Ashe prepares for an overhead smash. The ball is falling just in front of him. His left hand moves away as his racket head begins to rise from a very deep throwing position. He is on tip-toe, and will strike the ball partly off the back foot, the left foot aiding his recovery as he follows through.

Basic smash

Power smashing, both off the ground and in the air, is a vital part of the modern player's armory of strokes. It is the essential back-up to all net attacks, allowing attacking players to take up more adventurous volleying positions. Consistently effective overhead play stems from the development of a technically sound basic smash. The popular smashing style today combines the use of a Continental serving grip with an abbreviated version of the basic service take-up for a fast preparation to the stroke.

Stefan Edberg plays a typical action smash. A determined opponent has played a lob over Edberg's left shoulder, but he has moved swiftly across and behind the ball to smash it decisively away towards his opponent's backhand corner.

Virginia Wade, opposite, displays the prerequisites of good overhead play – early preparation and sound positioning. The perfect balance of Miss Wade is always desirable but not always possible in match play.

Orthodox style

A Left arm sighting ball
B Eyes fixed on ball
C Diagonal line made from shoulder to shoulder
D Deep throwing position
E Upper arm right angles to body
F Weight poised on back foot

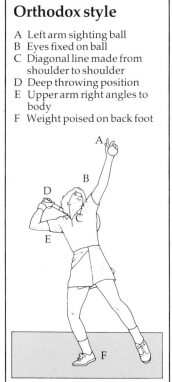

Jump smash

The jump smash is probably the most used variation of basic overhead play. A serve and volley player who can leap high in the air can press home an attack from the most aggressive volleying court positions, knowing that only the most perfect lobs are likely to cause concern. Mobility and timing are all-important with this stroke, for jump smash situations normally occur when a player has to back-track from the forecourt to tackle a surprise lob. Regular practice will enable you to extricate yourself from difficult situations, enabling you to hit balls which you could not otherwise reach.

John Newcombe has been caught facing the net with no time to turn or retreat. So he leaps up and, adapting his smash technique, opens his wrist and lays the racket head back. He will claw the ball out of the air and back into his opponent's court.

Frew McMillan plays a well controlled and timed jump smash. Study the perfect grip and exact wrist action. A well-timed jump keeps the ball in front of you, for once it is dropping behind it is difficult to make an effective return with any real force.

Agility

Agility is essential for a strong net attack allowing you to jump smash counter-lobs aimed to force you back.

A Nastase has brought his racket over the top of the ball, to smash it down into court.

B Upper body thrust counter-balances lower body perfectly.

C The scissor-kick leap off the back foot is a main feature of this stroke. Nastase will land on the other foot, ready to move forwards again.

Ilie Nastase leaps to execute a text book jump smash. He moves his legs in a scissor-like way, while thrusting his bodyweight upwards – two key features of this stroke. He has met the ball well in front, and his wrist action adds power to the smash as he projects the ball accurately into his opponent's court.

Tony Roche's outstanding competitiveness is reflected in his attitude towards this lob, as he leaps up to perform a flawless jump smash. He combines his upwards thrust and scissor kick with positive racket action and sound basic technique. Roche's concentration on the ball ensures the success of this shot.

Backhand and windmill smashes

Rarely can any great power be generated in executing either the backhand or the windmill smash. Players try to avoid these strokes in favour of the basic smash and the jump variation. Opponents deliberately lob balls over your non-playing shoulder to force a weak backhand smash, so that they can wrong-foot you or attack the opposite side of your court. The main essentials of the backhand smash are wrist, arm and shoulder strength, plus perfect timing. When power is lacking then accurate placement is the key, if the initiative is not to be lost. The windmill smash is really a desperate shot, when a lobbed ball has all but dropped behind your playing shoulder. When there is no other alternative, the stiff, round-house swing with late wrist action hooks the ball up and back over the net. Some players have developed both accuracy and power with these unusual variations of overhead play. Lew Hoad could produce a backhand smash that made the ball bounce over his opponent's outstretched reach.

Stan Smith completes a remarkable backhand smash with his back to the net. The flexibility of his Continental grip, plus wrist strength, provide enough power to return the ball from an almost impossible position.

The "impossible" retrieve

The diagram, below, shows how difficult an angle Smith attempts with his smash, turning defense into attack.

The arrow marks the probable flight of the ball down into court.

John McEnroe uses the windmill smash, hooking the ball back into court from behind him. He gathers impetus and racket head speed to apply some pace to the ball, thus keeping the point "alive" and possibly maintaining his attack.

191

BACKHAND AND WINDMILL SMASHES

Sue Barker finishes a difficult backhand smash. The ball would certainly have gone beyond her reach if she had attempted a high backhand volley. She has pivoted well, and has aimed her shot down the sideline.

Vitas Gerulaitis, below, plays a rarely used jumping backhand smash. He has been drawn very wide and, unable to develop enough pace for a crosscourt or through the center winner, has aimed a deep placement down the sideline to avoid giving away an easy angle.

Strategy

First principles

Strategy in a tennis match must promote your own strengths in attack, counter-attack and defense, while blunting an opponent's strengths, exposing and exploiting his weaknesses and undermining his morale. Tactics in tennis are the methods of playing and positioning which you use to secure an objective which is part of your strategic plan. The strategies available to a tennis player (for example, winning through attacking ploys or winning through tireless defense) have remained largely unchanged. New techniques of play and new equipment, however, bring about the refinement of old, and the development of many new tactics.

Every match which you play should be planned as to how you intend to deploy your own strengths against your opponent's resources. The more that you know about your opponent's capabilities the easier it will be for you to select the right strategy, but remember that your own strategy must be flexible. If you know your opponent well then your plan will probably be right first time and you must simply work out the tactics to implement it. But if you find that your match policy is failing, no matter which tactics you use, then you must alter your strategy or go down fighting. Sometimes your strategy for winning is correct, considering your opponent's weaknesses, but your chosen tactics fail to achieve your aim. In this case you must be able to recognize how your opponent is successfully counter-attacking and to change your tactics to meet the new situation.

The stronger your own game, the more likely you are to succeed with any selected plan in a tennis match. After learning how to play each stroke you will have seen its basic uses. The next step is to study the tactical use of strokes, both singly and in combination, and to see how they can be used to best advantage in singles and doubles play to bring about victories which might otherwise not have been yours.

Types of tennis player

There are various types of match player and you will find yourself developing, or will have developed, into one of, or a combination of, these types according to your physical and mental attributes. Most players fall into one of the four categories described below.

Retriever A player who has excellent control, mobility and fitness, and can scramble the ball back but has no match-winning stroke which an opponent needs to fear.

Baseliner A player whose groundstrokes are technically sound and is adept at moving in the backcourt along the length of the baseline. This player wins by encouraging a groundstroking game played from baseline to baseline, and then tiring and forcing errors from his opponent. The baseliner will only approach the net to play certain, winning shots, or when lured there by an expert opponent.

Serve and volleyer A player who prefers to volley than to play groundstrokes, and is strong enough both physically and technically to serve and, immediately, volley with power and accuracy. The serve and volleyer's strategy is to always attack from the net, crushing his opponent with varied serve and volley tactics. If inept they are labelled "netrushers". Players of this type are often able to rally from the baseline but may well have an unreliable drive on the forehand or backhand side which they need to hide.

All-court player A competent all-around player who combines skills from each of the three types above without being a brilliant exponent of play in any category. The all-court player is not weak in any tactical situation and applies mental, physical and technical abilities expertly from any part of the court, and so is perhaps everyone's ideal type of player.

Some players combine different aspects of each of the above types and their best method of play is not easily spotted. Good match players work hard to develop their game and do as much as possible to cover shortcomings. You must discover how better players prefer to play and then provide the right counter tactics.

Knowing the tennis court

Think of your playing area, on either side of the net, as being divided into three, as shown in the diagrams below. The area behind and up to the baseline is known as the backcourt, and the area between the service line and the net, the fore-court. Play from within each of these areas is distinctive – groundstroke rallying from the backcourt, and quick-fire volleying from the fore-court. Between these areas is no man's land, so-called because it is disastrous to remain in this area beyond the time it takes to play a stroke in it.

Backcourt Defensive play is your major concern when rallying from the backcourt but as a base-liner, an all-court player or a serve and volleyer you should be rallying with purpose – the base-liner to tire and upset the rhythm and timing of his opponent, the all-court player and serve and volleyer both trying to force poor length returns so that a net attack can be set up. From the backcourt, the depth of your opponent's shot dictates the type of reply which you make.

No man's land After playing a stroke from this area you should either move forwards to volley in the forecourt, or backwards to recover your rallying position behind the baseline.

Forecourt As you approach the net, your shots will have less distance to travel and an all out attack is the natural choice. Approach shot play from this area is nearly always successful as you will certainly be close to a good volleying posi-tion. Crosscourt drives can also be attempted with confidence. You will only have to exercise caution when the ball falls below net level.

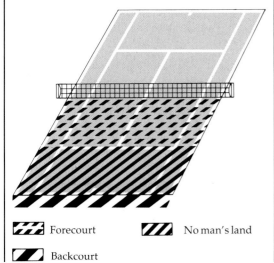

Forecourt	No man's land
Backcourt	

Center point theory

The center point theory determines the best posi-tion to move to after playing any of your strokes. By returning to a position about a yard behind the centermark before your opponent hits his next shot in a baseline rally or after serving, you will be in the basic position to cover the reply. This central position between the two extreme replies open to your opponent applies to all play, not just baseline rallies, and should always be your goal when moving about the court from returning service onwards. When you select your service return, and every subsequent shot, it is vital that the center point position is as close as possible. The diagram below shows a wide service to a right-handed receiver's forehand and how a deep crosscourt return puts the receiver's next center point position relatively close. If the receiver had selected a down-the-sideline return, the position midway between the possible re-plies would have been a yard or more beyond the center mark.

S Server
CP Centerpoint
R Receiver

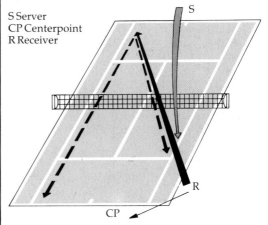

Countering spin

Assessing and countering spin is vital strategical-ly (see pp. 42-44). High topspinning balls can be played with an underspin chop shot, or a blocked return, to keep the ball low over the net. Low topspinning balls can be effectively countered with your basic drives, or your topspin drives hit with considerable forward thrust. High under-spinning balls can be countered by using a flatter basic drive while a very low underspinning ball may require a severe topspin action to counter the spin. Countering the effects of sidespin re-quires very firm strokemaking allowing for the fact that a ball travelling through the air and off the court with right-hand or left-hand spin will leave your strings with the opposite effect.

SINGLES – Serving

Your serves must be deep and accurately placed at all times, and in addition, either sufficiently powerful or spun. The combination of these elements will put most of your opponents on the defensive.

Compared with your second service, the first ball which you serve on each point has enormous strategic potential which you must exploit. The average player wastes many first service opportunities whereas the good player delivers 70 per cent of his first serves, not only into the court, but deep to areas which force defensive returns. To achieve this percentage of successful first services, you must settle for less than your very fastest delivery for most of the time. Reducing speed means that you can add more spin to increase your margin for error. By varying the amount and type of spin which you apply, and saving your very fastest delivery for situations when you have points in hand or as a calculated risk when you are love-40 down, your opponent will seldom be able to plan a specific return.

Top players say that you are only as good a player as you are a second server. Whichever spin serve you use as your main second delivery, you must develop it until you can serve it deep to your opponent's weakest side whenever your first serve misses. If you can master both topspin and slice serves you will be able to swerve your delivery away from, or into, your opponent's body as you require.

Left and right court stances

In the strokes section (see p.99) you learned that you should stand within a yard of the centermark when serving into left or right service courts in a singles match. As the effectiveness of your serving becomes more critical, however, you will find that the position of your service stance when serving into the right service court should be different in relation to the centermark than when serving into the left court, as shown right. These basic positions will enable you to start midway between the extremes of your opponent's likely returns and also to aim the ball as effectively as possible.

In the right court, moving very close to the centermark allows you to serve almost down the center of the court to a right-handed receiver's backhand – usually the weaker stroke. When serving into the left court, standing 1-2 feet further from the centermark will allow you to make your service to a right-handed receiver's backhand as angled as possible.

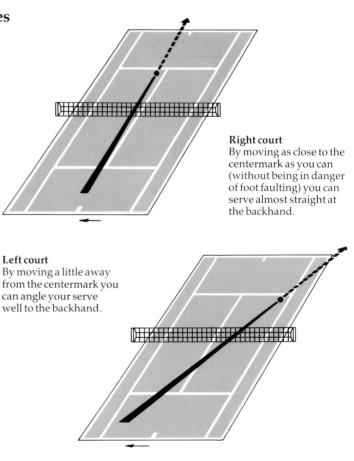

Right court
By moving as close to the centermark as you can (without being in danger of foot faulting) you can serve almost straight at the backhand.

Left court
By moving a little away from the centermark you can angle your serve well to the backhand.

Disguising your intentions

Surprise is a vital element of serving at higher levels of play. Learn to keep your serving intentions disguised. When adjusting your stance to serve to the forehand from the right court, for example, do not make an obvious move from your basic stance very close to the centermark. It is better to keep your opponent thinking that the ball is more likely to come to the backhand than to achieve a little more angle on your delivery. The unorthodoxy of some players' service stances is often a useful disguise in itself. John McEnroe's extreme stance, shown right, is indicative of his strong slice service, but it also often keeps the exact direction of his attack from his opponent until it is too late to make an effective return.

The importance of serving deep

The diagram, below, shows how deep serving (to the forehand, backhand, or at the body) will make sure that the receiver keeps well behind the baseline and so in a defensive position. If you serve short of the dark band you will allow the receiver to advance and receive from inside the baseline. From this position a counter-attack is far more likely and you could find the attacking initiative taken from you. The importance of depth applies to both first and second serving alike. Both serves must be deep and accurately placed. The reliability of your second serve must come from its controlling spin, not from aiming short.

Forcing the receiver to stand back

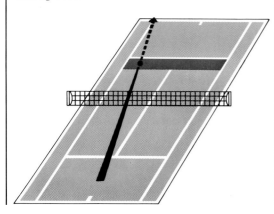

The spin alternative

You always have two alternatives once you have chosen which part of the service court to aim for. You can either use a basic flat serve hoping that the pace of your delivery will combine with your aim to produce a difficult shot for your opponents to deal with, or you can use a spin service to increase the angle of approach before and after the bounce. You can see, below, how a topspin serve to the backhand corner of the left service court will break even further to the backhand than an equivalent flat service. Similarly the nature of a slice serve to the forehand corner of the right court will swerve the ball further to the forehand of a right-handed receiver.

A Slice
B Basic

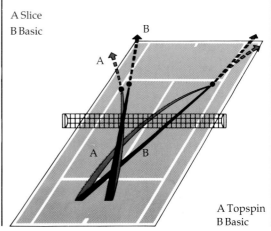

A Topspin
B Basic

Serving to the backhand

If there is no striking feature of an opponent's strengths and weaknesses which forces you to do otherwise, 80 per cent of all your serves should be aimed at the backhand. The four diagrams, below, show right-handed services attacking the backhand. In each case, a flat serve is shown together with the spin serve which you can use as an alternative means of attack. You will see that as a right-handed server the left court service stance (suggested on p.196), a little away from the centermark, leaves your forehand court more open to your opponent's return than the backhand. This disparity is usually insignificant as you will be facing in the forehand direction as you serve and the forehand stroke is likely to be your stronger.

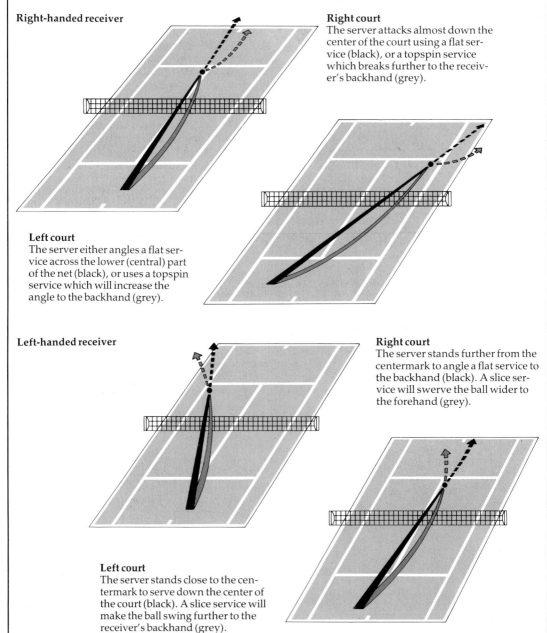

Right-handed receiver

Right court
The server attacks almost down the center of the court using a flat service (black), or a topspin service which breaks further to the receiver's backhand (grey).

Left court
The server either angles a flat service across the lower (central) part of the net (black), or uses a topspin service which will increase the angle to the backhand (grey).

Left-handed receiver

Right court
The server stands further from the centermark to angle a flat service to the backhand (black). A slice service will swerve the ball wider to the forehand (grey).

Left court
The server stands close to the centermark to serve down the center of the court (black). A slice service will make the ball swing further to the receiver's backhand (grey).

Serving to the forehand

The success of serving to the forehand depends on surprise. You must choose your opportunity with care and disguise your intentions well. It is best to risk attacking the stronger side when you have at least a one point lead.

If you notice that your opponent is taking up a receiving position nearer to the centermark in order to attack your less accurate serves to the backhand by running around the ball and hitting a forehand, a serve wide to the forehand, as shown right, may well be effective. It should force a short defensive crosscourt reply, opening up the court for your forehand attack. From the left court you can vary your backhand attack by serving deep to the forehand down the middle of the court. If you can surprise the receiver, the ball will tend to come back to you in the middle of the court, or slightly to your forehand side, allowing you to maintain the attack.

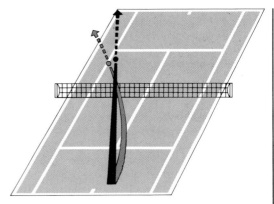

Right court, right-handed receiver
The server attacks the forehand with a flat service (black) angled to penetrate deep and wide after the bounce, or with a slice service which will swerve wider still, well beyond the sideline (grey).

Serving at your opponent's body

Your last attacking option is to serve directly towards your opponent's body. This tactic will sometimes force a weaker return than an open attack to the weaker stroke, especially if your opponent is a little slow-footed. Trying to make a backhand return when the ball is swinging into your body is one of the most difficult returns to play effectively, especially when the receiver is not sure when to expect the in-swinging action.

As with the other service attacking options, you can either use the speed of a flat service, or the movement of spin services for your purpose. The slice service is particularly useful for swinging the ball towards the receiver's body in an unexpected fashion. Serving at your opponent's body can be equally effective from both left and right courts, and your intentions can easily be disguised as no change in stance is necessary.

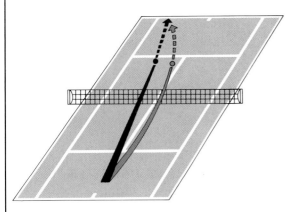

Right court
The server aims a flat service (black) to the central edge of the right service court, to bounce straight at the receiver, or slice serves to swing the ball in from the receiver's backhand towards the hip (grey).

Left court
Similarly, the server aims at the receiver's body using a flat service or curves a slice service in from the receiver's left. The slice will cramp the receiver's backhand.

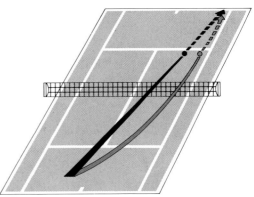

Returning service

Next to serving, the service return is your most important shot. The average tennis player makes approximately 10 unforced errors when returning service in every set of a match.

Keeping the ball in play underlies all service return tactics. It is far better to provide the server with the chance of making a mistake on the third shot of a rally than to lose the point outright by going for a winner off a very difficult service. Most service return errors arise from trying to hit the ball too hard.

Returning service begins with taking up the best possible receiving position according to your opponent's serving strengths and to your own abilities in groundstroke play. If, as I recommend, you use a different grip for forehand and backhand groundstrokes you must decide in advance which one to stand ready with. As your opponent starts the service stroke, speed of reaction and flexibility are required to move and play a stroke which must often be modified to be executed in a fraction of a second.

Being ready

The diagrams, below, show the basic receiving postions midway between the extreme angles of service possible from a right-handed and a left-handed server. The slight shifts in receiving position are recommended because a right-handed server can angle a serve more sharply to the forehand from the right court, while a left-hander can do the same to the backhand from the left court. When returning fast serves you should stand 3 to 4 feet behind the baseline so that you can play a strong return off a slightly falling ball. For a spin service stand inside the baseline so that you can take the ball early before the spin can

swing the ball away. In your ready position (see p.37) you must be totally alert. Do not stand tall and upright but bend your knees and your waist slightly getting well down so that your eyes will be nearer the level of the ball. You must be ready to move so keep your weight forwards over the balls of your feet. If you feel tense, relax your face muscles by slightly dropping your chin. Study the server's movements before he strikes the ball, and listen. With practice you will instinctively know the type of service about to be unleashed and its intended direction.

Right-handed server

Left-handed server

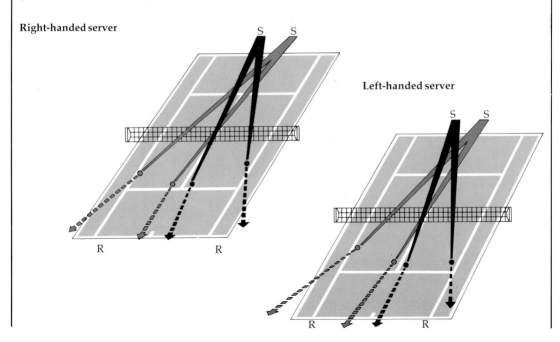

Choosing your grip

As an Eastern style player you will have to make the choice of whether to stand ready with the forehand or backhand grip. You can either stand using the grip to match your stronger stroke so that you are ready for an opportunity to use it, or you can stand using your weaker stroke grip confident of an adept change to your stronger stroke grip if it is necessary. If you decide to start off with your stronger stroke grip, you can ease the position of your ready stance left or right so that you can take more serves on your stronger side. This movement is shown in the diagrams, below, in both right and left courts. To favor your forehand, move slightly towards the backhand side. Conversely, to favor your backhand, start with your backhand grip and edge towards the forehand side away from the sideline.

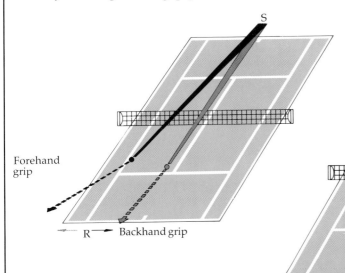

Forehand grip

R → Backhand grip

Backhand grip

Forehand grip ← R →

Modifying your strokes

As the ball is served you must pivot sideways and get your racket back before the ball crosses the net. You must see the ball bounce or your chance of making a good return will be slim. From this point the stroke which you play will be as close as possible to the relative groundstroke which you learned in the strokes section modified by the pace of the oncoming ball. Most likely, you will have to abbreviate your forehand and backhand swings considerably. However much you reduce your take-back, it is imperative that the racket stays with the ball in the direction of its flight for the first 3 to 4 feet after the hit. The block return (a basic volley-like stroke with a short take-back) is useful against fast serves and some spin deliveries. The chip return, shown right (simply an abbreviated forehand or backhand slice drive) is especially effective against high kicking serves, returning the ball to the service line area.

Stan Smith

Playing flat serves

To play a fast flat service successfully anticipation is vital otherwise you will lose three to four tenths of a second before you start to react, time you cannot afford to lose when you consider that a ball served by an average junior player at 60 miles per hour will arrive at the receiver's racket in approximately one second. A very fast flat service, served accurately at 120 miles per hour or more, by a world class male player, is almost unreturnable. You must stand far enough behind the baseline to allow more time and some of the service speed to dissipate before you contact the ball just after the top of its bounce. Unless the serve is short use a short take-back getting the racket behind the ball at hitting height, and simply block forwards with a basic volley-like stroke.

Playing spin serves

Topspin will rebound off your racket strings as underspin, and make the ball fly up higher than you might have thought (see p.44). Prevent the ball from flying too high over the net by playing a an aggressive stroke down and through the ball as it rises, at waist height or above. Stand just inside the baseline and take the ball before it breaks too far to the left on the backhand, or too close to the body on the forehand.

Sidespin or slice services will rebound from your strings with the opposite effect. This has to be allowed for when making forehand or backhand returns. Stand inside the baseline so that you can play the ball before it swings wide on the forehand or into your body on the backhand.

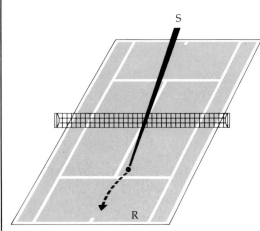

Spin service receiving position
When playing either topspin or slice services stand further forwards just inside the baseline, as shown above, where the receiver faces a topspin service to the backhand. This allows you to play the ball early.

Choosing the best return

The six diagrams on the opposite page each show returns against the three major types of service (basic flat service, topspin service and slice service), from both the right and left courts, when the server prefers to stay back. Each return is graded according to the quality of the serve to be returned. A very deep effective service, either flat or spin, demands return A in each case. A moderate service will allow you to try return B as an alternative, while a poor service will allow you to use option C. Each option will put the server under as much pressure as possible.

You will notice how the down-the-sideline return is used sparingly against the server who is staying on the baseline, and not at all against serves angled wide. This is because of the difficulty of achieving a good court position after such a return according to the center point theory (see p.195). You will have difficulty in moving far enough quickly enough.

1 **Left court, flat serve** to your backhand is best returned firmly along the flight of the service. A moderate service gives you the opportunity of playing a sliced crosscourt backhand, while a weak service may allow a winning crosscourt drive.

2 **Left court, slice serve** to the forehand which swings away from you should be played firmly back to the baseline center. If the service is not so strong, a deep drive to the backhand will be effective. A weak service can be driven wide of the server's forehand.

3 **Left court, topspin serve** which bounces deep and then breaks sharply to your backhand is best played back along the flight of the service. Weaker services can be played to the backhand corner or even on a half-court angle.

4 **Right court, flat serve** at your body with good depth and pace should be returned deep along the line of the service. A moderate service of this type can be played hard crosscourt, while a short service might be returned down the sideline.

5 **Right court, slice serve** to your forehand has to be played as early as possible and returned crosscourt. A less difficult delivery will give you the option of playing firmly back at the server and a poor service the chance of a half-court angled winner.

6 **Right court, topspin serve** to your backhand should be played firmly to the server's feet. If the service is easier to deal with you can angle the ball deep to the right-handed server's backhand or even play an angled winner if the service is weak.

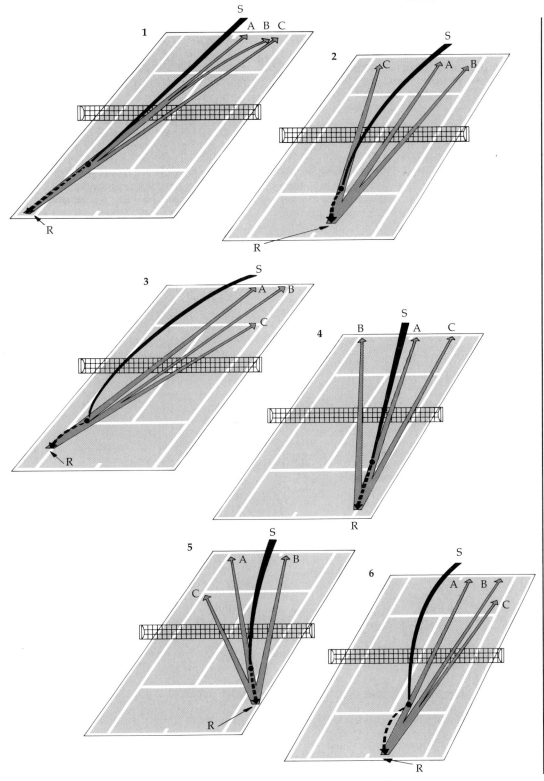

Serve and volley play

Following your serve to the net with the intention of making a winning volley is a major tactic in modern tennis. The serve and volleyer's aim is to dominate the rally from a position close to the net from where he can hit volleys beyond the reach of his opponent. This attacking tactic complements the advantage of serving. Its success depends on selecting the correct type of service, moving quickly enough to reach or cross your own service line to make the first volley, and then moving forwards again for subsequent volleys if they are necessary. Serve and volley play puts opponents under pressure to return your service fast, low and out of your reach, if they can, in order to foil your first volley. Success, however, also depends on good planning and a lot of practice, for mistakes quickly show how vulnerable the net position can be. Opponents provide more effective returns of serve when presented with an oncoming volleyer to avoid.

The serve and forward run

The aggressive quality of serve and volley play often prompts the server to charge the net after fast first serves. If your opponent is returning serve competently, fast services will tend to come back faster when you follow them to the net. To give yourself enough time to reach a sound court position from which to make an effective first volley, choose your second service (topspin or slice) to volley behind. Its higher, dipping trajectory will give you more time to move forwards. If you wait to see if you have made a good service before running forwards, you will have left your approach to the net far too late. Your rear foot swinging through across the baseline as your service is completed should be the first step of your run towards the net, as shown right.

The direction of your run towards the net should always be exactly along the flight of your service. Keep to this line and you will be positioned in the middle of the possible angle of returns available to your opponent and so be in the best preliminary position ready to move to either side. You should cross your own service line in about seven steps reaching an ideal distance from the net for your first volley (see diagram opposite). Exactly how far you can advance depends not only on your own speed and the depth and accuracy of your service but also on the speed and accuracy of your opponent's return. As your opponent's strings make contact with the ball you must ease your forward run and momentarily plant your feet as for the ready position – (known as split-stepping). From this position you will be able to move which ever way may be necessary to meet the oncoming ball, and play the necessary volley on balance.

Boris Becker

Hitting the first volley

The direction and length of your first volley depends on the quality of your opponent's return of service. If your opponent's return is slow and above net height you may feel that you can move on quickly and hit an outright winning shot across the court or down the sideline, out of your opponent's reach. A good quality return, however, will come across the net low and fast and your objective must be to punch your first volley deep to the baseline into a corner of your opponent's court. The maximum angles of return open to a receiver when you serve into right and left courts are shown in the group of three dia-

grams, below. As for approach shot play (see p.214), volley down the same side of the court to which you have been forced by the direction of service return. If, for example, the return is played wide to your forehand, volley down your forehand sideline to your opponent's backhand corner. A good, low return of service will be difficult to hit before the ball falls to net height or below so you will have to hit through the ball as much as you can with a more open racket face applying underspin for control. If you have to apply too much underspin, however, the ball will not penetrate and your opponent will have a chance to recover.

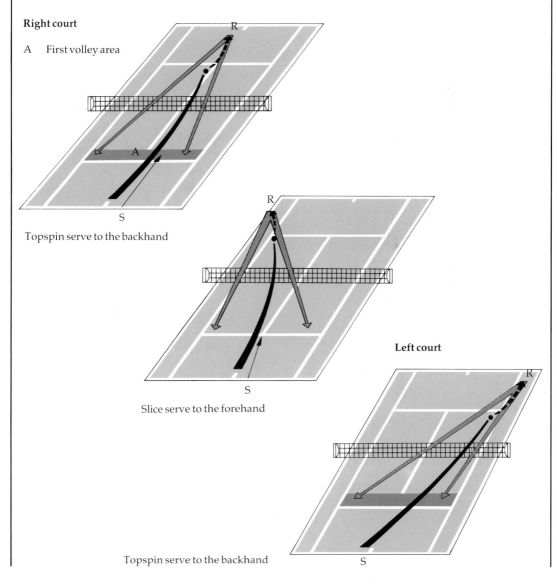

Right court

A   First volley area

Topspin serve to the backhand

Slice serve to the forehand

Left court

Topspin serve to the backhand

Hitting the second volley

As soon as you have made the first volley (see diagram 2 below) follow it, moving quickly up court again to within 10 feet of the net – the second volley area (see below). From here you can punch down through the ball from above net height. If you do not finish the rally from here, however, and your opponent has a chance to play the ball, your proximity to the net may turn into a huge disadvantage and you will be very vulnerable to a lob or a passing shot. As for your run towards the first volleying position, move towards the center of the possible angle of returns open to your opponent (positioning yourself marginally towards covering the straight passing shot) to give yourself the best chance of playing your volley. Providing your first volley is deep enough an angled second volley away from your opponent will often win the point.

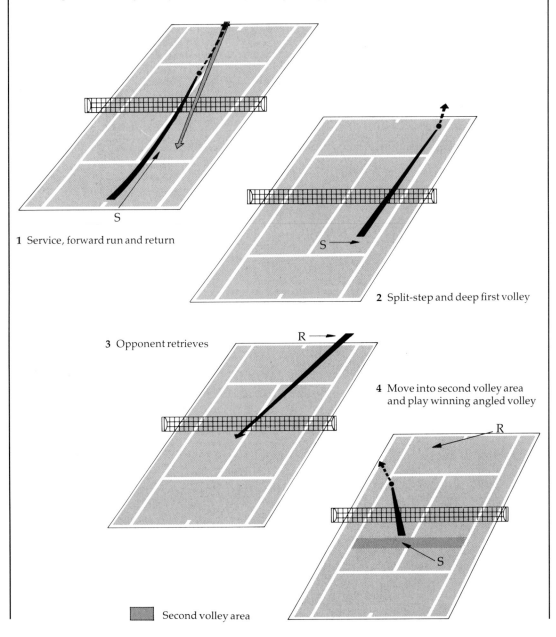

1 Service, forward run and return

2 Split-step and deep first volley

3 Opponent retrieves

4 Move into second volley area and play winning angled volley

Second volley area

Crossing your opponent

Although a bold and lightning-fast tactic, serving and volleying is, nevertheless, a pattern of play which can be anticipated by your opponent. If your opponent manages to anticipate an angled second volley you can occasionally cross him by playing the second volley back to the position that he has moved from, as in diagram 2 in the sequence below.

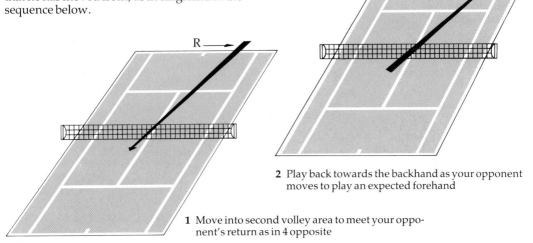

2 Play back towards the backhand as your opponent moves to play an expected forehand

1 Move into second volley area to meet your opponent's return as in 4 opposite

Practicing with a partner

On court, practice combining your second, spin serve with the run to the net. Counting your back foot following through after the serve as step one, count how many steps you need to reach the first volley area. When the number remains constant and you feel that your action is fast and smooth, have a partner time your forward run with a stopwatch. Try to improve your speed while maintaining rhythm and balance and the quality of your service.

Once you feel confident of your approach, try the drill shown below with your partner. Using half the doubles court only, your aim is to play the serve and volley pattern, winning the point with your second volley. As server you should take up the service stance behind the baseline between the centermark and the corner of the doubles court and serve straight into the service box opposite you. Use numerical scoring applying the following rules. The server must not allow returned shots to bounce between his service and baselines, and his first volley must land between the receiver's service and baselines. The receiver may not lob his first return. Play the drill to 10 points then reverse roles. This practice gives the serve and volley player a chance to build confidence and develop feel and depth while the receiver has a limited court to aim at and so must

seek to put the server in difficulties rather than risk going for outright winning shots. This is an ideal competitive practice for developing percentage play.

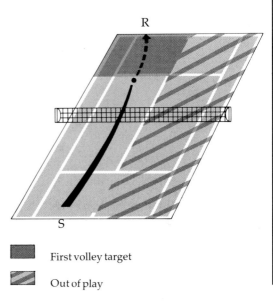

First volley target

Out of play

Playing the netrusher

The sensible serve and volleyer will only approach the net behind a deep, well-placed service, whereas the netrusher follows every service to the net hoping to pressurize you into sending back the sort of returns which can be easily dealt with. Your best weapons against such a player are the passing shot, the chip shot and every type of lob.

If you keep a cool head you can play passing shots against the inevitable short service which the netrusher will make and follow to the net. If the serves are repeatedly weak you may be able to step forwards and hit crosscourt passing shots before your opponent has gained a good first volleying position. Alternatively, move around the ball as it approaches and play passing shots down the sideline off your stronger side.

The opportunities for hitting a winner with your return of service against better quality serve and volley play will not occur so often as the pace, depth and spin of the service will limit your swing at the ball. A chipped return to the sidelines or at your advancing opponent's feet may be very effective, not winning the point outright, but forcing a non-aggressive reply from an opponent who is intent on attack. When you are under extreme pressure from a net attack your final recourse is to lob.

Playing passing shots

In the diagram, below left, a netrushing opponent is attacking behind a short service which lacks both pace and spin. As receiver, you can move up court to make your return at the same time as the server starts to move forwards to the net. Contacting the ball before the server has reached the service line, you can choose whether to hit a passing shot down the sideline or to play a crosscourt shot.

With experience you will be able to counter more efficient netrushers by applying spin to your passing shots as in the diagram, below right. By hitting around the outside of the ball you can swerve your groundstroke return so that the ball crosses the net in the doubles alley before swinging back into court near your opponent's baseline for a down-the-sideline passing shot. This stroke has to be modified to cope with service spin.

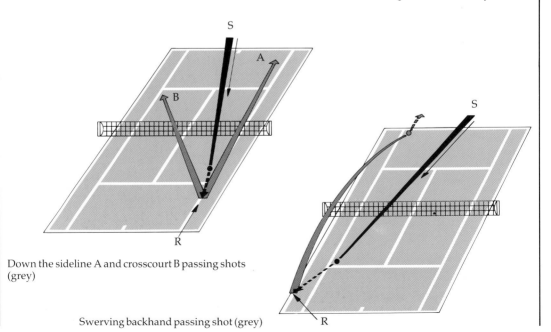

Down the sideline A and crosscourt B passing shots (grey)

Swerving backhand passing shot (grey)

Chipping your return

To prevent a serve and volleyer from continually smashing the return which remains above net height in the forecourt, you can elect to chip your returns low to the feet or low to either sideline, as shown in the diagram below left. If you can force a weak half-volley return you might well be able to run forwards and win the point with a passing shot. In a rally, if you are drawn wide by an approach shot, as in the diagram below right, a dink shot (see p.76) angled over the net and outside the netrusher's angle of retrieve, can turn defense into attack. The net attacker has to leave a section of the court unguarded. If you find it with your return you may win the point outright.

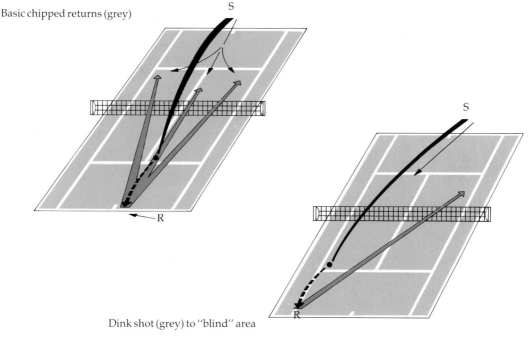

Basic chipped returns (grey)

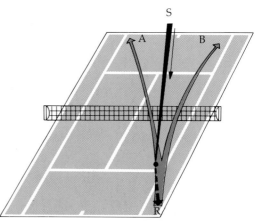

Dink shot (grey) to "blind" area

Lobbing

A deep basic or underspin lob, either crosscourt or down the sideline, but particularly over the backhand shoulder of the net player, will discourage even the most ardent netrusher. Playing the lob against a proficient netrusher is not only the correct tactical solution, but it is also the safest return you can possibly make, so, if you have developed a good lob, use it with confidence to counter-attack.

In the diagram, right, the serving opponent has forced you, the receiver, back and to the right with a penetrating service. The server is inside the service line and is split-stepping as you play your reply. The percentage return to make must be a lob, the safest being crosscourt, along the longest line possible within the court. A lobbed return will drive your opponent from the net and allow you time to recover your next center point receiving position.

Lobbing crosscourt or down the sideline
The crosscourt lob A is the safest return but lob B, down the sideline, may win the point outright if you can disguise your intentions.

Baseline play

If you serve and stay back, or return service and stay back you are electing to play from the baseline or back court. By contesting most points from the backcourt you will become known as a baseliner. This approach to tennis can be very successful as baseline play is founded on putting and keeping the ball in play and, even at the highest levels, more points are gained by opponents' mistakes than by winning shots which beat opponents outright. Even though playing from the backcourt means taking up a defensive position, it need not mean that you run to and fro returning every ball into court in the hope that your opponent will make an error. A good base-line player attempts to play forceful, attacking groundstrokes using the length and width of the court to tire and force errors from his opponent. Your service must be deep, accurate and reliable, and your return of service positive and effective. You must always keep the center point theory (see p.195) clearly in your mind.

The mirror reply

A crosscourt reply to a crosscourt drive from your opponent is the surest way of keeping the ball in play in a baseline rally. By hitting such a reply you are not changing the line of flight of the ball and by hitting back across the diagonal you are using the longest line on court as well as hitting the ball over the lowest point of the net. You are safe in the knowledge that if your opponent tries to change the line of flight with the next shot by hitting down the sideline, you will have the crosscourt or down the sideline option available to you – both of them safer than the shot your opponent has just played with its change from crosscourt to down the sideline. This tactic may not wrest the attacking initiative from your opponent but it will always maintain your position.

Changing the line of flight

Your two main objectives when playing from the baseline are to make your opponent run and to expose any weaknesses in your opponent's baseline game. You should aim to achieve both of these objectives whenever your opponent plays a crosscourt drive which is short of a good, deep length. In this situation you can safely move around the ball playing it with your stronger stroke and if necessary, changing the line of flight to send a penetrating drive wide towards your opponent's weaker side, usually the backhand. If you have changed the line of flight with a positive drive your opponent will have to cross the full width of the baseline to make a return. Combining shots in this way will lead to successful baseline play.

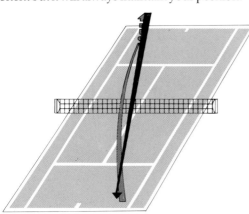

Playing a crosscourt drive
In the diagram, above, your opponent has played a good length crosscourt drive (grey). Your surest return is back along the same line (black) across the lowest part of the net.

Attacking the backhand
In the diagram, above, your crosscourt drive (black) has drawn a poor length return from your opponent (grey), giving you the opportunity to move forwards and drive hard to your opponent's backhand corner.

Crossing

Trying to move your opponent from one side of the court to the other will provide opportunities for crossing. This entails playing the ball back to the corner your opponent has moved from in anticipating your next shot. Successful crossing depends on making your opponent move a long way to reach the center point between the angles of your next return.

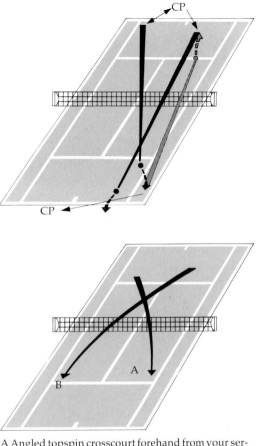

Playing back to the forehand
Your opponent, right, is stranded, being committed to moving beyond his centermark to reach the center point (CP), which covers your expected reply wide to the backhand as you play back to the forehand (black).

Varying your attack

When rallying from the baseline in a match, vary your drives not only in pace and height, but also in length, angle and type of spin. The diagrams, right and below, show a selection of shots which you might use singly and in various combinations. Note carefully the court areas the shots are played from as well as where the ball is played to. If you look at the diagram of court areas on page 195 you will be able to judge whether these baseline play shots are attacking or defending. Some of the shots are played from well inside the baseline. You must be ready when your opponent plays poor length drives or shots which are designed to tempt you forwards. Try to develop your game so that you can take full advantage of shorter balls making full use of the geometry of the court.

A Angled topspin crosscourt forehand from your service line to your opponent's right service court.
B Angled crosscourt backhand slice from your service line to your opponent's left service court.

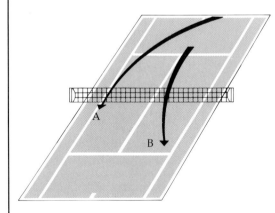

A Acutely angled backhand dink shot which will draw your opponent forwards.
B Fading backhand sidespin shot to your opponent's right service court.

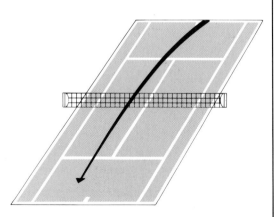

Deep baseline to baseline drive down the middle of the court which lands just to the backhand side of your opponent's centermark.

211

Playing the baseliner

Playing the baseliner from your own baseline will lead to long rallies as you both launch deep and accurate drives at each other from secure defensive positions. To counter baseline play effectively you should learn how to break an opponent's rhythm, and how to use an opponent's entrenched baseline position to your advantage.

If you know your opponent to be your equal, or your better, at groundstroke play, mix your basic drives with deep semi-lobbed drives, or "nothing" balls, which will force your opponent to hit the ball hard to generate pace. Make it difficult for your opponent to play deep angled drives by returning balls deep to the baseline only a yard or so to the right or left of the centermark. Introduce slower, sliced backhand, or sidespin forehand, drives, to further upset your opponent's rhythm and timing.

Using the "nothing" ball

When your opponent is timing well your penetrating basic drives which bounce to waist level, an effective way of upsetting his rhythm is to introduce a semi-lobbed return. This return should have little pace and should bounce to about shoulder height providing a very different ball for your opponent to hit, forcing him to alter his timing radically and upsetting his weight of shot. Whereas faster basic drives can be returned with little effort, an opponent has to strike a "nothing" ball with a slower timed swing to generate pace. Few players at any level can deal with this hanging paceless ball as well as they can harder hit balls. Play your "nothing" balls deep so that there is no chance of your opponent playing the ball at a comfortable height when it has fallen below shoulder height. Choose your opponent's weaker side and aim the ball to bounce to that side of the centermark.

Using slice and sidespin

A very effective baseline rhythm breaking tactic is to introduce slower, slice backhand or sidespin forehand drives. Try to play such drives every fourth or fifth shot and occasionally play the ball to the sideline corners of your opponent's service courts rather than deep into the baseline corners. This variation in speed, spin and length may well spoil concentration and timing no matter how well your opponent has been hitting the ball. Using the sidespin forehand drive reply to an angled drive gives you a double advantage in that your opponent will not only have to deal with the spin which takes the ball away to his backhand before and after the bounce, but also have to cover the width of the baseline to reach the ball. If this tactic is successful, keep changing your sequence of drives so that your opponent cannot settle into a new rhythm by anticipating your cycle of shots.

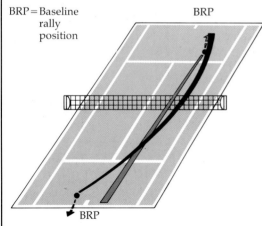

BRP = Baseline rally position

Breaking rhythm
Your opponent plays a baseline drive (grey) to which you make a semi-lobbed return (black), attacking your opponent's backhand.

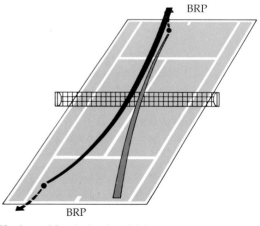

Playing a sidespin forehand drive
Receiving a center court reply (grey) from your right-handed opponent, play a sidespin forehand drive (black) making the ball swerve to his backhand.

Using the dropshot and drop volley

Played skilfully, the dropshot or drop volley can leave the baseliner stranded in the back court with no chance of reaching the low-bouncing ball close to the net. The dropshot can be attempted during a baseline rally when you are presented with a shorter length drive from your opponent hit from a wide position down the sideline. You can then play your stroke crosscourt, clearing the net at its lowest point and falling in the service court furthest from your opponent. Playing the drop volley requires strong approach play (see p.214) enabling you to keep your opponent back on his baseline while you position yourself close to the net for the winning shot, as shown in the series of two diagrams below.

Playing the drop volley

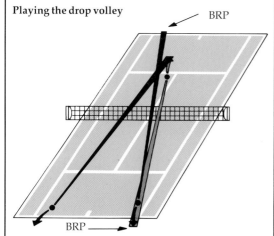

1 Your crosscourt forehand drive (black) forces a weak mid-court reply (grey) which you drive to the backhand corner (black) with your stronger stroke.

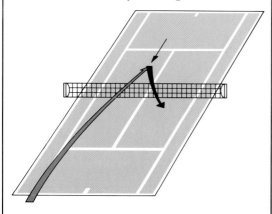

2 As your opponent rushes the length of the baseline move forwards to drop volley (black) the inevitably weak reply (grey).

Extending your attack

Now that you have seen the basic tactics for countering entrenched baseline play, you are ready to consider further means of attack. If your style tends towards baseline play you will be concerned with graduating towards all-court play, in itself a way to beat the proficient baseliner. You need to further develop the use of the dropshot and drop volley, and to add the passing shot and the lob to your attack. You may be technically competent to play the necessary strokes but introducing them at precisely the right moment in match play requires experience, concentration and considerable nerve. Practice realistically with your partner to gain familiarity and confidence at playing sequences of shots culminating in dropshots which will lure the baseliner from his strategic stronghold in the backcourt.

When you have mastered this ability to bring the baseliner out of the backcourt use passing shots to leave him stranded, hitting the ball beyond his reach with good margin for error and sufficient depth and pace to win the point. Your passing shots become more critical against the netrusher (see p.208) who will be much more determined to volley your reply than the baseliner who has advanced because there is no alternative. However, in the two diagrams which illustrate the use of the drop volley, left, a passing shot would have been a point winner if the final drop volley had gone too far with your opponent retrieving from the mid-court area.

Arantxa Sanchez-Vicario is a developing all-court player.

Approach play

Approach shots are groundstrokes played with the intention of following them towards the net to gain a good volleying position. The diagram, right, shows from which areas on court you can play approach shots. All short balls must be attacked with approach shot and volley play, even if you are a baseliner. Constructive baseline play is designed to force a short return from your opponent, so you should never ignore it and return to your baseline without taking advantage. In approach play the ball is often taken on the rise after the bounce.

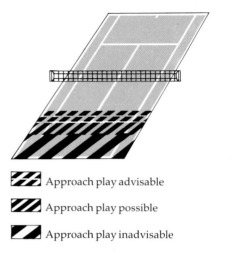

Approach play advisable

Approach play possible

Approach play inadvisable

Modifying your strokes

You can play your approach shots flat, with topspin, underspin or sidespin, all according to the height at which you are able to play the ball and your court position at the time. Modify your strokes by simply shortening your take-back. As you advance up court the distance your shot will have to travel diminishes rapidly so the shortened take-back will control the power in your stroke to match. If your approach shots are repeatedly flying out over your opponent's

baseline, or you are consistently netting your approach shots, check the take-back, racket face angle, and degree of spin which you are applying.

Do not form the habit of always slicing your backhand approach shots and topspinning your forehands. Try a modified slice on your forehand side sometimes. Shorten your basic slice stroke, taking the ball earlier than usual and slice through and under the ball for depth and control without loss

of speed. Short sliced strokes do not require the precise footwork of longer strokes and are easier to move forwards behind.

As you move forwards both to play your approach shots and the subsequent volleys, make sure that you slow down before making your strokes so that you can move quickly in any direction on balance in order to play your opponent's shot. If you are still running forwards when your opponent hits the ball, you will not have time to react.

Approaching from near the center line

You can play your most effective approach shots off balls that land within your service line and near the center line. The higher such balls bounce, the easier they are to attack. Although it is marginally safer to hit to the nearest corner with your approach shot (the center point of your opponent's possible angle of return will be a little closer for you), your central position allows you to play deep to either corner as shown in the diagram, right. If you have moved up court quickly and can take the ball at, or about, net height, you can attack crosscourt, perhaps crossing your opponent who may expect a down-the-sideline approach shot. If the ball is lower it is wiser to play to your opponent's backhand, then move forwards to volley the less forceful backhand return.

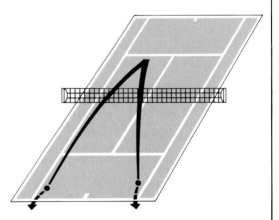

Attacking either corner
The approach shots, above, deep to the corners of your opponent's court, are both possible if the ball which you are attacking bounces near the center line. Either angle should make your opponent defend.

Approaching from nearer the sideline

From near the sidelines it is tactically sound to play most of your approach shots straight, parallel to the sideline nearest to you. If you play a crosscourt approach shot from near a sideline you will open up the court for your opponent to make a passing shot by making your next court position at the center point of your opponent's

angle of reply more distant, below left. The diagram, below right, shows how playing straight will maintain your advantage as the next center point will be closer. The exception to the rule might occur if your opponent is particularly strong on the backhand. In this case, play a crosscourt approach to the forehand.

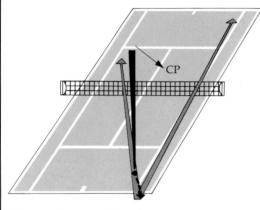

Crosscourt approach (black)

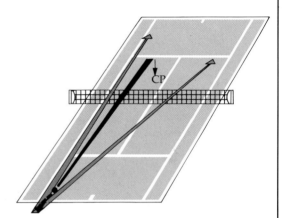

Down the sideline approach (black)

Playing an attacking approach sequence

Any down the sideline return from your opponent which falls short and does not force you too wide can be turned to your advantage by playing the sequence shown in the two diagrams below. The sequence starts as you can take the advantage of your opponent's particularly wide position by playing a crisp crosscourt forehand approach shot to the corner of the right-hand

service court. Your opponent may reach this shot but will have had to run hard and will probably manage a mid-court down the sideline reply (grey). You can then play a backhand drive or slice (depending on the height of the ball), deep crosscourt. If your opponent manages to retrieve this shot, using an angled drop volley will help you win the point.

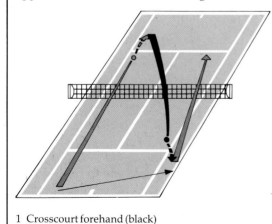

1 Crosscourt forehand (black)

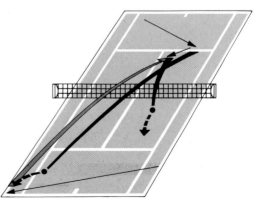

2 Backhand drive (black) and drop volley (black)

Lobbing

The lob, in all its forms, has a major role to play in any singles match but it is often neglected and only used as an emergency shot. The basic lob can be used to counter any offensive while the underspin lob can be impregnable as a last line of defense. The topspin lob can be used to initiate an attack.

The major strategic use of the lob is in defense. In a rally where you have made a tactical error and find yourself out of position and desperate to retrieve the ball, the basic or underspin lob will slow your opponent's attack, forcing him back towards the baseline. The length of time that the ball stays in the air gives you the chance to regain your centre point position. The defensive lob played from the back court is the only means of guaranteeing a successful return against a hard-hit smash.

The lesser, attacking use of the lob occurs during a rally where you take the initiative to use the lob in a rally playing the ball over your opponent's head either to win the point outright, or to force a weak reply.

Defensive lobbing

At some time or other, every player is forced into the situation where the lob has to be used or the point is lost. If you can only just reach a hard-hit drive or smash with a desperate lunge, then a high, deep, underspin lob is the only shot which gives you the sort of margin for error and the time for recovery necessary. In less critical tactical situations the high, defensive lob will allow you to recover your best center point position in a rally after a tactical error on your part, or an outstandingly good shot from a strong opponent

as shown in the sequence, below. The lob can sometimes provide the drastic change of pace necessary to break an opponent's baseline, or serve and volley rhythm. If you detect a weakness in your opponent's overhead game, then higher, defensive lobbing can become an attacking ploy.

It is best to lob over the backhand shoulder of your opponent, if you have time to pick your target, making him run around the ball, or attempt the difficult backhand smash.

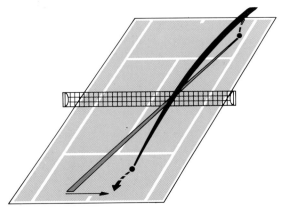

1 Your opponent plays a strong crosscourt backhand drive (grey) which you return down the backhand sideline (black).

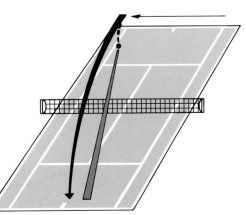

2 Your opponent has anticipated your shot well and plays a powerful crosscourt forehand (grey) which you can only just reach. Your lob (black) is directed towards the center of the baseline.

Offensive topspin lobbing

The topspin lob can be used as an effective alternative to the passing shot to attack your opponent. In the sequence, below, you can see how to take advantage of an indecisive volley. Your opponent's service is good and he has gained a solid volleying position behind it. However, your return prompts a weak volley. If you can introduce a surprise topspin lob at this point, to the most distant corner of the court, your opponent will have little chance of a reply.

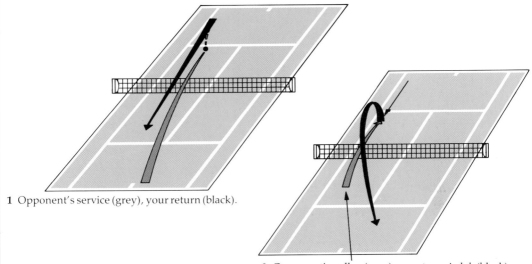

1 Opponent's service (grey), your return (black).

2 Opponent's volley (grey), your topspin lob (black).

Testing your opponent's stamina

Using the lob allows you take full advantage of the depth of your opponent's court, and so it is an effective weapon to use when your strategy is to sap his stamina. In the sequence of shots shown below, you can see how to combine a deep baseline drive and a dropshot with a basic lob to exhaust even the fittest competitor. You will see how your opponent is forced to run sideways, then diagonally forwards, and then, as he recovers and hopefully advances a few steps to volley, diagonally backwards to chase the lob. Your movement will be slight.

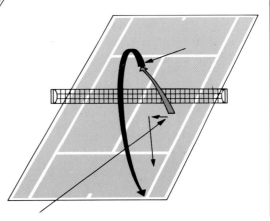

1 Your down-the-line forehand drive (black) elicits a weak cross-court reply (grey) against which you play a dropshot (black).

2 Your opponent has to run the length of the court to return (grey), and expects a volley, not your topspin lob (black).

Overhead play

The closer you get to the net in an attacking serve and volley sequence of play, the more likely your opponent is to lob. Be prepared for a lob once you have crossed your service line. If your overhead game is strong you should treat this as an advantage knowing that the smash can often be an outright point winner. Weak lobs can be forced by exerting pressure in a match from both the baseline and the forecourt particularly by attacking an opponent's weaker groundstroke side. Sometimes the one stroke a one-sided player can play on his weak side is the lob, learned and practiced as an emergency measure. In such an event, you may well find that the weak lob which you were looking for turns out to be quite a good one and you will then have to change your attack accordingly. Lobs which you force from a defending opponent

that would land in your forecourt or no man's land must be dealt with aggressively. Smash deep to the baseline from no man's land. If the lob falls towards your forecourt you can safely play your smash at an angle to avoid your opponent. Attacking overhead play from the forward areas of your court will often entail playing the jump smash if you are not to be sent scampering back to your baseline to retrieve the ball.

When playing against opponents who are capable of using the lob for attack you must be able to use your smashes as effectively as possible so that, at the very least, you maintain the attacking initiative in a rally. Good quality lobs will sometimes take you into your backcourt and have to be played after the ball has bounced.

Maintaining service initiative

When playing serve and volley tactics your opponent is likely to use the lob to deter you from approaching the net. The two diagrams, right, show how you should smash your reply depending on the quality of the lob. In both cases you are serving and your first volley has elicited a lob from your defending opponent. The first diagram shows how your strong, well-played first volley has brought a weak lob reply. You can reach the lob in your forecourt with little effort so the point should be yours with an angled smash away from your stranded opponent. In the second diagram the lob reply to your volley is deeper, forcing you to retreat into no man's land to play the smash. Your best overhead reply is deep to your opponent's backhand side, then advance again but be ready for another lob as you again exert pressure on your opponent, so keeping him on the defensive.

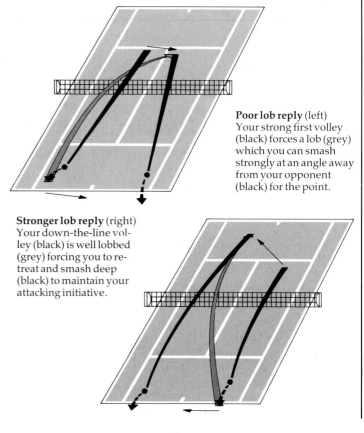

Poor lob reply (left)
Your strong first volley (black) forces a lob (grey) which you can smash strongly at an angle away from your opponent (black) for the point.

Stronger lob reply (right)
Your down-the-line volley (black) is well lobbed (grey) forcing you to retreat and smash deep (black) to maintain your attacking initiative.

Countering an attacking lob

If your opponent is a good baseliner it is possible that you will have to deal with unexpected lobs which force you back from a good net position to your own baseline. The diagram, right, illustrates your best options when countering such play. After playing your second volley crosscourt from a strong net position your opponent, who anticipated your volley well and managed to react quickly enough to cover nearly the width of the singles court, hoists an exceptionally good, high, underspin lob. If you hesitate at this unexpected turn of events you are lost. You must get back to be able to play the bounce smash. Power is not important, your aim is simply to regain your attacking advantage by smashing deep with good placement. Your best option is to hit the ball crosscourt (the longest line available) and this could cross your opponent, who may well be expecting a smash or drive down the sideline and will therefore be caught unawares if you can play the stroke successfully.

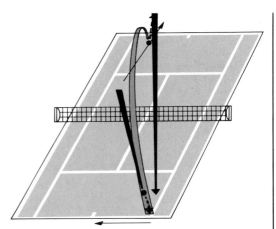

Making the surest bounce smash recovery
After a good volley (black) your opponent plays a very difficult crosscourt lob (grey). You sprint for the baseline and play a crosscourt bounce smash (black) for maximum safety as the diagonal line across the court allows the best margin for error.

Vitas Gerulaitis jump smashes from his service line area. In the top class game overhead play is generally strong and lobs which fall to the forecourt area are treated as opportunities to win the point outright. Because of Jimmy Connors's agility, however, Gerulaitis must choose his court placement carefully.

DOUBLES

Match-play doubles is a team game. Strategy and tactics must be agreed upon by both partners before play gets underway and the match plan jointly reviewed while the match is in progress. Because of the importance of your teamwork, the most successful partnerships are those who have played together over many years of competitive play. When players come together and have immediate success because of their rapport they usually go on to become a lasting and highly successful doubles team.

Try out different partners until you find a player whose game complements your own and who is a friend both on and off the court. If you prefer playing the right court your partner should favor the left, or vice-versa. With two players at either end of a court, the easiest place to win points from is the net area, as shown opposite. There is little point in a dedicated serve and volley player part-

nering someone who only goes to the net when he receives an invitation. The prime strategy for any team is to gain the best net position first to secure victory. The pair showing the best combination of tactics and strokes should then triumph by dominating the play from the net more often than their opponents.

In doubles play the advantage is always with the serving team because it has the first chance of establishing both players in a fore-court volleying position. Your aim should be never to lose your service games and to go all out to break your opponents' service games once to seal each set.

Your doubles game will mature with your ability to position yourself effectively while your partner is playing. You must be where you know you can do the most good after he has made his play.

Individual requirements

In order to be a successful doubles player you need to have developed an aggressive spin service for both first and second deliveries which you can follow to the net safely. Your service returns have to be reliable; they will mostly be crosscourt and ideally should force the server to volley from below net level while not exposing your partner to a volley attack. You should be agile and have excellent volleying ability from anywhere in the forecourt and your overhead play should be reliable and strong. In the fore-court doubles play is often spectacular and you will have to display good anticipation and excellent reflexes to play the ball as all four players position themselves only 15-20 feet apart.

Doubles play will involve some groundstrokes which you must be able to keep low. When your opponents are able to dominate the net position, you will need to defend or attack with the lob. However, the percentage of groundstrokes to all shots in a match decreases as the quality of doubles play increases until in a top class doubles game you can expect a repeating pattern of serve, return, volley, volley, volley. In this style of doubles play, confidence in your service control, your service returns and net play is vital.

Partnership requirements

Most top doubles partnerships combine a power player with a consistent player who is a sound tactician and can maneuver the opposition into situations from which his partner can win the point. This contrast should not be too great, however, because with both teams seeking similar objectives, a great deal of joint effort is required to gain and keep the attacking initiative. You must combine your efforts against a weakness or the weaker player. In an unbalanced doubles team, or one which has one out-of-form partner, the stronger player must endeavor to take more than a half share of the play.

Ideally, the right court player should possess a strong crosscourt forehand return of service and an excellent backhand volley, while the left court player should favor backhand returns and be equipped with a strong forehand volley. The left court player should have a really good overhead game for he will have to play lobs in the middle of the court as well as on his own side. He should also be the stronger player for most of the crucial points in a match are played against the left court receiver, for example, 15-30, 30-15, 30-40, 40-30 and the advantage point for or against. If you are left-handed, then, almost without fail, you should play in the left court where you can use your crosscourt forehand to greatest effect.

Basic doubles court positions

The two diagrams below show the basic court positions before the start of each point.

Server (S) Almost halfway between the center-mark and your doubles sideline providing the best opportunities for serving and a sound advance towards the net.

Server's partner (SP) About 10 feet from the net, about 8 feet from the center line and 10 feet from the doubles sideline.

Receiver (R_1 R_2) When on the defensive, the normal singles receiving position (R_1) is usual but I recommend that the receiver should try to play offensive returns from R_2.

Receiver's partner (RP) An unenviable position just inside the service line and 6 to 8 feet from the center line. The receiver's partner will often have to rely on quick reactions.

Advantage of the net position

Although defensive tactics often win singles matches at all levels, doubles matches are usually won by attack. The reason for this is illustrated by the diagrams, below. These show the great advantage of assuming the net position in doubles play, whether you are serving or receiving. If the serving team manage to force both receiver and receiver's partner behind their baseline the areas of the court left undefended, and so possible target areas, are considerable (below). From the defenders' point of view (bottom), the target areas are very limited: difficult passing shots are available down the sidelines or through a narrow gap between the opposing netmen. A slightly wider target area exists along the baseline which can only be reached by effective lobs from the defending pair.

◣ Targets from the net

◺ Targets from the baseline

Right court

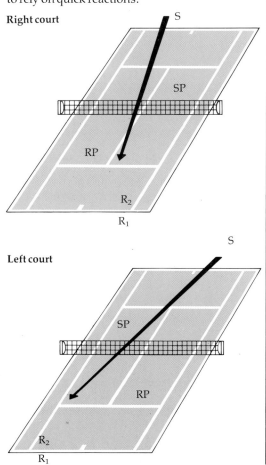

Left court

Serving

Whereas when playing a singles game you need to strive for a 70 per cent success rate with your first serve, in doubles you must aim even higher with 75 per cent as your minimum target. This figure is very high because of the need to gain the net position behind all of your serves. If you miss your first serve you still must follow your second service to the volley position from where you and your partner have the best chance of winning points. The tactical balance remains in your favor if you have to rely on your second service to initiate such serve and volley tactics, but far fewer points are won behind second serves when compared statistically with successes achieved with first serves.

As with serving in the singles game, it is sound practice to serve the majority of balls deep to your opponent's backhand, the naturally defensive stroke. How often you use other services depends on the strengths and weaknesses of your opponents and the score, but your aim must always be to force a defensive return which you can volley aggressively to maintain the initiative.

Which type of serve to use

As the major tactic of doubles play is serve and volley, the same guidelines for choosing the type of service to use apply as for singles serve and volley play. The safest serve to use is a spin delivery which is struck with more speed and less spin than your normal second service. You can modify your topspin service best for this purpose and I recommend it as the ideal service for doubles play. Simply place the ball slightly further in front of you and not so far over towards the left shoulder and you will produce a more attacking topspin delivery. On your second service you must risk less but still elicit a defensive return. Use the same spin service hit with enough power to maintain your attacking initiative. As with all second serving, let increased spin give you a greater margin of error rather than hitting the service weakly and so giving your opponent a chance to counter-attack.

Who should serve first

If you win the toss, always elect to serve first, just as in singles, so that, having won the opening game, you will remain a game ahead through the set with your opponent serving to get even. As a pair, you should always open with your strongest service game. This need not proceed from the strongest server, but from the service which suits best the serve and volley tactics of doubles play. If you start with your best service game you will play the maximum number of games in that formation. Remember that you can end one set on your strongest service game and then open the next set serving the same way (you may, however, prefer to do this only when it does not involve a change of ends for either partner).

Stan Smith and Bob Lutz assume orthodox positions, with Smith serving from the left court. Smith's first service may be similar to his second in singles play.

Serving to the right court

Although the modified topspin service to the backhand is your main service for doubles, you should not miss the opportunity of using your slice service to the right court wide to the right-handed receiver's forehand.

The two diagrams, right, show the different positions the server and server's partner must take up when serving through the middle of the court to the receivers' backhand, or wide to the forehand. The server maintains his usual doubles serving position for both services. If he were to stand nearer the center of the court to improve the service angle to the backhand the receiver would be warned of the server's intentions. By holding his ground the server makes the receiver maintain his position for a possible wide service to the forehand. His net approach after serving should be closer to the middle of the court than usual when serving wide to the forehand. The server's partner stands further towards the sideline for the wide slice service.

Backhand
The server aims deep to the backhand corner of the right service court using a topspin service. Do not warn your opponent by standing too near to the centermark.

Forehand
Wide slice service to the forehand corner of the right service court. Server's partner moves closer to the sideline.

Serving to the left court

When serving to a right-handed opponent in the left court, most of your serves should be aimed deep to the backhand corner, as shown in the diagram, right. Again, the modified topspin service is ideal for the purpose. Whether purely for variety or to attack a specific weakness in an opponent, you should reserve some alternative means of serving attack. If your opponent is standing nearer to his sideline and is attempting to run round your service to play a forehand return, occasionally serve down the middle of the court, wide to the forehand. A flat or slice service may well prove more effective than the topspin. The forehand alternative should be used more regularly if your opponent is disproportionately strong on the backhand side or is left-handed. The slice service can be a useful alternative on the backhand side too, allowing you to swerve the ball into the right-hander's body, thus making it extremely difficult to return effectively.

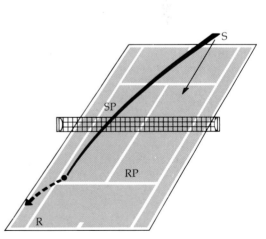

Backhand
Topspin service deep to the backhand corner of the left service court using the sharp angle made possible by the doubles service stance. The server's partner protects the sideline with his forehand as the server makes his forwards run.

Returning service

It is a common occurrence in top doubles play, where the serve and volley game is so good, that stalemate is reached when neither side is able to break their opponents' service games. Prior to the introduction of the tie-breaker, sets sometimes became very protracted until one team played enough high quality attacking returns to break service.

As in the singles game your first priority as receiver must be to keep the ball in play. However, to win doubles matches your team's service returns have to be of high quality, forcing defensive volleys from the incoming server which allow you and your partner to wrest the attacking initiative from the serving team.

Doubles receiving positions

You will have seen on page 221 how the usual singles receiving position behind the baseline is not always the best position for doubles play. In good quality doubles, the threat of the big first service is not such a vital factor. Your serving opponent will be concentrating on making sure of the success of his first service and will most likely be using a spin service to follow to the net. To allow you to make attacking returns when it is possible, you should take the calculated risk of standing just inside the baseline to receive service. This will give you the chance of playing the ball early, before spin takes the ball too far away and perhaps catching the incoming server a little off balance and too far from the net when he makes his first return.

If the first service fails, and the server has to rely on a second service, stand in a little closer.

Crosscourt or down-the-sideline returns

Although there is a higher success rate of returns made down the sideline than is commonly thought, the percentage return in doubles is crosscourt.

Playing down the sideline against the net man can result in the immediate loss of the point because it provides an angled shot between you and your partner for the opposing net man. However, a successful down-the-line return can be an outright winner. You will have the highest chance of success in the right court where you will be able to play a forehand return against the opposing netman's backhand volley. The two diagrams, right, show how the best opportunity for attacking the sideline occurs with wide-swinging services which take you beyond the sideline to make the return. From this position a triangular target area beyond the netman increases in size the wider you are.

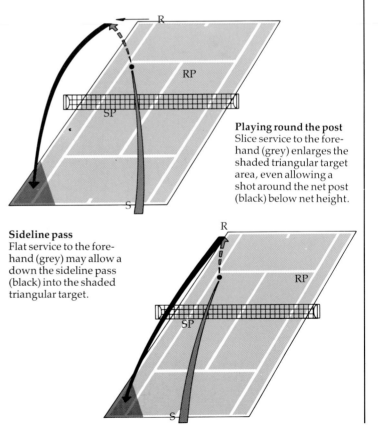

Playing round the post
Slice service to the forehand (grey) enlarges the shaded triangular target area, even allowing a shot around the net post (black) below net height.

Sideline pass
Flat service to the forehand (grey) may allow a down the sideline pass (black) into the shaded triangular target.

Choosing the best option

The four diagrams below show services to the forehand and backhand in both right and left courts, and the options for service return which are open to you as receiver. Compared with returning service in the singles game there is less choice of counter-attacking returns open to you in doubles play, especially when the quality of service is consistently high. As can be seen below, the good service gives you no alternative but to play return A, back low over the net into the server's court. Less effective services will allow you to play return B, or even return C in some cases to attack a specific weakness.

Your choice of return in doubles also depends on the strengths and weaknesses of the server's partner. Returns which attack the net man will obviously be more attractive if you can take advantage of a weakness.

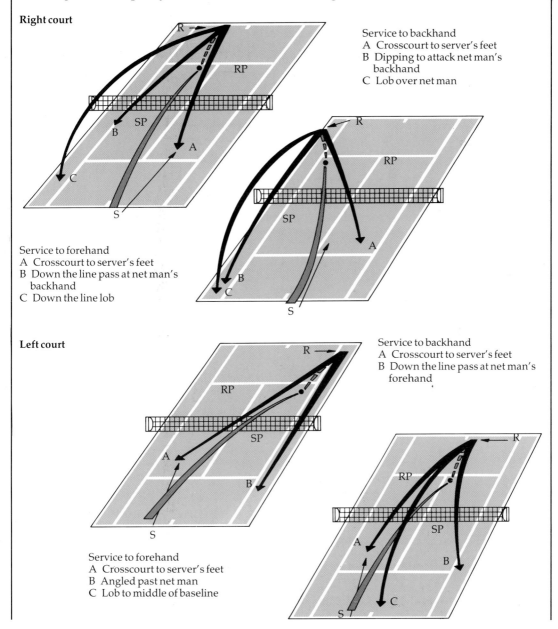

Right court

Service to backhand
A Crosscourt to server's feet
B Dipping to attack net man's backhand
C Lob over net man

Service to forehand
A Crosscourt to server's feet
B Down the line pass at net man's backhand
C Down the line lob

Left court

Service to backhand
A Crosscourt to server's feet
B Down the line pass at net man's forehand

Service to forehand
A Crosscourt to server's feet
B Angled past net man
C Lob to middle of baseline

Net play

Net play is at the heart of doubles strategy and your success from the forecourt after serving or receiving will usually determine the outcome of a doubles match. The server's first volley should initiate the serving team's net attack, as shown below. If the receiver has opted to play to the server's partner then that player, already in the net position, is in the best position to win the point. Any ball played to him by the opposition which is not a good shot should be put away for the point, as shown below right. When the service is to the right court, a right-handed net man should cover up to the center of the court for his server with his forehand volley. In the left court, an agreement must be struck as to which type of ball the net man leaves.

The receiver's partner has a similar role to play as the server's net man if the receiver can make a good enough return to take the attacking initiative. The receiver's partner must then move forwards to volley any weak reply in his half while the receiver moves forwards to join him in the forecourt.

Server's role

If the serve has forced a defensive reply from the receiver the server should be in a good first volley position (see p. 205) in order to press home the attack. The server's forward run should not be directly along the line of the service as in singles, but should be towards the center of his half of the court, veering a little towards the center line. The server's first volley should be punched deep into the receiver's court, as in the diagram below, where the receiver is still in the backcourt, or, at best, advancing through no man's land. A strong volley will pin the receiver back or fall awkwardly at his feet as he advances. Such a volley will allow the server to move forwards again.

Role of the server's partner

The server's partner's primary role is to cover his forecourt as completely as possible with emphasis towards the center of the court. This is why he should stand slightly nearer to the middle of the court, from where he can cut off any crosscourt drive which passes on his side of the center of the net. If the server's partner does this efficiently the server will have more confidence to make his net approach. The server's partner too should always be prepared to intercept the receiver's return, especially from the right court where, as a right-hander, he can forehand volley the ball before it falls below net height. Never intercept, however, unless you are sure of making a volley which is likely to win the point.

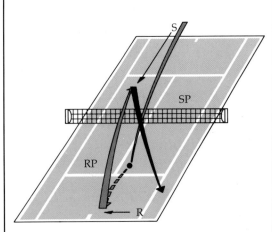

Server's first volley
Serving to the backhand in the right court the server runs forwards keeping to the right court to meet the return which avoids the server's partner (grey). The best volley is deep and angled crosscourt (black).

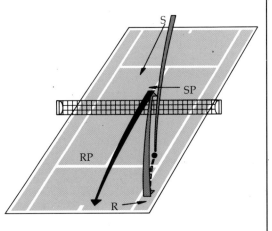

Basic interception
A deep, wide service to the forehand has elicited a hard crosscourt reply (grey). The server's partner judges the receiver's intentions and intercepts volleying between the opposing pair (black).

Role of the receiver's partner

The receiver's partner is always in danger of being caught off guard (as in the case of server's partner intercepting, opposite) if he does not keep alert to the course of play and move with purpose while his partner and the opposing pair plays. Just as the server's partner should intercept when the opportunity arises, so should the receiver's partner be alert to the possibility of an interception, especially when a strong shot from his partner wrests the attacking initiative, as in the example right. Suddenly changing defense into attack requires considerable presence of mind. As the receiver's partner you will not be in a position to make an attacking volley unless you move forwards to a more aggressive net position. Your success depends on judging when this move will be effective and, the decision made, timing your move so that the interception can be hit effectively as possible.

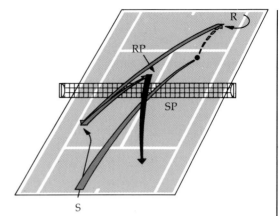

Receiver's partner intercepts
A shorter length service allows the receiver to hit an aggressive, sharply angled topspin return (grey). The receiver's partner sees the opportunity to move forwards and intercept (black) the server's reply.

David Lloyd and Mark Cox in tandem at the net in sound volleying formation. Both men cover the center of the court well, but the right-handed Lloyd positions himself to take a smash as Cox watches intently. Cox is ready to retreat if a deep counter-lob is forthcoming from the opposition.

227

Four players at the net

With both pairs trying to attain strong forecourt positions, it is often the case in top class doubles play that all four players converge at the net. The speed at which volleys will cross the net in these situations limits the length of such encounters to a few seconds at the most, as all players strive to find a gap to play through or force an error. In these situations it is often possible to play the ball at an opponent's body. However, this play sometimes backfires when your victim plays a volley successfully which results from a purely reflex action, as in the example, below. Most effective reflex volleys are played on the backhand so aim your shots to the forehand hip of your opponent's body, or you may face unexpected difficult returns.

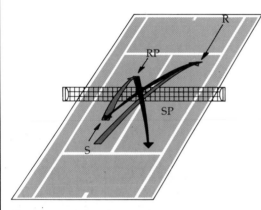

Receiver's partner makes a reflex return
The receiver's partner has moved forward, anticipating an interception. Server's first volley is strong, forcing a weak reply from the receiver. Receiver's partner plays a reflex volley off server's hard second volley reply to win the point.

Reflex volleying

Most tennis strokes are produced through reaction, when the brain responds to an opponent's shot and provokes the body into action. When you play a reflex volley you are simply making an involuntary response in the same way as you blink to protect your eyes. When a tennis ball is hit hard at you, your body responds with a reflex action, a response initiated by your nervous system fractions of a second before the information reaches your brain. You can most easily fend the ball off with a backhand volley movement.

Faking

Deceiving the opposition is part of advanced doubles tactics. The fake move is a useful ploy for the server's partner to use against the receiver, as in the series of two diagrams, below. By moving a step towards the middle of the court, or even by simply swaying on to the foot nearer the middle of the court, the server's partner tempts the receiver to play the ball down the sideline thinking that the net man is anticipating a crosscourt reply. The server's partner's intentions, however, are to move swiftly back to volley the sideline return crosscourt between his opponents. Faking a move in this way can be very successful as long as the movement involved is not overdone.

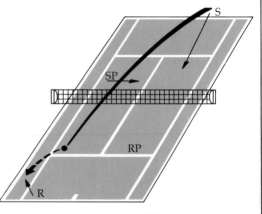

1 As the server runs to the net following his service, server's partner fakes a move towards the backhand, anticipating an interception. Receiver notes this as he makes his stroke.

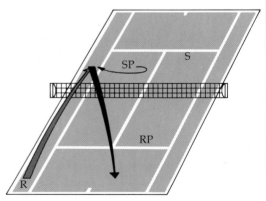

2 Receiver directs his shot down the sideline (grey), but server's partner times his return to take the forehand volley perfectly and makes an angled winning shot (black) between the receiver and the receiver's partner to win the point.

Marginal balls

As most of the play in doubles is across the middle of the net or directly through the center, it is important that you do not get in each other's way at the net and that the best positioned, or better equipped, player takes the ball.

A ball coming straight through the middle of the court should most often be taken by the player who can use the forehand. Crosscourt shots should be taken by the player opposite unless an interception has a high chance of success. Lobs to the center of the court should be taken by the left court player providing he is right-handed. Otherwise the nearest or better overhead player should take the ball. When either player could take the ball, as a general rule, the player who last played the ball should play the next shot rather than the "cold" partner stepping in. The cardinal sin of doubles play is for both players to leave the ball for the other to play. It is better that you clash rackets as long as one player returns the ball. You will find, however, that as you improve your doubles play rapport, such dangerous measures will prove unnecessary and you will develop a "feel" for who should step in to take marginal balls.

Calling

In the best doubles teams each player will know automatically what the other's intentions are in the majority of situations. While you are developing this sort of rapport you should form the habit of calling to clarify your own intentions, especially in tight situations at the net. You should call: when you want to play the ball or when you want your partner to play the ball in situations where there is any confusion; when you want your partner to leave the ball because it will land out of court, and when you want your partner to change position.

Use one word commands only and decide on your terminology before starting to play. I would recommend calling "mine" if you think you have a better chance with a certain ball, "yours" when you want your partner to take a ball, "out" when the ball will bounce out of court and "change" if play necessitates swapping sides. The more experienced player can prompt his partner to advance or retreat in attack or defense with calls of "up" or "back". He can also call "stay" when his partner makes an interception and the cross-over should stand, or "recover" if he wants him to return to his own side.

John McEnroe and Peter Fleming show good teamwork at the net as McEnroe takes a central ball played by the opposition and plays a deft drop volley. There was no danger of Fleming trying for the ball and he remains in a good covering position as McEnroe plays the dominant role.

Lobbing

The lob is not only the safest but in its various forms is also one of the more versatile strokes used in the game of doubles. As with singles, the lob can be used in attack and counter-attack, but its major use is in defense. As doubles play is so orientated towards attack from the net area, having to play defensive lobs from your baseline means that you have been badly out-maneuvered. Your purpose in resorting to the lob is to buy time while you recover so that you can perhaps regain the attacking initiative and return to the net. When lobbing in defense, the partner who does not make the first lob must retreat with the lobber to present a tandem defense to the opposition who are smashing from their forecourt. You might elect to lob defensively as a tactic designed to break your opponents' morale if you judge one or both of them to be inconsistent in their overhead play. Used with skill, the deep defensive lob can very easily become a means of destroying the confidence of all but the best of overhead players.

The counter-lob is a useful reply with which to drive your netrushing opponents from the net. Your purpose is to elicit a weak defensive lob from your opponents that you can smash to win the point. The purely offensive lob, hit with topspin and used to win points outright, should not be used from too far back in your court or it may dip before it clears the opposition.

Defensive lobbing

Defensive lobbing in doubles play should be high and deep for success and you should work as a pair. As can be seen in the diagrams, right, the defensive lobbing formation is both players back behind the baseline to cover the likely overhead play from the opposition. Once in this position it is likely that the point will be played out with one team lobbing, and the other smashing. The two examples of defensive lobbing, shown right, illustrate the most effective lobs to play against services in both the right- and left-hand courts. In both cases, lobbing has been adopted as a tactic and the receiver has opted to stand further back than usual to play the aggressive serving. Receiver's partner joins receiver behind the baseline as receiver makes the lobbed return. In the right court, aim deep down the sideline from the right court over the left shoulder of the net man. In the left court you should still lob down the sideline rather than risk a crosscourt lob against the incoming server.

Right court
Service (grey) is taken late and the lob is played (black) deep over the server's partner.

Left court
Service to the backhand (grey) is lobbed (black), again, over the server's partner, deep to the right-hand corner.

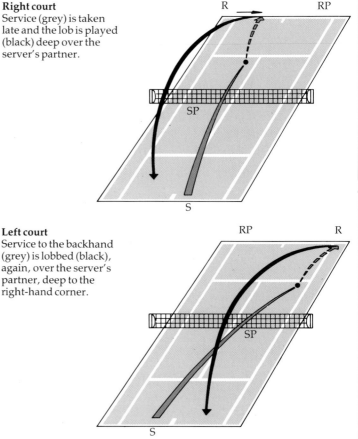

Counter-lobbing

Counter-lobbing can be an effective tactic to employ against a netrushing doubles team. It is especially useful when your return of service is ineffective. A counter-attacking lob is a far better reply against a net man than a weak, high drive or cut which can be easily attacked. A successful counter-lob will allow you and your partner to move up court into the volley position. From here, you will be able to deal with the probable defensive reply from your opponents. The diagram, below, shows the basic lob being used to counter-attack in place of the driven return. The aim is to send the net man running back to play the ball after the bounce. As soon as your partner sees that the net man is unable to smash the lob, he should move forwards to the net position. When the server sees what is happening he will have to halt his forwards run and move back behind the baseline to line up with his partner in defense, as you join your partner at the net. The counter-lob as a return to a service in the right court works well in that your lob can be played over the right-handed net man's backhand shoulder.

With so much emphasis placed on gaining the net position in doubles play by using low returns of service, switching to a counter-lob return contains a useful element of surprise. This type of shot can also cause team confusion for your opposition as it is most likely that the server will be in the best position to play your lobbed return. To do this he must cross over the court and his partner must cover the server's side – a maneuver that can sometimes cause problems.

Offensive lobbing

The offensive lob hit with sharp topspin can, like the counter-lob, be played as a service return, but only against poor, short-length services. The offensive lob is more usually played against short balls which you can advance on and take at about waist height. Playing such a shot will surprise the attacking team who think that they have the court well covered, as in the illustration, below. The serve and volley pair are perfectly positioned at the net after well-executed serve and approach play. However, server plays a mid-court volley (grey) which lacks penetration. The receiver, who has been previously pinned back close to his own baseline, is able to advance to take the ball. He notices that his opponents are both a little too close to the net and so plays a topspin lob, angling the ball over the server's left shoulder for maximum effect, to win the point. Even if the right-handed server had been able to reach the ball, an effective smash would have been very difficult to play as he was forced to jump backwards, and wide to his left.

The offensive lob has to be played well or not at all. If you simply give your opponents an easy smash winner, you will not only lose the immediate point, but you will also give the opposing team's confidence a considerable boost. This goes for defensive lobbing and counter-lobbing too, but it is with offensive lobbing that your margin for error is smallest.

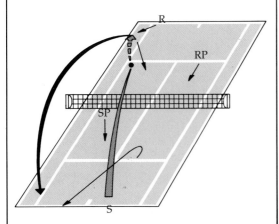

Counter-lobbing your service return
Service to the forehand (grey) which server starts to follow to the net. A deep lob (black) over the net man's shoulder, forces opposition to retreat and allows your net approach.

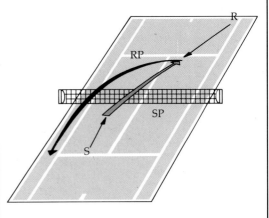

Receiver lobs to win point
Server volleys weakly during a net exchange (grey) allowing receiver to run forwards and play a surprise topspin lob (black) angled to just clear the server's racket and land in the alley.

Overhead play

When you and your partner are at the net in the basic volleying formation (both of you 6½ to 10 feet from the net and 8 feet from the center line) you will be in the ideal position to cope with most shots directed at you in a frontal attack. As you saw on page 221, only narrow strips of court between you, and down each sideline, exist as targets. However, this situation changes as soon as your opponents decide to lob. Your basic volleying positions must then become mobile ones. You must be on your toes, alert and studying your opponents so that you can anticipate their intentions and react early. When there is no specific need to move apart you should keep level with your partner, so, as the lob goes up from your opponents, take a couple of steps backwards in tandem, both being ready to smash. At this point the two golden rules of smashing in doubles apply:

do not let any lob fall over your head without smashing it, and always smash your own lobs (those which fall in your half of the court). As you smash, remember that it is the deep smash and the angled smash, shown opposite, that win most points in doubles play matches.

The reason for thinking positively that no lob should go over your head is that once the lob has beaten you, your team is automatically on the defensive even if you can run back and retrieve the ball – your vital net position is lost. Being responsible for your own lobs will make sure that both players remain alert at the net and will avoid any misunderstanding as would result from changing positions by running in diagonal lines. In a few exceptional circumstances only is it advisable to cover for your partner, one example of which is shown opposite.

Anticipating lobs

Good forecourt play depends on anticipation so that you can present the most effective foil to your opponents' play. The two diagrams, right, show how you must work together, moving in parallel to face your opponents' attack. When a lob is played at you, retreat together, as shown in the diagram, above right, but it is the player who is covering the side on which the ball lands that must hit the smash. If the ball falls between you, the same rules for who takes the ball apply as for net play (see p.229).

If play takes your opponents to one side or the other of their court, make sure that, as a team, you continue to present a united front. This will entail wheeling so that an imaginary line joining you and your partner remains perpendicular to the direction of play, as shown in the diagram, below right. In this way you remain in the best position to play angled overhead shots that will leave your opponents stranded.

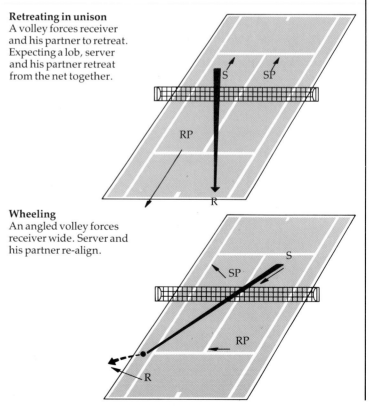

Retreating in unison
A volley forces receiver and his partner to retreat. Expecting a lob, server and his partner retreat from the net together.

Wheeling
An angled volley forces receiver wide. Server and his partner re-align.

Covering for your partner

There are some exceptional situations where covering the lob which is falling into your partner's side of the court is the only sensible solution. One of these situations is shown in the series of diagrams below. Remember that if you do have to smash in your partners' court, your partner must also cross over and cover your original side.

The play, below, starts with the receiver playing a poor, short ball which server thinks his partner will make a winning stroke against from very close to the net. However, server notices that receiver is recovering and will probably hoist a deep defensive lob so he moves back slightly to cover this expected lob and is ready to cross over. Server's partner retreats diagonally to take up server's baseline defensive position.

Positioning your smashes

All the types of smash which you have learned in the strokes section have their place in doubles play. However, the most effective positioning for your smash strokes is sharply angled, preferably into the alleys, or deep to the baseline, between your opponents. Examples of both these replacements are shown below.

The effectiveness of your smash placements depends on how you seek to avoid both of your opponents. The sharply angled smash is often the only way of playing away from two lobbing opponents entrenched at their baseline as shown below. The opportunity of splitting your opponents with a deep smash will reveal itself if you can catch the opposition moving into the net position. A good lob volley can often achieve this (see bottom diagram).

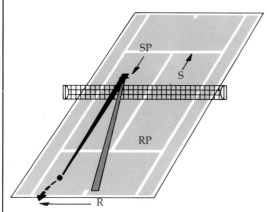

1 Receiver plays a weak return (grey) which server's partner moves forwards to meet and volley (black). Receiver starts to recover so server moves back.

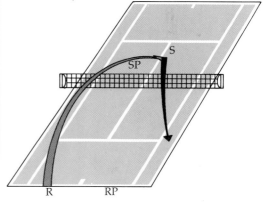

Angled smash winner
A short lob (grey) from defending receiver allows an angled smash winner (black).

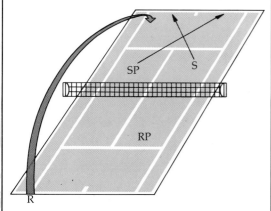

2 Receiver plays a desperate deep defensive lob (grey), server continues diagonally to play the lob. Server's partner changes sides.

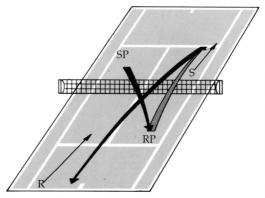

Deep smash winner
Lob volley (grey) encourages receiver to advance. Server smashes deep through the middle (black) leaving the receiver and his partner stranded.

233

Formations and tactical situations

The idea of using different formations in doubles play is either to exploit a weakness in the opposition, to block their strengths, to cover up your own weakness or to use your own strengths to the full. In the first doubles formation in the history of lawn tennis both players stood back at the baseline. Today this is considered an out and out defensive configuration and is only used as an extreme measure, or for possible use to break opponents' confidence. It was the British Doherty brothers who, at the beginning of this century, introduced the now internationally accepted formation of one player at the baseline and one just inside the service line.

The variations of formation and planned tactical ploys available are almost endless. However, the most successful and common-

ly used alternative formation is the Australian formation, described below and opposite. This formation, together with the signalling associated with poaching and the bluffing, shown on the following pages, is known and used by most players at championship and tournament level, but they could be experimented with and used more at school and club level where they would achieve successful results while enriching and developing match play.

There is a danger of attempting too complicated ploys in doubles play, and you should remember that the success of any formation or method of signalling depends on its simplicity. If it is too involved it will confuse its practitioners as soon as the ball leaves its planned course.

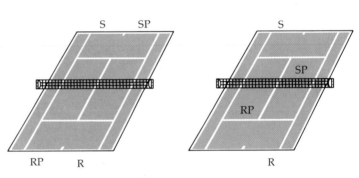

Normal and defensive formations
The two diagrams, right, show the first doubles formation with both players at the baseline compared with the usual one up, one back formation of today. The both-players-back formation still has a limited use when completely defensive play might win the day with both players prepared to start lobbing as soon as possible.

Australian formation

The Australian, or tandem, formation, can be adopted by a doubles team when serving. Instead of the server's partner standing in the opposite court to the server at the outset of the point, he stands in the same court as the server. This formation can be particularly effective against a player who has a strong shot, but only in one direction, or against a player with a weak stroke who only manages to return the ball high across the net.

In the Australian formation the left or right court is deliberately left open while the other

court is strongly guarded by the net man. This formation is designed to attract a specific shot and deter the strong reply which has prompted the change. Because the server and his partner are positioned in the same court, server must stand as close as possible to the center-mark so that he can move swiftly into the empty court. The server's partner takes up a net position that is slightly further back than normal and a little closer to the center line. This positioning allows the net man to counter crosscourt returns while covering a potential attacking lob.

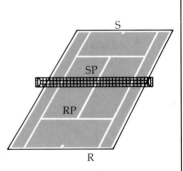

Australian formation in the right court
The right-handed server stands close to the centermark while his partner takes up the net position in the same court opposite the opposing team's net man.

Using the Australian formation

The three diagrams below show the Australian formation being used in different situations In the first diagram the receiver is right-handed and has been beating the incoming server with a powerful crosscourt backhand return and never plays down the sideline. Adopting the Australian formation, the server's partner is now directly in the path of the crosscourt return and will have a good chance of dispatching it. The receiver is forced to play a weaker stroke down the sideline to the incoming server's strong forehand volley. Receiver does have the alternative of playing a crosscourt lob (often the downfall of the Australian formation), but server's partner should be covering this by standing a little further from the net than normal.

The second and third diagrams, again in the left court, show the Australian formation used against a left-handed receiver who has a weak slice stroke only on the backhand. The server slice services to the backhand and follows into the net expecting to force an easy volley at the net on the forehand, or an easy volley for his partner. The returns which server's partner must beware of are the lob and the dink shot, or slice, angled wide to the backhand.

Right-handed receiver
Slice service to the backhand (black) with serving team in the Australian formation should force a down-the-line return which server can volley (grey). Server's partner must beware the crosscourt lob (dotted).

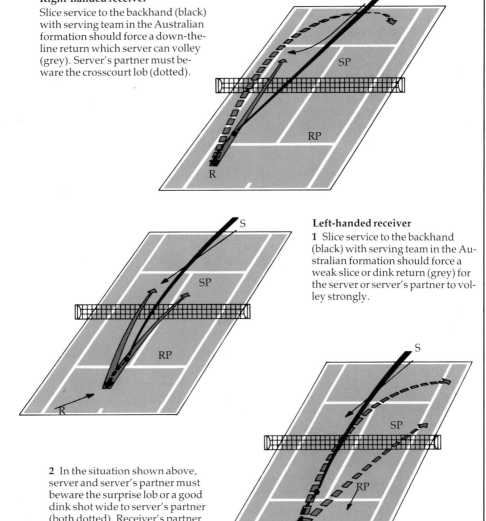

Left-handed receiver
1 Slice service to the backhand (black) with serving team in the Australian formation should force a weak slice or dink return (grey) for the server or server's partner to volley strongly.

2 In the situation shown above, server and server's partner must beware the surprise lob or a good dink shot wide to server's partner (both dotted). Receiver's partner may retreat if the receiver can manage neither, as shown right.

Signalling

The net man in a doubles team is in an ideal position to relay signals behind his back to his serving partner without disclosing them to the opposition. Signals are useful to indicate poaching and bluffing, as shown opposite. You can invent your own method of signalling to your partner, just make sure that the signals are sim-ple and that your opponents cannot see or decipher them. When Bob Hewitt and Fred Stolle were winning all their doubles titles, their signalling caught the public's interest. A clenched fist behind the back meant that the net man was staying put, two fingers pointing downwards in a "V" meant he was going to intercept.

John Newcombe serves with his doubles partner **Tony Roche** in the net position. From this viewpoint you can see how the net man can signal to the server while shielding the signal from the opposition. Any signal which uses the non-playing hand behind the back is suitable. The system which you work out with your partner should be clear and simple. Once you have signalled your intentions, never change your mind and so confuse your partner.

Poaching

Signalling your intention, as net man, to intercept the receiver's return, although the ball may return in your partner's half of the court, is called poaching. When poaching, you should carry on across into the server's half of the court. The server must veer across to the poacher's court.

Poaching allows the net man to use a particularly strong volley. The two diagrams, below, show poaching in the right and left courts. The top diagram shows a poach by a right-handed net man. In the bottom diagram the poacher is left-handed and intercepts a left court return.

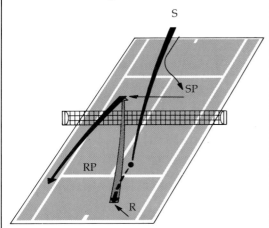

Right-handed net man's poach
Server's partner signals the poach. Service to the backhand and server starts on usual course. Server's partner moves across to volley return strongly into the tramlines. Server changes course to left court.

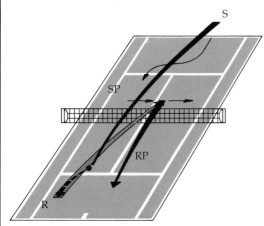

Left-handed net man's poach
Server's partner signals poach. Service to receiver's body and server starts on usual course. Server's partner volleys strongly between receiver and receiver's partner and exchanges position with server.

Bluffing

If poaching becomes a feature of a doubles match, then the bluff (where you make your opponents think that you will intercept, but you intend to regain your usual position) can be an effective tactic. The bluff can elicit a down-the-line reply if you judge that this will provide an easy stroke to attack. Whereas in the faked interception (see p.228) the deception is solely the job of the net man, when you signal a bluff to your serving partner he can help to carry through the plan. As shown in the top diagram, below, the server can add to the deception by starting his approach to the net as if a poach were indeed to take place. As the server knows the plan, however, he can swiftly move back to the normal net approach as his partner returns to volley the elicited return. The diagram, bottom, shows how the poach or bluff can backfire on the serving team if a poor service gives the receiver a chance to make a strong down-the-line passing shot.

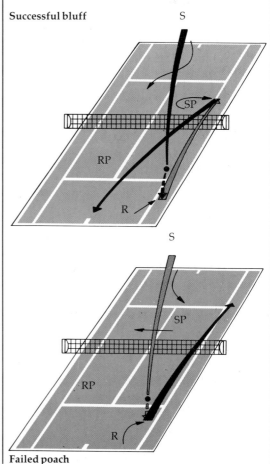

Successful bluff

Failed poach

Mixed doubles

In many respects mixed doubles should be played in the same manner as other doubles with both players in the net position. But even though top women players take their fair share of net play, if the woman's service or return of service are not strong enough to follow to the net, she must play from the back court and only come to the net on a short ball. The man must still play up at the net.

The rule in mixed doubles is that you play the woman partner. To present as strong a combination as possible the man should take the left court but if the woman is left-handed, she will most likely be more effective in the left court, providing her game is almost as strong as her partner's.

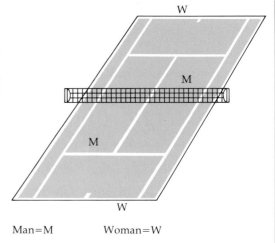

Man=M   Woman=W

Orthodox mixed doubles formation
The court positions, above, show the usual configuration of right-handed men and women players at the beginning of a point in a mixed doubles match.

Woman serving

When the woman is serving from the right court she should try to serve down the middle to the opposing woman's backhand so that her partner at the net has more chance of an interception. He must volley at every opportunity against the woman opponent, poaching on his partner's side of the court whenever it is intelligent to do so. If, however, the net man does not intercept, the weaker backhand reply will be easier for the server to take on her stronger forehand. Depending on her mobility, the server might try standing near the centermark when serving from the right court, as shown in the diagram, above right.

When in the left court the woman should also serve to the man's backhand to elicit the most defensive replies. To facilitate this she can stand nearer the sideline than usual so that her backhand is protected. From this position she will again be able to make better use of her stronger forehand drive against the return.

Right court
The woman should serve mostly to her opponent's backhand down the center of the court from a position close to the centermark.

Left court
Serving, again, mostly to the backhand, the woman can adopt her service stance closer to the sideline.

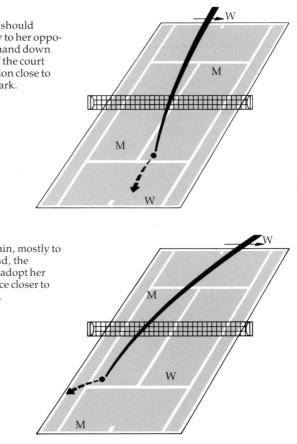

Woman at the net

With her partner serving it is more important that the woman covers the sideline return of service rather than the center of the court and she should stand slightly nearer the sideline to do this. The server can then confidently serve and volley in the middle of the court. The woman should be alert for any lob which the receiver might direct over her head. The serving man's net attack should take this possibility into account and he should cover any balls his partner cannot smash while she crosses over to his side of the court. If an angled shot is not possible, he should play to the opposite court.

Woman returning service

As long as the lady partner is returning service effectively, the man should remain at the net and volley. If the woman has difficulty with her return, her partner should retreat to the baseline from where they can mix drives and lobs to engineer an opportunity for the man to move up court and finish the point.

As a rule, the woman should return service crosscourt and deep, away from the net player. If the opposing woman is at the net, the lob can be used, keeping the man back and running. After a successful lob return, the man should be ready to move in and win the point.

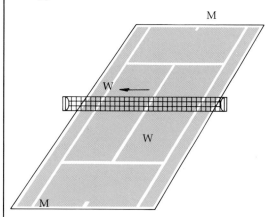

Woman's net position
With the man serving, the woman at the net should modify her position in mixed doubles so that she is closer to the sideline and so better able to defend against a sideline return.

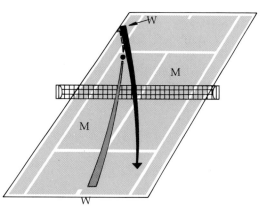

Crosscourt return
It is particularly important to play most of your returns (black) crosscourt (especially when returning the opposing woman's service) avoiding the net man as in the diagram above.

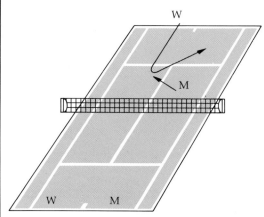

Crossing over
Crossing over every time that your partner does is essential in mixed doubles. This mostly occurs when the net woman is lobbed and must change courts as her partner moves to retrieve the ball.

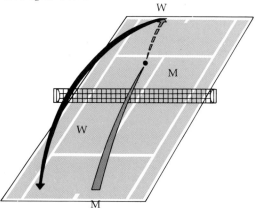

Lobbing the net woman
As the woman partner facing the man's service, you should lob your return when possible, aiming the lob over the opposing net woman so that the server has to retreat and cross over to return your lob.

Tactical situations

The two pairs of diagrams below, are representative of the variety of ploys available when serving and receiving in mixed doubles play.

In the top pair, the woman server is left-handed and the serving team decide to use the Australian formation (see p.234) from the right court. The service is deep down the center court to the backhand forcing a poor length backhand return. The server, on her strong forehand side, hits a sidespin reply swerving the ball into the tramlines. The receiver recovers, but only in time to play a crosscourt forehand which is easily intercepted by the serving team's net man. In the bottom pair, the receiving team attacks a weak service, the woman receiver running round the ball to hit an aggressive crosscourt forehand. This forces a defensive lobbed reply which the receiver's net man can deal with easily.

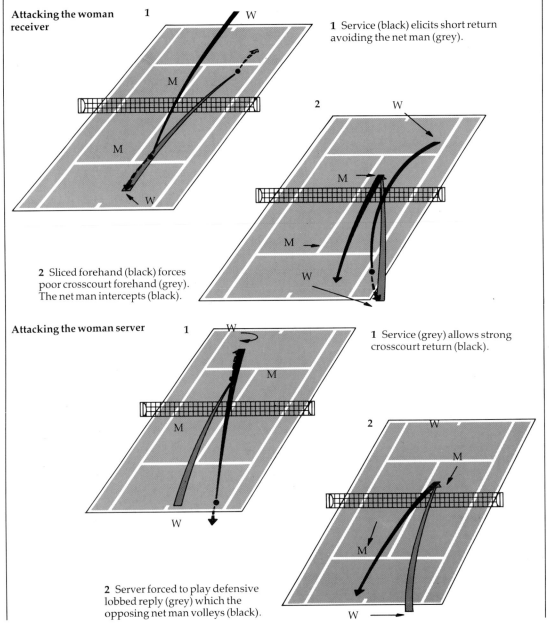

Attacking the woman receiver

1 Service (black) elicits short return avoiding the net man (grey).

2 Sliced forehand (black) forces poor crosscourt forehand (grey). The net man intercepts (black).

Attacking the woman server

1 Service (grey) allows strong crosscourt return (black).

2 Server forced to play defensive lobbed reply (grey) which the opposing net man volleys (black).

Adapting your game

All weather play

If you are playing tennis outdoors, weather conditions will rarely be ideal, and, more often than not, you will have to adapt your game, if only slightly, to suit the particular conditions under which you are playing. When playing in windy conditions, you will have to judge exactly how the wind is going to affect play from either end of the court. This will vary according to whether you are playing with the wind behind you, against you, or across the court. The position of the sun in cloudless conditions, and rain during play are the other factors which must be given careful consideration.

If you are really serious about your game, it will be just as vital to have the right attitude towards adverse weather as towards different types of opponent (see p. 245).

Playing with the wind behind

It is generally thought to be easier to play against the wind than with it because the wind will hold your shots in court, but this need not be so if you adapt your game correctly when playing downwind. Although playing with the wind behind you will add easy power to your shots, and so give your opponent less time to prepare his return shots, this extra power may well work to your disadvantage as your shots can tend to fly out over the baseline, particularly when you are going into the net to volley. You will not need to manufacture as much pace of your own, but you will have to improve your control by modifying your normal stroking. Use shorter take-backs, apply more spin (sidespin and underspin will give maximum control in windy conditions), and lengthen the follow through of your strokes.

Gain the net position whenever possible, since volleying is less likely to be disrupted by a following wind than groundstroke play and the wind slowing up your opponent's passing shots should work particularly to your advantage. Vary your approach shots and, if forced on the defensive, use passing shots, not lobs.

Playing into the wind

The main advantage you will have when playing into the wind is the feeling that you can hit the ball as hard as you can without worrying that it may go out of court.

You will, however, have to generate more pace or your shots will have little effect. Early positioning before playing the shot is important so that the extra speed of the ball arriving with the wind does not catch you out of position.

Aim to gain the net position by playing lobs. Your own passing shots will be slowed up by the wind, so, when your opponent appears at the net, hit a high lob deep to his baseline and then prepare to follow it up to the net. Use topspin rather than underspin when lobbing.

Force your opponent into his back court with deep drives and use drop shots.

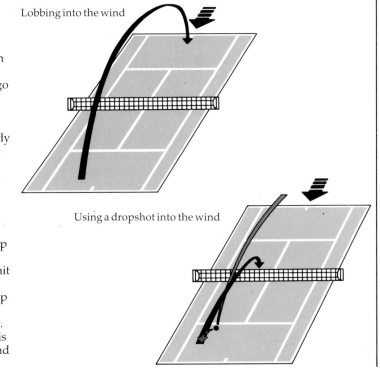

Lobbing into the wind

Using a dropshot into the wind

Playing in a crosscourt wind

When playing an attacking game, use the direction of the cross wind to help you; in a defensive game, play into the wind. For example, if you are serving from the right court with the cross wind blowing from right to left, use your slice service so that the wind combines with the spin to make the ball swerve wide of your opponent's court. With approach shots, use the wind to swing the ball away from the baseliner with sidespin. Alternatively approach the net by playing sidespin drives into the wind.

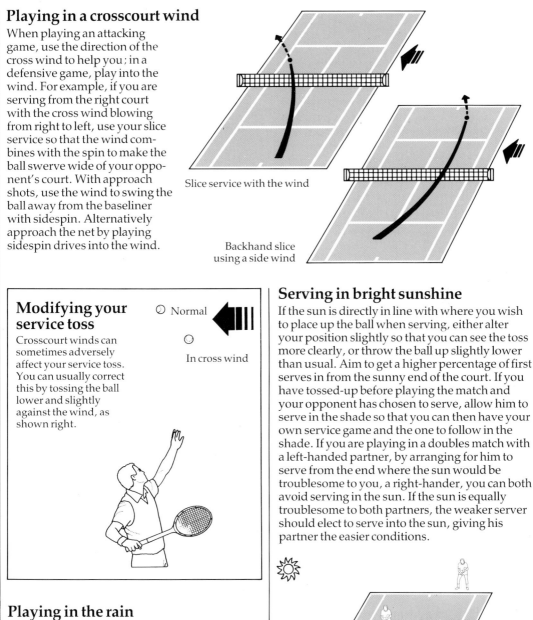

Slice service with the wind

Backhand slice
using a side wind

Modifying your service toss

Crosscourt winds can sometimes adversely affect your service toss. You can usually correct this by tossing the ball lower and slightly against the wind, as shown right.

⊘ Normal

◯

In cross wind

Playing in the rain

Rainy conditions will affect gut racket strings adversely, so make sure at least one of your frames is strung with a good synthetic stringing. Dampness will also affect the playing surface: grass or painted asphalt courts will become slippery, and shale and clay courts will get soft and heavy. In either case, precise footwork may be difficult. You will generally have to prepare for your shots lower down and lengthen your racket follow throughs for greater control. When the court is slippery use spin shots.

Serving in bright sunshine

If the sun is directly in line with where you wish to place up the ball when serving, either alter your position slightly so that you can see the toss more clearly, or throw the ball up slightly lower than usual. Aim to get a higher percentage of first serves in from the sunny end of the court. If you have tossed-up before playing the match and your opponent has chosen to serve, allow him to serve in the shade so that you can then have your own service game and the one to follow in the shade. If you are playing in a doubles match with a left-handed partner, by arranging for him to serve from the end where the sun would be troublesome to you, a right-hander, you can both avoid serving in the sun. If the sun is equally troublesome to both partners, the weaker server should elect to serve into the sun, giving his partner the easier conditions.

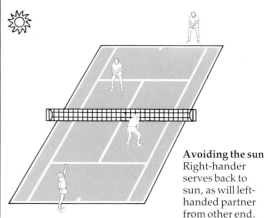

Avoiding the sun
Right-hander serves back to sun, as will left-handed partner from other end.

Playing on different types of court

A smooth court surface and dense, resilient substructure (see p.268) will make the ball bounce lower and farther. A rougher surface and less dense substructure are both features which make the ball rise at a steeper angle, and not travel so far, after the bounce. Any court on which you play will have a combination of these characteristics and will play faster or slower accordingly.

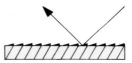

Slow surfaces
A more spongy court, with a rough, high-friction finish will slow the ball and make it bounce up more sharply.

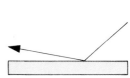

Fast surfaces
A hard, resilient court surface, with a smooth, low friction finish, will make the ball bounce far and skid low.

Knowing court characteristics

Asphalt and other all-weather materials These are versatile outdoor courts used in many schools and parks. They have a macadam type of surface which provides a slow game. If the black surface is covered with a specially prepared green paint it will convert the court into a medium-speed playing surface so that the ball stays fractionally lower after the bounce. Porous concrete provides a good slow court game, which can be played on immediately after it rains.

Cement These fast-playing courts favor the serve and volley type of game. When the top surface is left rough, play will be considerably slower than when it has a polished finish or where the surface is painted.

Clay Courts made from red hard court materials (usually called clay or shale courts) have similar characteristics, all consisting of several layers beneath a loose top surface. The top surface has to be frequently watered and rolled in order to provide a good playing surface. Rain can adversely affect these courts, making the surface very soft and muddy. In good condition, however, they provide a slow to slow-medium surface which is relatively easy on the feet but inflicts considerable wear and tear on balls and strings. A loose surface will grip the ball so that it bounces up slowly to a comfortable height for hitting, favoring a baseline game (see p.210). Play steadily from your back court, introducing your all-court game at every opportunity, but avoiding the net position unless you are certain of success. Vary your service on these slower surfaces. Probe for an opening and aim to force a short return for a net advance (see p. 214). Because your opponent will be able to retrieve your shots more easily, pace with accuracy is all-important if you are going to put the ball away successfully to win points on these courts.

Grass Grass court surfaces vary considerably in texture. Some are hard, with short cut grass, and will play fast, while others have longer grass, and are therefore more spongy, slowing the game down considerably. On the whole, however, grass courts are fast-playing, suiting the serve and volley game (see p.204) rather than baseline play. As for all fast-playing courts, it is preferable to use a tightly strung racket for grass court play, but not so tight that you lose control of the ball.

Synthetic materials Courts with synthetic surfaces are the main type of indoor tennis court and the outdoor court of the future. They are often carpet-like and portable. When laid outside, synthetic courts are particularly resistant to rain, snow and frost, and, indoors or out, provide a perfect, even bounce. The exact playing characteristics of a synthetic playing surface depend on the density of the underlying court-structure and the type of surface finish. A hard, close-textured mat on concrete will produce a medium-fast surface while a dense-piled carpet finish on wood may produce a slow court. Most synthetic surfaces are non-slip and care should be taken to accustom oneself to the change in footing when transferring from a surface on which you can slide, such as grass or clay. If you are unsure of your footing you will lose points. Too much grip can initially be as unnerving as too little.

Artificial grass This surface is widely used in clubs, colleges and schools. Its playing characteristics are similar to grass but the speed of the court varies according to the sand level. The bounce is medium high and the pace is fast, unless the level of sand has been raised. Matchplay approach should be in line with the grass court game (see above) but leaning toward all-court play. Generally, the ball tends to come off the surface a little quicker than you would imagine.

Playing different opponents

It is always important for players to develop their own game, no matter how much they may then have to adapt this to suit different conditions. As your game matures you should be able to adapt it without losing your own identity as a player.

Junior players may either be too cautious, or will hit every ball like a bullet. Both extremes are bad: the cautious player must develop his ability to attack when the opportunity presents itself, and the hard-hitter must still move about quickly and attack the ball, but must concentrate on hitting with control and with reliability.

Once you have developed your own game, you are then in a position to adapt this to suit the different opponents you may play against, as described below.

Adopting the right approach

Playing a strong opponent If you know your opponent's game is stronger all around than yours, resist the temptation to have a crack at everything, but settle down to play your own game first. As the game progresses and you get more used to the faster pace, you may find you can raise your speed of play.

Playing a weak opponent The main danger when playing a weak opponent is that you may subconsciously drop your game to the same low level. Always apply pressure against a weak player by playing slightly faster than he can and maintaining your concentration. Always treat your opponent with respect, and beat him by the best score you can.

Playing an equal opponent Playing against someone of the same standard will require concentration if you are to play your own game according to the tactics upon which you decide. If your opponent is of a similar standard, yet always wins when you play, do not be over-concerned. Keep developing your game using the strategy section (pp.194-219), and use a different tactical approach each time you meet. You can do this by introducing strokes which you have not used a great deal in previous matches.

Playing a negative opponent This type of player, who concentrates on retrieving every ball you play, is a very difficult opponent to beat. Come to the net whenever you can and, when rallying from the baseline, play the drop shot and lob. The retrieving player has no armory with which to hurt you, so if you are patient and do not try to finish the rallies too quickly, you should win. A negative player will hit shots that lack speed, but do not try to play your returns too hard, just hard enough to keep your opponent running.

Adapting your footwork in an emergency

You may sometimes be in a position where you will find it difficult to return an opponent's shot because you have no time for basic footwork. When trying to return a fast wide service, or when you are crossed by your opponent's shot, you will often only recover in time to play the ball off the wrong foot. In situations like this you may have to adopt open stance footwork as shown below. Reach the ball with the foot that is nearest to its line of flight and swing your racket, rotating your body about the hips. Your other leg will support some of your bodyweight.

John McEnroe

Playing left-handers

If your opponent is left-handed you will have to change your general approach. Instead of attacking the left court more than the right and facing a defensive backhand from that side, you will now probably have to deal with a topspin drive, hit either crosscourt or down the line from your opponent's left court. Your opponent's forehand will be a particular danger and your main tactical ploy should be to hit the ball to his backhand, which will probably be his main weakness, as in the diagram below. When playing from the back court hit your forehand crosscourt and your backhand down the line consistently. Adopt the general tactic of serving balls wide to his backhand from the right court and down the center to his backhand from the left court. Use your slice service, using the swerve and bounce to swing the ball away.

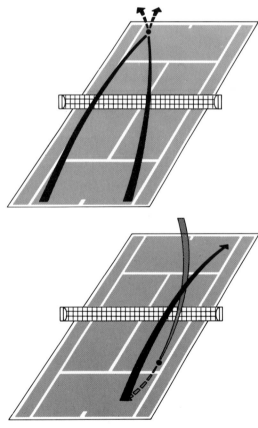

Countering service spin
If your left-handed opponent slice serves to your forehand from the right court, the approaching ball will be travelling with sidespin, so aim your return more towards the center of the court.

Playing double-handers

When playing a good double-handed opponent remember that the increased strength from the use of both wrists will give more power to his strokes. Whenever possible try to make him use a one-handed grip – which will probably be weaker – by hitting the ball wide and making him stretch to hit it. A particular way of doing this is to hit short, low balls to the backhand. Since this type of ball usually needs sharp underspin to deflect the ball over the net and the two-handed shot is not good in this respect, it will usually force your opponent to release the support hand.

Hitting a low short ball to a double-hander's backhand

Natalia Zvereva finishes a backhand drive which illustrates the potential strength of two-handed play and the importance of countering it effectively.

Winning

Improving your attitude

Winning seems to come naturally to some players while others can only produce their best form on the practice court. For the majority of players, however, match-play tennis is an unpredictable mixture of winning and losing, with maintained success an illusive goal.

It is just as important to develop the control of your mental attitude as to improve your physical ability as a winning attitude is often the sole distinguishing factor between winning and losing in closely contested matches. Although attitude is regularly manipulated by changing external circumstances, it is nevertheless possible to change your mental attitude at will by understanding and following some of the forms of mental control described below.

Being determined

Although your attitude to winning and temperament forms the solid mental base on which winning is founded, determination will provide the key to success. Determination involves striving 100 per cent at all times to reach your objective, which will require both mental and physical stamina. You must decide what you want from your tennis, and become determined and dedicated to achieving your ambition. Set out a success chart, planning each step separately, and, as soon as you reach one goal, start working towards the next. Never be satisfied with your achievement.

Focusing your imagination

Reactions to certain situations are often affected by imagination and, conversely, your imagination can be used to control these reactions. A tennis example might be when an opponent has a habit of bouncing the ball six or seven times before serving. If however, you regard this as a deliberate act of gamesmanship you will, as a result, be distracted from making a good return. If, however, you imagine he is doing it because he is anxious about his service and needs to calm himself, and that by this action he is providing you with more time to focus your concentration, you will probably remain calm while he bounces the ball, and your concentration will be heightened as a result.

Visualizing improvement

Imagination can be used to visualize improvement by helping you to create pictures in your mind of how you would like to play and to see yourself playing in this way. If you have difficulty in winning important matches, or have a defeatist attitude to them, start setting aside 15 to 30 minutes every day for visualizing the success you desire. When you lack confidence in a particular stroke, see yourself performing it perfectly in match-play situations.

Controlling your temper

Losing your temper on court is to be avoided at all costs, not only out of courtesy to your opponent and any spectators, but also because it will distract you and waste your mental energy which will ultimately make your performance suffer. It may even provide a psychological boost to your opponent who may interpret the outburst as a sign of nerves.

Just before you lose your temper there will be a split second when you are aware of what is about to happen, and at this precise moment you can decide to use the energy you were going to waste on losing your temper to play better tennis and beat your opponent.

Achieving good match-play temperament

Good match temperament is founded on sound stroke play. If you tend to get nervous, the problem lies in lack of confidence in a particular stroke and this can always be remedied by practicing and perfecting the stroke in question. Develop a sound temperament by perfecting reliable techniques and skill which will encourage you to play with relaxed confidence.

Gamesmanship and fair play

There is an unwritten code of fair play in tennis, upholding the true spirit of the game. A few players do not follow this, and many of them regard gamesmanship as part of the game, and seek to gain an advantage by means other than racket and ball.

Deliberate gamesmanship is cheating, and is therefore to be deplored. It can range from simple delaying tactics, like doing up your shoe laces when they are perfectly all right, to an all-out verbal attack designed to intimidate, distract and totally confuse an opponent who might otherwise have provided tough opposition.

Ann Hobbs leaps for joy after winning 4-6, 6-4, 6-2 in 1980 against the world's tenth-ranked player Kathy Jordan. Such a win against a high-ranking opponent will increase confidence immeasurably as believing in your play becomes knowing that you can win at a higher level of competition.

Concentration

Concentration in tennis means not merely looking at the ball, but focusing your complete attention on it so that neither eye nor mind are distracted by outside pressures. This can sometimes be difficult in match play, where tension and anxiety tend to distract your mind at an important moment. There are ways of improving concentration.

Concentrating during rallies

One method of counteracting the tendency to get distracted when rallying, is to count. Counting keeps the conscious mind occupied and will aid your rhythm and timing as well as your concentration. When practicing your baseline rallying with a partner, count "one" when he hits the ball, "two" when the ball bounces on your side, and "three" when you hit the ball. In practice your coach or a friend should count for you, but practice counting as well to yourself as you rally; it will help you to prepare early, move rhythmically and time the ball perfectly. Another way of using this basic method of improving concentration would be to say "hit-bounce-hit".

There is a danger, if using the "1-2-3" method, that you may start to count automatically instead of consciously, and become distracted. One way to overcome this may be to count "3-2-1" instead.

Jimmy Connors shows just how the world class player focuses all his attention on the ball. His eyes will never consciously leave the ball during a rally, allowing his skills of anticipation the best chances of success.

Concentrating during the change-over

The change-over is a definite time for relaxing physically and mentally priming yourself for the task ahead. Plan consciously exactly what tactics you are going to pursue to fulfil your overall strategy for the successful outcome of the match, then, when it is time to go out again, fix your eye and mind on the ball and let yourself get on with the job. In this way you do your thinking about what you are going to do before you do it, not while you are doing it and so initiate your different tactics and patterns of play as automatically as you play your strokes.

Conserving mental energy

In general match play when you feel mentally fatigued, you are either genuinely tired, or only think you are tired. More often than not, your lethargy will be due to your imagination taking over – conjuring up visions of tiredness because your attention has been diverted to how badly you are playing. You are probably also imagining how super-fit your opponent seems to be compared with how you feel. If you allow this situation to continue, your fatigue will grow, you may get angry about decisions, and your mental energy supply will soon be drained. Mentally, as well as physically, you have what is known as a "second wind". We have all known the feeling of being really tired and then, when given a new task or somebody suggests doing something different, becoming filled with a new surge of energy. It is quite similar in match play: you need to refocus your concentration and gain fresh motivation for victory. Do not wait for an external circumstance such as a superb passing shot to revitalize you – this may never happen – but concentrate on bringing your mind back to the present. Winning the next point is always the task which you must apply yourself to. Use the experience which you collect from each point played to help in your decisions for the best tactic to employ for the point ahead, whether you are serving or receiving.

The key factor to bear in mind is that far more mental energy is used up when you allow your mind to wander aimlessly into the past and future than can ever be used up by concentrating your mind totally on something in the here and now, namely, the ball. Thinking about points in the last set that you should have won, or that unfair decision in the fifth game, are not only obviously distracting but will also drain your mental energy at a much faster rate than normal.

Improving attention

You can train your mind to resist distraction by deepening your ability to concentrate on one thing at a time. Studying the seam of the tennis ball as well will be helpful. Playing chess is an excellent off-court concentration exercise.

There are several exercises you can practice to focus your attention and improve your eyesight. Examples are trying to read car number plates, road signs and billboards from further and further away. Even when the numbers and words are only a blur try to see them clearly through concentration of eye and mind.

Two more exercises are described below. You can invent others yourself, and practice them.

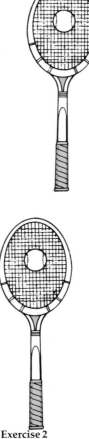

Exercise 1
Concentrate on the racket and ball, left, but try to see only the ball on the strings without the racket frame.

Exercise 2
Place a thin book, about 4 in. wide, between the right- and left-hand rackets shown, on this page. Rest your forehead and nose against the book so that your eyes are about 4½ in. from the page. Try to make the balls merge in either racket head.

Improving your chances of success

However good your physical and mental fitness, take advantage of every aid to your success in match play. Warming up before each match and being able to relax are both mentally and physically important. When to attack and when to defend – how to play the percentages (see below) – underlies all the strategy which you have learned.

Warming up

Except under special conditions the warm-up period should last for only four minutes. If you need longer to get ready you can arrange private practice with another player before you are due to go on court with your opponent. Use the warm-up period to acclimatize yourself to the balls, court and your opponent's individual method of striking the ball. Before you start warming up it is wise to spin up first, so that you can go straight to the end you will play from first. Look for weaknesses in your opponent's game and disguise weaknesses of your own, but do not show your full strength and power till the match gets under way. He may try to make you believe that he has a certain weakness because he wants you to play on it, so weigh up his game carefully. After you have exchanged groundstrokes take turns to volley and smash at the net. Spend at least one minute of the four warming up your service strokes. Many opening service games are lost because the server is not ready to serve competitively from the first point.

Percentage play

Percentage play basically means playing the right shot at the right time. You must be fully aware of your own strengths and weaknesses, and plan your tactics accordingly.

Important points in percentage play are match, set and game points, followed by points which will create game point either for you or against you, such as when the score is 15-30 or 30-15. Some players attach definite psychological advantage to winning the first point in each game. As the majority of matches are won by the player who makes the fewest errors and not by the one hitting the most winners, control is vital and playing to the score essential. This means covering your weaknesses by using your stronger strokes to play percentage shots on the most important points, and only taking risks when you have points in hand.

Percentage play also consists of selecting the right reply to your opponent's shots and this may outweigh selecting the one that is easiest for you. This choice is thoroughly examined in the strategy section on pages 194 to 240.

Relaxation

Strokes must be played with relaxed precision for maximum effect and minimum energy loss. Casual play, on the one hand, results in loss of control and lack of purpose, while tension stiffens stroke play movements and speed, using up unnecessary amounts of energy. On court you must be mentally alert, yet physically relaxed enough to swing your racket and move about the court fluently. If you feel yourself tightening up at a critical point – say, when waiting to receive a service – relax your jaw muscles and let your chin down a bit. If you feel your grip tightening up, deliberately relax it in between shots. If you just need to relax at the change-over, sit down and relax every muscle, and keep perfectly still. Practice relaxing and conserving energy by sitting absolutely still in a straight-backed chair, in front of a mirror. Watch yourself all the time for the slightest little movement, apart from blinking. Keep adding a minute until you can sit still for 15 minutes at a time.

André Agassi

Fitness and training

FITNESS AND TRAINING

In order to play tennis at the highest levels of competitive performance you must be in peak physical and mental condition. Slack muscles will tighten during play restricting leg and arm movements, while uncontrolled nerves could result in loss of sleep before an important match. Successful players, therefore, will aim to reach their peak in the tournaments which are most important to them, and their training and playing program will be planned with those events primarily in mind. Correct preparation for overall match-play fitness requires training in stamina, speed, strength and mobility, dealt with below and on the following pages.

Stamina

A long, hard-fought tennis match requires a strong heart, efficient lungs and leg power, all indications of stamina. The best way to develop stamina is by running, which will improve your capacity to take in and efficiently use more oxygen.

Running

All running training programs should involve steady running for stamina over reasonable distances together with a program of short fast runs to develop speed and the ability to recover quickly between periods when maximum effort is required. Provided you have been passed as medically fit you can start running a mile several times a week, at a comfortable speed.

Measure out a mile route in your local park or, if you must run round the block, wear a pair of cushion soles or heels in your training shoes. Take a stop watch with you so that you can record your times from the outset and your improvement over a period of time. Step up your runs gradually to distances of 2 miles and beyond, or simply to runs of approximately 30 minutes each, at least two or three times a week.

Breathing

Deep breathing for a few minutes every morning and before and after considerable effort, such as between hard-fought rallies, is of psychological benefit as well as aiding physical recovery and helping you to use your lung capacity to its full. Breathe in deeply, using your diaphragm and not simply raising your chest. Feel that you are breathing through your stomach before finally filling the chest for the best possible effect.

Pulse rate

Pulse rate – the rate at which the heart beats in order to pump blood – is an indication of your overall fitness. It can be measured by placing three fingers above the center of the inside of your wrist and counting the number of beats per minute (b.p.m.) with the help of a stop watch.

The average pulse rate is between 70 and 80 b.p.m. It can be affected by many factors – it will decrease after resting and increase quite dramatically during exercise – but, as a general rule, the fitter you are the lower your pulse rate will be. An example is Bjorn Borg, whose resting pulse rate was reported to be about 40 b.p.m.

If your pulse rate is normal, build your fitness steadily; if in the low 60s you are probably fit enough for more strenuous activity if you warm up first. Try to achieve and maintain a pulse rate of between 140 and 150 b.p.m. during your distance runs. Take your pulse before and after each run, and then again 10 minutes after that. Your pulse rate should return to 100 b.p.m. within this time – back to normal if you are particularly fit.

Speed

Once your stamina training is well under way, you can then concentrate on developing the ability to produce a constant maximum effort, or speed endurance. The body must be trained to cope with tiring situations and learn to recover quickly.

The best way to develop speed endurance is to perform regular speed and recovery training exercises, such as shuttle sprinting and non-stop sequences, with the emphasis on striving for maximum effort with increasingly short rests between sprints.

Shuttle sprinting exercises

Shuttle sprinting exercises are a useful way of training for speed and recovery. They can be practiced anywhere, such as a park or between lamp posts, as long as you measure out a distance and time your efforts. Rest briefly between exercises reducing these rest periods as you improve.

Three-ball shuttle Using the width of a tennis court, place three balls on a singles sideline, slightly apart, and stand behind the opposite singles sideline. With a friend timing you, run across the court as shown below, pick up one of the balls and bring it back to the sideline you started from. Repeat the process for the second and third balls, placing each ball on the line. Boys and men should aim for a time under 12 seconds; girls and women under 13 seconds. Gradually step up these sprints, using six balls and then nine. When you have progressed to the latter, try and complete the exercise in 40 seconds.

Alternative shuttle Place an empty bucket on the centermark and place one ball at each of the junctions of the sideline, service line, centerline and baseline. Starting from the centermark, run forwards to get one ball at a time, returning to place each ball in the bucket running backwards.

Non-stop sequences

Tennis-playing routines on court demanding alertness, fast footwork and early reactions form a good basis of pressure training. As long as maximum effort is made by the trainee, any stroke, or combination of strokes, can be used to rapidly put the player under physical stress. After a short recovery period, the routine should be repeated, the emphasis being on speed rather than accuracy or technical perfection.

Non-stop smashing One player at the baseline with a basket of balls can pressurize the skill of another at the net by continually lobbing balls to be smashed by the net player, who must run forwards and touch the net band with his racket between each smash, as shown below. Allow five minutes for this exercise.

Smash and volley A player at the net must smash and volley to counter continuous alternate drives and lobs fed by two baseliners.

Non-stop volleying Players at each side of the court feed balls alternately which the net man must volley. The net man is under continuous pressure as he covers the width of the singles court to play each volley.

Three-ball shuttle

Non-stop smash sequence

Strength

Physical strength is a prerequisite for all good tennis players and is dependent on good muscle tone, endurance and power. Muscle tone (responsiveness of muscle fiber) and muscular endurance will be improved through circuit training or a weight training program based on the use of light weights and high repetitions. Power is dependent on the number and size of the muscle fiber groups within the muscle tissue. These fibers will grow larger according to the demands of progressive weight training.

Circuit training

Work out a schedule so that no two exercises for the same body parts are practiced consecutively. Perform as many repetitions as you can of each, resting 45 seconds between each exercise. Half of each maximum will be the right number of repetitions for each exercise in your program. Run through the circuit twice without rest, keeping a record of times to gauge your progress. The chart on the right shows a typical schedule that might be followed, at three possible levels of fitness.

Typical program

Exercise	Repetitions (three levels)		
Push-up	10	25	50
Sit-up	10	25	50
Step-up	8	20	40
Leg-raise	10	25	50
Jump	10	25	50
Back-arch	3	5	10
Squat thrust	15	30	60

1 **Push-up** Adopt the front support position, with palms under shoulders, body straight. Bend and straighten your arms without your legs touching the floor.

2 **Sit-up** Lie flat and anchor your feet, legs outstretched, hands behind your neck. Sit up and bring your head to your knees. Lower yourself slowly without your back touching the floor.

3 **Step-up** Step on to a bench about 20 in. high and step down again with the same foot. Start half of your repetitions with the left foot and half with the right foot.

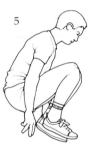

5 **Double knee jump** Stand with your feet together. Crouch before leaping up in the air, bringing your knees up to your chest. Repeat without pausing.

4 **Leg-raise** Lie on your back, hands clasped behind your neck. Lock your knees and raise your legs till they are at about right angles to your body. Lower them slowly.

6 **Back-arch** Lie on your stomach, hands by your sides and palms up. Slightly raise your head and chest off the ground and at the same time your legs off the floor.

7 **Squat thrust** Adopt the front support position, knees between arms. Thrust backwards, straightening your body and legs, and then forwards again.

Weight training

Correct weight training equipment is important for your safety. Basic equipment includes a barbell 5 to 7 feet long and weighing 20 lb, together with a pair of dumb-bells and a range of weight discs weighing a total of 174 lb. You will also need a firm bench. A pair of supporting stands is also useful, but not essential.

Never pick up weights in an unprepared, bent-backed fashion and always try to work with a training partner who can support heavier weights in and out of stands. As with circuit training, the completion of one exercise is called a repetition. Repeating a given number of that exercise is called a set. Sets of many repetitions with light weights are excellent for muscular endurance, and so are ideal for the tennis player.

Always warm up before lifting sessions and get into the habit of finishing each exercise with a fast set of eight repetitions, using about one third of your maximum weight. The chart which follows the exercises below shows a possible schedule with recommended repetitions and sets the amounts by which to increase the weight on the bar as you progress from a light starting weight.

1   2   3   4   5

1 **Starting position** Stand up straight with your shoulders back and your feet shoulder-width apart under the barbell. Bend your knees, keeping your head and your back straight, until your hands reach the bar. Your arms must be outside your knees and, as you overgrasp the bar (hands over the bar), keeping your arms straight, check that your back is flat.

2 **Clean** (Back, legs). Take up the starting position. Then stand erect, pulling the bar up to your chest in one fast movement. Lower the bar first to the waist, then to the floor.

3 **Overhead press** (Upper body). Push the bar upwards from the clean position until your arms are straight. Hold it steady for a second, then lower the bar to the clean position again. Repeat the press, then lower to the waist and then to the floor.

4 **Dead lift** (Back). Start position, one hand overgrasps and the other undergrasps (hand under the bar). Keep your back flat with your shoulders well back. Stand erect, arms straight, pulling the bar up to rest against your thighs as you straighten your legs.

5 **Semi-squat** (Upper leg). For the semi-squat the weight is supported across the shoulders, directly on the trapezius muscles which join your shoulders to your spine. Your back must be straight and as you bend your knees they should go forwards and slightly outwards. Your knee bend should stop when your thighs are at right angles to your shins.

257

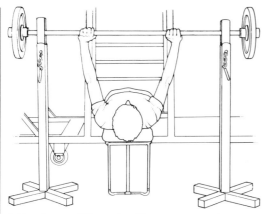

6 **Bench press** (Chest, shoulders, arms). Lie flat on your exercise bench (with knees bent and toes touching the floor either side of a free-standing bench). Overgrasp the barbell across your chest with a wide grip. Repeatedly push it away and lower it.

7 **Barbell curl** (Abdomen, back, arms). Stand, feet apart, undergrasping the barbell with your hands shoulder-width apart and arms hanging down. Keeping your back straight, curl your arms upwards bringing the bar up to your chest. Keep your upper arms by the side of your body as you bend at the elbow.

8 **Barbell bendover** (Lower back). Stand, feet apart, holding a barbell across your shoulders behind your neck. Bend forwards until your straight back is almost parallel to the floor. Stand upright again and repeat the exercise.

9 **Chinning** (Arms, shoulders). Adopt the "dead hang" position from a beam or bar, overgrasping the bar with a wide grip. Pull your chin above the bar, lower and then repeat.

10 **Heel-raise** (Calves, ankles). Stand with your feet apart, and the barbell across your shoulders. Step on to your two thickest weights leaving your heels resting on the floor. Rise up as high as you can on your toes and then lower your heels to the floor. Really stretch your calves.

11 **Barbell tricep press** (Arms). Support the barbell overhead with your palms forwards and a narrow grip. Keep your upper arm straight and close to your head while you lower the barbell behind your head.

12 **Inclined sit-up** (Abdomen). Anchor your feet under the strap at the top of an inclined bench (if available) with your knees slightly bent and the barbell held across your shoulders as you lie back. Sit up and lower yourself repeatedly.

13 **Wrist and forearm strengthener** Suspend a weight on a piece of rope from an old racket handle. Overgrasp the handle on either side of the rope at arm's length. Wind the weight up by turning with one hand at a time. Lower the weight in the same way.

Typical program

Exercise	Sets	Repetitions	Weight increase
Dead lift	3	4,3,2	10lbs
Bench press	3	4,3,2	10lbs
Semi-squat	3	4	5lbs
Inclined sit-up	3	6	5lbs
Clean lift	3	4,3,2	10lbs
Heel raise	3	6	10lbs

Mobility

All regular training programs should include a series of stretching exercises. Work out a routine that you can perform before and after every practice, training, and match-play session. Warming-up or warming-down should take about fifteen minutes. These exercises will not only prepare you for hard physical effort without fear of injury, and increase the suppleness and flexibility of your muscles and joints, they will also help prevent stiffness from setting in afterwards, and enable your body to recover more rapidly. Once you have established the stretching habit you will want to stretch every day regardless of your training program or matchplay schedule. Here are some stretching exercises, incorporating the three outlined below, which you can use as part of your regular fitness program. Remember to breathe normally during the exercises and never force but 'feel' the stretch for about six to ten seconds.

Upward stretch (Arms/Shoulders/Back) – Stand, feet apart, hands by sides. Raise hands above head, intertwine fingers and turn palms uppermost. Stretch upward and hold for 6 to 10 seconds. Lower arms to sides. Repeat 4 times.

Side stretch (Upper body/Side) – Stand, feet apart, hands by sides. Raise hands above head, intertwine fingers and turn palms up. Stretch out and bend to the right, hold for 6 to 10 seconds. Come upright, then repeat for left side. Come upright and lower arms to sides. Repeat 4 times.

Hip circling (Pelvis/lower back) – Stand, feet apart, hands on hips, (do not lock knees). Circle left 5 times and right 5 times. Keep your head and upper body still as you circle.

Alternate knee raise (Lower back/Legs)– Lie flat on the floor. Raise your right knee toward your chest, pull it gently from below the knee with clasped hands. Hold for 6 to 10 seconds, lower leg. Repeat with left knee, 4 repetitions, alternating each leg.

Leg stretch (Front upper leg) – Stand close to a wall, placing your right palm against it for support. Bend your left knee and grip your left toe with your left hand behind you, pulling your heel toward your left buttock. Repeat with right leg. Repeat 4 times. Now try exercise using opposite hands and feet.

Calf stretch (Calf/Achilles) – Stand close to a wall and lean forwards on to it, resting your forehead on your crossed forearms. Let your right knee bend and stretch your left leg backward keeping your left heel on the floor. Move your hip forward to 'feel' the full stretch at the back of your leg. Switch legs, alternating 4 times. To stretch the Achilles and lower calf, bend your front knee more and lower your hips as you stretch further back with your rear leg.

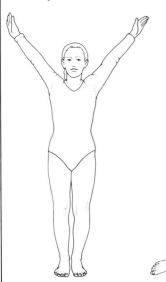

1 **Arm circle** Feet shoulder-width apart, arms by your sides. 5 full arm circles forwards, 5 backwards.

2 **Lunge** Feet well apart. Lunge right, bending your right knee and straightening your left leg. Stand, then lunge left. Repeat.

3 **Ankle stretch** Toes and balls of feet on a 2 in. block, arms by your sides. Slowly raise and lower heels 5 times.

Weight and diet

Fitness is closely associated with correct bodyweight, and a fairly constant bodyweight can only be achieved by maintaining a balance between energy intake (food eaten) and energy output (metabolism, movement and exercise). The rate at which calories are burned up is known as the metabolic rate. This will increase whenever exercise is taken and energy therefore used up.

The correct proportion of nutrients is also important if this balance is to be effective. Broadly speaking, a balanced diet should contain adequate amounts of protein, vitamins and minerals, and carbohydrates and fats. Examples of foods in these categories, together with their basic proportions of required consumption, are shown in the table, below left, and diagram, below right.

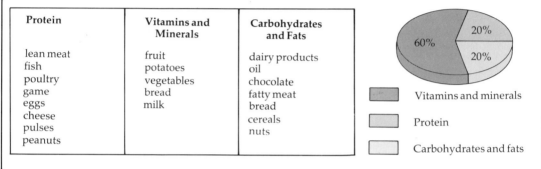

Protein	Vitamins and Minerals	Carbohydrates and Fats
lean meat	fruit	dairy products
fish	potatoes	oil
poultry	vegetables	chocolate
game	bread	fatty meat
eggs	milk	bread
cheese		cereals
pulses		nuts
peanuts		

Before the match

As a general rule, do not eat within two hours of a match. If you have eaten a good breakfast, then a light lunch between 11:30 and noon should provide sufficient intake before a competitive match programmed for a two o'clock start. This light lunch should include some carbohydrate food for energy (avoiding fatty foods) and plenty of fluids, such as milk or soft drinks. If you tend to get nervous before a match and are prone to sickness, then avoid food altogether and settle for a glass or two of skimmed milk. Remember, you will play better on an empty stomach than on one that feels a bit too full, to say nothing of the cramps and indigestion you will probably be avoiding by abstaining.

If you are having a specific diet problem, it is advisable to consult a nutrition expert to see exactly what your food requirements are.

During and after the match

Temporary weight loss frequently occurs during hard, competitive matches. During strenuous exercise like this, the metabolic rate can rise by as much as 10 times its normal figure, and up to 600 calories per hour can be used. Weight loss is mostly made up of fluid loss, which can be adjusted to a certain extent during play, and, of course, completely replenished when the match is over. Players nowadays take in extra fluids regularly during the change-overs, drinking water, soft or carbonated drinks. Glucose tablets can also be eaten during the match as, like all sugars, they are readily absorbed into the bloodstream, and provide almost instant energy for your muscles. Remember, though, that sugars themselves contain no vitamins or protein. In hot climates, or if you have a tendency to perspire a great deal, taking salt tablets during play may help you avoid cramps and dehydration, but these tablets can sometimes upset the digestive system. It is better and safer to take adequate salt in your diet, especially in extra fluids, hours before an important match. As a general guideline, avoid fried and fatty foods.

It is common practice among competitors to restore food loss and rebuild energy supplies for the following day by eating their main meal in the evening. Otherwise, there are many different diets and schedules for players to follow. One such schedule involves following a high protein, high fat, low carbohydrate diet for the first three days, and a diet rich in carbohydrates for the next three days. The aim of this particular diet is to increase glycogen (the glucose-producing chemical) in the muscles above the normal level, and to provide the player with the ability to perform at his peak over a series of strenuous matches.

Injuries and treatments

INJURIES AND TREATMENTS

You will always be more prone to injury when you are tired, so physical fitness is a priority to the serious match player. Although a regular fitness program will help to protect you from serious tennis injuries, you are still likely to suffer relatively minor injuries, particularly if you play on cement, asphalt or synthetic courts which have no give, rather than on the softer clay and grass courts. Surfaces with no give will put more strain on your knee and ankle joints, and will jar your spine.

Injuries suffered by tennis players range from harmless but troublesome blisters to severe sprains of joints which require expert attention and time to heal. Whatever the injury, pain is an important warning sign and should not be ignored; always find its source rather than simply taking pain-killing

drugs. These will merely enable you to play when you should not, so possibly doing further damage.

If you are temporarily unable to play, due to an injury, try not to put on extra bodyweight, since this will put greater stress on the affected part. After joint or soft tissue injuries decreased mobility may arise from adhesions (the sticking together of tissue as a result of inflammation). Subsequent disability can be diminished by gentle stretching exercises of the injured part.

Below are some of the match to match injuries which you are likely to face, their prevention and some simple remedies. On the following pages you will find descriptions of injuries and treatments to joints and of the lower back – common complaints among tennis players.

Abrasions

Abrasions, or grazes, are probably the most common injury you are likely to encounter. Normally only the top layer of skin is broken, and the graze can be cleaned with an antiseptic solution and covered with some form of non-adhesive dressing. Deep cuts and lacerations may require further medical attention.

Blisters

These small, bladder-like cavities under the skin contain a watery fluid and are caused by moisture, pressure and friction. Wearing terrycloth pockets or wristbands to keep your hands and racket handles dry will counter-attack sweating palms as will sawdust or powdered chalk dabbed on to your racket handle. You can often get blisters from gripping your racket too tightly. In such cases tape your fingers, apply an adhesive bandage, or simply wear a tennis glove until your hand recovers. As a preventive measure, soft skin on the palms and soles of the feet can be hardened by soaking in an alum solution or methylated spirit, but protect your skin from becoming too hard by applying an emollient ointment if necessary. Given time, blisters usually dry up without any special attention. If you have to open up a large blister containing fluid, pierce the outer edge of the blister with a sterilized needle, press the fluid out gently, and cover the area with a clean, dry dressing. It is better not to

remove the lax skin as the underlying dermis may become infected. If it does, apply a mild tanning antiseptic, such as iodine or mercurochrome, and keep covered with a dry, absorbent dressing. If you have to use waterproof dressings, the lesion may become macerated. To avoid this the dressing should be changed often allowing time for the lesion to dry in the air.

Bruising

Bruising is normally brought about by blows, often against soft tissues, damaging blood vessels, muscle sheaths and fibers. Bleeding into the tissues causes swelling, discoloration and pain. Minor bruises can be treated by applying cold compresses, cool spray or ice packs. If there is severe pain, seek expert medical attention.

Cramp and stiffness

Cramp is the sudden contraction of muscle fibers, resulting in painful muscle spasms in the stomach, legs and feet. It can be caused by tiredness, incorrect training, loss of body salt and fluid in the system, excessive smoking or even a faulty diet, where the acid balance is disturbed. Sound training and pre-match preparation plus adequate intake of salt and fluids before play are good preventive measures and should be of particular concern where climatic conditions promote excessive sweating, especially when a hard fought match is probable.

If you are prone to cramp you may find the perfect solution in biochemic tissue salts These inorganic salts are mixed with lactose, and are available in tiny molded tablets that dissolve under your tongue in about four seconds. They can be taken at virtually any time and are immediately absorbed into your bloodstream. Three tissue salts are of special interest: sodium and potassium, which are essential for maintaining the electrolyte balance of the body and the muscle and nerve impulse transmission that is vital to the tennis player; and magnesium, which, as well as being good for your heart, can have quite a magical effect on cramp, often eliminating its occurrence altogether. Tissue salts can be bought in health food stores and some drug stores. They are safe to take, unless your body is sensitive to lactose. If you have any doubts you should seek advice from your doctor.

If cramp does occur during a game, on-court treatment can be very effective. If cramp affects the thighs, calves or feet, lay the player on his back and stretch the affected muscle by straightening the leg with the toes raised and the heel pressed down. For cramp in the hand, pull the fingers straight firmly. For stomach cramp place the heels of your hands on either side of the abdomen and knead the abdominal muscles with your fingers together.

If you feel stiffness in your legs, lie on your back and let the thumbs and fingers of each hand meet round your leg below the calf muscle, then draw them upwards with slight but firm pressure, ease off over the knee and then continue up the thigh. If your stiffness develops several hours after activity has ceased, there could well be some inflammation in the affected joint. Do not try to straighten or bend the joint with force in such cases; seek expert medical attention.

A "stitch" occurs when a small group of adjoining muscles goes into temporary cramp. These minor cramps can be treated on court – gentle massage of the affected area and deep breathing should provide fast relief.

Hematoma

This is severe bruising under the skin, or bruising of the muscle due to it being partially torn. Apply a cold compress to the affected part, and rest it in a raised position. This should be followed by exercise and, according to the degree of injury, expert physiotherapy perhaps including ultrasonic treatment for rapid healing.

Sprains

The physical demands of tennis can sometimes lead to the injury of joints. Generally speaking, a sprain occurs when a joint is subjected to stress which forces it beyond its normal range of movement. This will damage ligaments (the bonds between adjoining bones which normally enclose and support joints) and cause pain which can sometimes be intense. The degree of injury will depend on how far the joint was wrenched. Severe sprains require specialist attention.

Most muscle injuries require movement to stimulate recovery, but injuries to joints most often require rest or even complete immobilization. The supports and strappings shown are suggested as aids to recovery. They should not be used to facilitate a premature return to competitive tennis.

Ankle

The likelihood of spraining your ankle can be kept to a minimum by wearing tennis shoes with good supports (see p.19) and perhaps two pairs of socks. If your feet tend to move about inside your shoes, insoles and heel pads may be useful. A support sock (see p.264) underneath your normal tennis sock is an alternative combination.

In the case of less severe ankle sprains, cold applied immediately will reduce pain, prevent excessive swelling and help to prevent bleeding within the tissue. If ice is used it should not touch the skin directly because it may "burn" the skin. Bandage the ankle using a crepe bandage and starting underneath the foot, bind the ankle using a figure-of-eight pattern and fasten the bandage on the outside of the ankle.

Bowls of hot and cold water can be beneficial in the treatment of ankle sprains so stimulating the blood supply for the most rapid healing, and reducing swelling. Immerse your ankle in a bowl of water as hot as you can bear it for about 15 seconds. Then transfer it to a bowl of cold, but not icy, water for five seconds, and so on.

Ankle sprains, even when mild, can be extremely painful and swelling usually results. Mild ankle sprains should feel better within two or three days. If there is little, or no obvious swelling but your ankle is still very painful, do not discount the injury lightly but seek expert help. Such sprains can be serious as there may be bleeding within the joint itself.

Knee

The knee is the joint most commonly injured in all sports. It is a complex joint and it is prone to a number of injuries. Any swelling of the knee should be treated seriously, as wrong diagnosis and poor attention will lead to incomplete recovery and the gradual degeneration of the joint and its supporting muscles. Always fix in your memory how the injury occurred, remembering what strains were exerted on your knee and how it was forced to move beyond its normal range of movement. These facts will help an expert to diagnose your injury correctly. As a general rule, immediate swelling at the time of the injury which stops you in the middle of a match and prevents you from continuing, indicates that there may be blood in the knee joint—a sign of a severe knee injury. If the swelling grows more slowly then the damage to the joint is probably less severe and the same treatments described for rapid healing of an ankle sprain will help. When binding a swollen knee, start bandaging below the knee and bind in a figure eight; pass the bandage behind the joint and cross on the knee cap.

Wrist

Treatment of wrist sprains must be based on getting full use of mobility back as soon as possible, even though you will probably not be able to play for a week or two. Rest your wrist completely for a few days, then start mobility exercises, rotating the wrist, followed by strengthening exercises depending on the amount of pain felt. You may be able to avoid further injury by strengthening your wrist and forearm with one of the exercises described on page 258.

Any mild sprain should clear up within two or three weeks. If it does not, consult a doctor for expert advice and attention.

Bandaging will help if enough support is given to the wrist without restricting circulation to the fingers. You may find the wrist strap, shown below, useful if you decide to continue playing with a very mild wrist injury, and as physical (and mental) support when you start to play again after a more serious wrist sprain. Many wrist strappings now available have an absorbent outer covering so that, in position, the support also serves as a sweatband wristlet.

Aids and supports

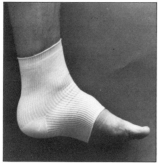

Ankle support

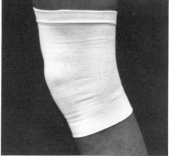

Knee support

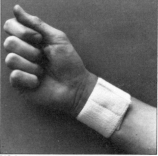

Wrist support

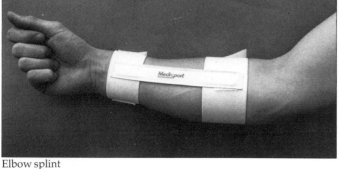

Elbow splint

Elbow support

Tendon damage

Tendons connect the muscles to bone and so enable the contraction of muscles to move limbs. Among tennis players, tendon injuries occur from over-use or unexpected stress. Damage takes the form of rupture, partial rupture, or inflammation of the tendon (tendinitis). Complete and effective treatment of tendon injury sometimes includes surgery. They take a long time to heal as the blood supply to them is generally comparatively poor.

Achilles tendon

The Achilles tendon, joining your calf muscle to your heel, can be injured if you descend awkwardly after playing a jump smash, especially if your bodyweight is falling backwards over your heels as you play the stroke. You can help to prevent this situation from causing an injury by wearing good shoes and a support sock. Inserting a shock-absorbing pad in the heel of your shoe can also be beneficial.

Coming down on the ball of the foot, putting extreme pressure on the tendon by not lowering the heel, can either rupture or partially rupture the tendon. A complete rupture will sound like a pistol shot as the tendon breaks like elastic band. There is usually complete loss of function and urgent surgical repair is the most effective solution. If a partial rupture is suffered some control of movement will usually be retained although pain will be acute. It will heal if treated conservatively with appropriate immobilization but the healing process will be slow and surgery is often needed to ensure full and more rapid recovery.

Persistent Achilles tendon pain can be treated with rest, ultrasonic treatment and other forms of physiotherapy, but as there are different forms of tendon damage, such as peritendinitis (inflammation of the tissue around the tendon) or central degeneration, it is vital to seek help from a qualified person so that a correct diagnosis can be made and the appropriate treatment administered. If you experience Achilles tendon pain while you are on court, keep the affected part immobile until a skilled examination can be carried out.

Tennis elbow

The most infamous elbow injury is probably tennis elbow, although far fewer people suffer from it than is generally supposed, since the term is used to describe most types of inflammation and pain felt over the outer part of the elbow. True tennis elbow is likely to occur whenever the forearm is continually involved in a rotary movement—as, for example, the backhand action made by some tennis players. Your chances of ending up with tennis elbow are increased if you tend to turn or flick your wrist and elbow sharply through the hitting zone, finishing with the palm aiming upwards and the racket face closed or completely inverted.

A common type of tennis elbow occurs when the attachment to the extensor muscles(which extend the wrist) is torn or pulled away from the ridge of the bone on the outer side of the lower end of the humerus, causing inflammation or epicondylitis. Other forms are annular ligament strain (the straining of the ligament linking the radius to the ulna) and radiohumeral bursitis (inflammation of the bursa, or pad, between the radius and the humerus).

Treatment

If your tennis elbow has developed through faulty technique, you can sometimes cure and prevent the condition from re-occurring through proper use of the arm, and avoiding over-contraction of the muscles or joint. Physiotherapy and ultrasonic treatment can sometimes be of benefit.

If you injure your elbow, aids and supports can often be useful to help you back to match fitness. Elbow bandages or warm-up sleeves, for example, are readily available in drugstores and sports shops. They provide support and warmth to the vulnerable area, and are flexible and comfortable, provided they are not worn too tight. They should be worn for 10 or 15 minutes before play, and removed after you have finished. Other splint-type supports are more restrictive but may well allow you to play when the elbow lesion should be rested. For a simpler type of support wrap a tourniquet-style bandage about an inch wide around your forearm in the hollow of your muscle just below your elbow (you can find this by holding out your hand and clenching your fist).

Lower back injury

Among the factors contributing to the increase of lower back injuries among tennis players is the fact that more and more matches are played on synthetic courts with insufficient give. Shock-absorbing heel inserts in your shoes will help to cushion your back.

The most common cause of lower back, or lumbar, injuries in tennis players, however, is the strain caused by excessive and unnecessary back-arching when playing the topspin service. Arching your back violently and throwing your upper body weight so far over that it has no support apart from the arched vertebrae, can not only cause severe stress, but will also continually aggravate any previous back condition you may have suffered. You can remedy this by pushing your weight forward on to the balls of your feet by bending your knees and raising your heels so that your upper body weight is completely balanced over your heels. Muscles and ligaments in this region can also be damaged, and sacro-iliac strain can occur amongst players who repeatedly step far across with their front foot when groundstroking instead of stepping forwards.

Treatment

Any back injury will require careful and expert consideration, for it can affect so many other parts of the body. Any injury to the muscles of the lower back region will normally respond to physiotherapy treatment and massage, according to the nature of the damaged tissue, but cold, heat, and massage may not always be the answer. If you develop pins and needles in the arms or legs after a violent jerk or fall, be particularly cautious as some nerve root damage may have been caused, and this should be treated only by an expert.

Many osteopaths can manipulate back injuries successfully and where a more serious injury seems likely an X-ray may be necessary to locate and confirm bone fracture or disc movement. Depending again on the exact nature of the injury, rest, immobility and possible surgery may be required. Neuro- and orthopedic surgeons may have to be consulted in extreme cases, followed by hospitalization, surgery and rehabilitation until the injury is completely cured.

Massage

Few top class players could survive the very strenuous globe-trotting circuit of championship tournaments without the aid of a skilled masseur. Massage is not only a necessary treatment in the case of some injuries; it also has a vital role to play before and after a tough training session or match. Many good players become expert masseurs and so can help each other and themselves. However, massage should not be practiced by an amateur because of the very real risk of causing damage. It is often erroneously thought that the more vigorous and violent a massage the more effective it will be, but it can cause further injury.

Before play

Massage can be used just before a match to loosen up and generally stimulate the player. It will provide a mental lift and often helps a slow-starting player to begin competing seriously from the very beginning. Two minutes of brisk stroking and kneading and some slow stretching movements are more than enough to prepare a player for the match. If the player is nervous and tense then the massage should be applied slowly and rhythmically to encourage mental and physical relaxation rather than stimulation.

After play

Massage after a tough match can help prevent stiffness developing in the muscles. Limbs should be raised and slow, easy stroking movements applied to disperse waste products and restore normal circulation. Massage limbs towards the heart and away from stiff areas in the body. As the stiffness eases, firmer massage can include stretching and kneading until the muscles are loose and the player relaxed.

If another match has to be played shortly, then the session should end with the brisker type of massage normally needed before play starts.

Appendix

Courts

Tennis courts can be outdoors or indoors, and can have a variety of surfaces, though these are being increasingly determined by economic factors. Grass courts, for example, which originally formed the basis of the outdoor game, are now too expensive to build and maintain and are being replaced by synthetic surfaces which are cheaper and easier to maintain.

Each court surface, whatever the type, is made up of several layers, including a drainage layer to counteract rain. The main types of court surface are described below.

Net, posts and sticks

The net is suspended from a cord or net cable, the ends of which pass across the tops of two posts. This cable can be cranked higher or lower as required. When a combined doubles and singles court with a doubles net is used for singles play, the net, must, in addition, be supported by two singles sticks.

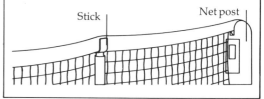

Stick | Net post

Grass courts

Grass courts are becoming less and less common because of the time and money needed to maintain them. They are dependent on good drainage. A cross-section of a typical grass court is shown in the diagram, right. It is made up of a top layer comprising 7.5cm (3in) selected loam and 15cm (6in) free-draining loam, two sheets of permeable non-woven fabric separated by a layer of coarse aggregate and a 44-cm (18-in) wide drainage channel above the subsoil. The perimeter is made up of a batten wear strip, concrete wall and footings.

Hard or clay courts

Hard courts need to be maintained regularly, and repairs can sometimes be costly. The diagram, right, shows a cross-section of a well-constructed hard court. It is made up of the following layers: a layer of surfacing material, which can be from 19mm (¾in) to 4cm (1½in) deep; a blinding layer made up of hard gritty clinker ash or coarse sand; a 12.5cm (5in) permeable layer; and a 7.5cm (3in) drain with an invert 22.5cm (9in) below base level, above the subsoil. The perimeter consists of a concrete edging.

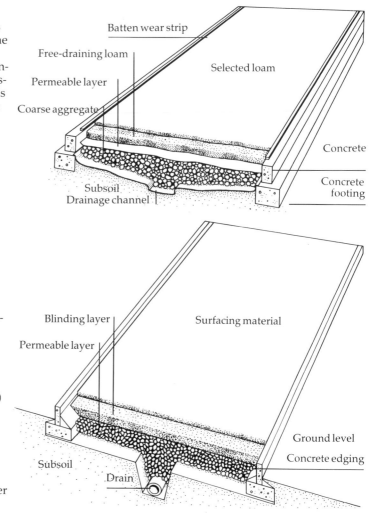

Batten wear strip
Free-draining loam
Permeable layer
Coarse aggregate
Selected loam
Concrete
Concrete footing
Subsoil
Drainage channel

Blinding layer
Permeable layer
Surfacing material
Subsoil
Drain
Ground level
Concrete edging

All-weather courts

Most all-weather courts require little attention other than brushing and are very popular. They usually have a macadam-type surface, which is sometimes covered with specially prepared paint. Two types of hard court are shown right. The Tennisquick court, top right, has a proprietary top surface, a second layer of cement-bound stone and a third layer of stone or gravel. The Grass-phalte court, bottom right, is also made up of three layers. The foundation consists of a 15cm (6in) thickness of stone or ash, or, alternatively, a combination of both. This is then rolled with a heavy power roller; a bituminous surface is subsequently laid in two coats, the top surface of which is slightly finer than the second.

Synthentic courts

Synthetic courts are becoming increasingly popular because they are so easy to maintain. A wide variety of synthetics is available. The Mercury Grass-phalte court, top right, has a surface which basically consists of a special grading of granulated rubber particles bound together with epoxy resins, sprayed with a polyurethane coating.

An artificial grass or sand-filled tennis carpet that was first launched in 1976 as an inexpensive replacement for natural turf courts is shown right. Astroturf, as it is sometimes called, is playable all the year round because rain drains through both the sand and the carpet into a sub-structure beneath. The tennis lines are tufted into the carpet and the courts are virtually maintenance free. The speed at which the court plays is adjustable through levels and graduations of sand.

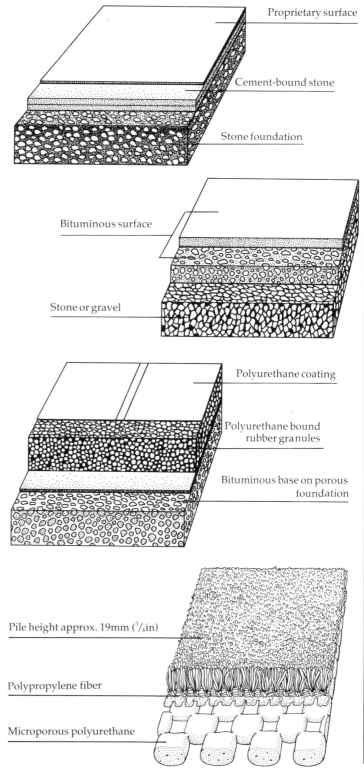

Proprietary surface

Cement-bound stone

Stone foundation

Bituminous surface

Stone or gravel

Polyurethane coating

Polyurethane bound rubber granules

Bituminous base on porous foundation

Pile height approx. 19mm (³/₄in)

Polypropylene fiber

Microporous polyurethane

Rackets

The selection of tennis rackets available today is greater than ever. In the 1970s, it was found that composite rackets – made of carbon, graphite, nylon, fiberglass, polyurethane, and other materials – had distinct advantages over wooden frames, because they could be made lighter, stronger, and with larger heads. Metal frames were also experimented with, and aluminum rackets are still produced, but wooden rackets became museum pieces as racket design and technology advanced.

Composite racket manufacture

A composite is a general term that has evolved to mean an article molded from plastic material reinforced by strong fibers. The plastic material is known as the matrix (or resin). There are several types of reinforcing fiber used in the manufacture of composite rackets. Glass fiber, or fiberglass, is inexpensive, heavy, relatively weak and rather flexible. Carbon fiber is more expensive, but lighter and stronger and also stiffer – in the sporting world it is known as graphite but this is not strictly accurate: true graphite comes in pencils and is used as a lubricant. Boron fiber is more expensive than carbon, but even lighter and stronger. Other substances which have limited use are Kevlar, which is used in making bullet-proof vests and of course in Kevlar racket strings in hybrid compositions, and ceramics, of which many varieties exist, all of them expensive.

All of these fibers are very strong, but they are threadlike in form, and consequently have to be bonded into a matrix in order to be used to make tennis rackets. Composites are much denser than wood, and a system which molds a hollow racket had to be used in the manufacturing process. Two different methods have been developed to accomplish this – compression molding and injection molding.

Compression molding The majority of composite tennis rackets are made by this system, which produces very high quality rackets. The matrix (the plastic material) is almost always epoxy resin, which is "thermosetting", that is, when heated it solidifies and cannot be re-melted. The longer reinforcing fibers are coated with epoxy and placed in the mold, which is then closed and heated. To make the racket hollow, internal pressure is created by inflating an inner tube or using an expanding foam. In the construction of the racket, normal percentages of materials are matrix 40 per cent and fibers 60 per cent. A mixture of fibers is often used so that a racket may not be too expensive – a common example would be matrix 40 per cent, carbon fiber 30 per cent, and glass fiber 30 per cent. A racket in which all the fibers are carbon is known as 100 per cent graphite, and, although this is not strictly true (since the 40 per cent that is made up of matrix is not carbon fiber), it is generally accepted for most trading purposes.

Injection molding The Dunlop Sports Company introduced their unique injection molding system in the early 1980s. The material used is "thermoplastic": that is, it melts when heated and solidifies when cooled. The matrix is nylon, and the short reinforcing fibers are entirely carbon fiber. To make the racket hollow, a core is produced from a metal alloy with a low melting point. This has the shape of the finished racket, but is slightly smaller in cross-section. It is fitted into the mold, leaving a small space between the mold and the core. The carbon fiber and nylon mixture is injected into the mold, and fills this space, sheathing the core. The molding is removed and then heated, causing the metal alloy to melt and run out, and leaving the hollow frame. In construction, percentages are matrix 60 per cent, reinforcing fiber 40 per cent. As with compression molding, a racket made from 40 per cent carbon fiber and 60 per cent nylon is referred to as being 100 per cent graphite.

Removing the core from the mold

Composite rackets

The most advanced composite frames are those of a wide-bodied design, constructed from combinations of graphite, glass fiber, Kevlar, Boron and other materials. All composite rackets have some vibration-dampening system to help to absorb shock waves at impact. Widebody rackets have a streamlined head, face-on, but a broader beam side-on. When widebodies first emerged they were generally very stiff and unyielding but manufacturers now produce a complete range of widebody rackets of varying widths and tapering beams. The average racket head size or strung surface of composite widebodies is 612–710 square centimeters (95–110 square inches). These rackets enlarge the "sweet spot" area – the central part of the stringing for sound hitting – and are therefore the most popular sizes. The widebody racket is lighter, more powerful, and easier to maneuver than any of the composite predecessors.

Aluminum alloy rackets

These rackets, made from ex-truded aluminum, are strong, light, and easy to handle. They captured a large corner of the market for a while, between the decline in the use of wooden rackets and the development of modern composite rackets. The modern aluminum racket can be produced using wide-beam technology and early problems with vibration have been, for the most part, overcome. The degree of flex makes it an ideal racket for players starting out and many companies manufacture a complete range of junior length aluminum frames.

Stringing

The problem of choice of stringing is no longer the simple decision of choosing between natural gut and synthetic stringing. Some top players still tend to prefer gut because of its resilience and the high standard of its playing characteristics. Synthetic strings, however, have improved tremendously during the past decade, and with the international popularity of the innovative but rigid widebodied racket, multifiber synthetic strings, which are both responsive and durable, are now generally used in competitive play. Selecting the right type for your game will require some experimentation.

Natural stringing

Natural gut is preferred by some professional players because its responsiveness and resilience remain superior to the majority of synthetic strings and it is ideal for both touch and power play. It is, however, much more expensive than synthetic gut (though this will vary according to the quality of the gut used) and is considerably more sensitive to atmospheric conditions such as damp and extreme heat. The stiffness of the modern frame also shortens the life of gut.

Natural stringing is processed from the intestines of sheep, cows or pigs, and is graded according to its quality: the top grade is known as "championship"; others are simply "second grade", "third grade" and so on. The best-quality gut is pale gold in color and, on close inspection, the twists in the string should be almost unnoticeable. It should also be free of fault marks and consistent in diameter throughout its length. The finest strings are Australian, but excellent gut strings are also produced in the United States, Europe and India.

It takes a 10.05m (33ft) set of gut to string a racket. This set usually comes in two lengths of 6.7m (22ft) and 3.35m (11ft) for easy handling. Since each string is made individually bulk spools are not available. Gut is bought in thicknesses of 15 and 16 gauge. In normal tennis racket stringing the heavier 15 gauge is used, which proves more than adequate for most standards of play. The finer 16-gauge stringing is even more resilient and feel and performance are improved accordingly, but playing life is short.

Synthetic stringing

Synthetic stringing is much less expensive than natural gut and it now provides the tennis player with feel and response. Its added advantages of durability and being impervious to moisture make it the natural choice for many players. Synthetic strings come in lengths of 11m (36ft), or in spools of 100m (328ft) or 200m (656ft).

The first man-made synthetic stringing for tennis rackets came from single-stranded or monofilament nylon. It was cheap and durable but performance and basic control were poor. Rayon and silk were also tried and found wanting, but the more sophisticated modern synthetic strings (multifilaments) are made from extruded materials which can vary considerably. Some synthetics have central cores with a series of mini-cores built around them, while composite core strings have a central structure made up of many fine strands. There are various types of string, but the best modern synthetics are multifiber.

The evolution of the widebody racket means that the strings, as opposed to the frame, now take most of the impact of the tennis ball, and this has led to a high number of premature breakages, even when the very best synthetics are being used. With the greater demand for durability, while maintaining optimum performance from the strings, many top players now use hybrid strings, which combine Kevlar stringing with synthetic gut. The very strong Kevlar is used for the main strings (where most breakages occur) and the synthetic gut is used for the cross strings. When stringing a tennis frame with hybrid strings the Kevlar mains should be strung to a tension of up to 20 per cent less than the cross strings in order to put less strain on the frame.

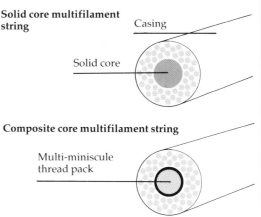

Solid core multifilament string
Casing
Solid core

Composite core multifilament string
Multi-miniscule thread pack

Restringing

In general, the tighter the stringing the more stress is placed on the frame, and the stiffer the frame the more stress is placed on the strings. The thickness of string that you should use, and the ideal tension at which to string it, may need some experimentation and advice to find. The tensions used by top players range from 20.4kg (45lbs) to 36.3kg (80lbs) depending on their game and racket type. As a rule synthetic strings are strung at lower tensions than gut strings.

When restringing, check wooden frames for lamination cracks. Flex them gently across your knee; too much give may result in warping if you have the racket tightly strung. Composite and metal rackets should be checked for cracks and worn or damaged grommets in the string holes. Tension the main strings first, working from the center outward. When interlacing the cross strings, start from either the throat or the crown, according to whether there are six or eight string holes in the throat bridge. Never pull the cross strings straight through the mains, as this may cause fraying: always pull them up or down as you work them through. To restring a racket you will need a restringing machine, stringing and cutting pliers, and a pointed and blunt awl.

Table top machine

The illustration, below, shows a restringing machine which is both portable and suitable for table top use, although traditional floor standing models are also available. It will restring or repair any type or size of racket. The best machines have a special locking device which prevents frame distortion, and a precise scale to give uniformity of string tension up to a maximum of approx. 29kg (64lb). The overall weight of such machines varies from 4kg (9lbs) to 16kg (35lbs).

Running repairs

These repairs cannot be carried out on wide-beam rackets, as the holes are too small. On other types, however, they can help to avoid a complete restringing. Make sure that the remaining strings are in good condition before removing a broken string. Any strings that may have become loosened can sometimes be tensioned before being tied off at the nearest hole, preferably at the throat, as tying off elsewhere can prove tricky. Select the same type of string as the original, and use the hitch knot as shown right.

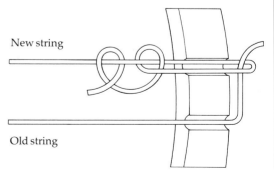

New string

Old string

Balls

Certain specifications govern the acceptability of tennis balls for tournament and championship play (see p.279). These, however, do allow some latitude in the actual manufacture of the ball, which accounts for the different playing characteristics of balls made by rival manufacturers. Some makes of ball bounce higher and seem, in general, to be more lively than others. This is due to a testing procedure that allows almost nine per cent variation in rebound – i.e., between 135cm (53in) and 147cm (58in) when dropped 254cm (100in) on to a concrete base. Balls can be pressurized (internal pressure greater than external) or pressureless (equal internal and external pressures). The step-by-step stages of manufacture of pressurized balls are laid out below.

Manufacturing process

1 Raw rubber is mixed with ingredients including sulphur and clay, to form a compound that will produce tennis balls of uniform characteristics.

2 The compound is cut up into pellets which will each form half of a ball.

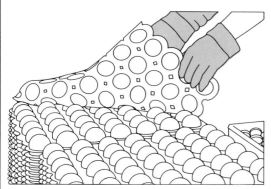

3 Hydraulic pressure is used to shape the pellets into hollow hemispheres.

4 These shells are trimmed and buffed and the edges are coated with rubber cement. An inflation pill is then added.

5 The shells are molded together and temperature controls bring the pressure inside the sphere to the correct compression.

6 The complete cores are then buffed.

7 Covers are automatically cut from a roll of tennis ball fabric spread with adhesive.

8 The covers, packed in frames, are dipped into rubber solution which will produce the seam of the finished ball.

9 The cores are checked for weight and size, coated with adhesive, and then each one is fitted with two interjoining covers.

10 Automatic presses mold the cloth around the balls and fuse the seams.

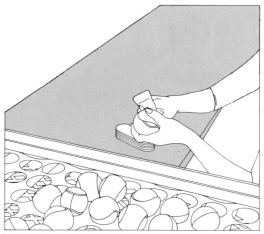

11 The balls are trimmed.

12 The compression of each ball is checked meticulously to see that it meets LTA and ITF requirements (see rule 3, p.279) before dating and packaging.

Practice aids

Sometimes it may be difficult to practice on a court or to find a practice partner at the right times. Several practice aids are available to help you overcome these difficulties. These will help improve your timing, co-ordination and reflexes as well as strengthen your muscles. Some of the most popular aids are described below.

Portable wall

The portable wall, right, consists of a steel frame, to which a playing surface, consisting of thick resilient foam, is attached. This has a white strip across it, approximately 1 yard from the ground, representing the net-top line. It measures 2.1 x 1.2 metres (7 x 4ft), and can be used singly and in pairs.

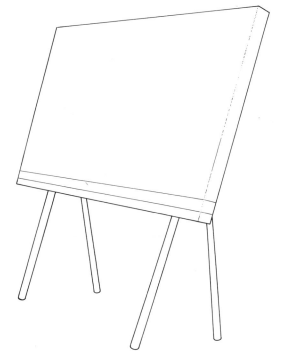

Ball machine

The large capacity ball machine, below, can be programed by means of a dial to feed balls at regular, or random, intervals at the speed and height required to your forehand and or your backhand. It is a good all-around practice aid for developing different strokes and perfecting timing (see p.165).

Short tennis

Short tennis can be used indoors or outdoors. Although smaller than a fully-sized court its dimensions are in proportion. The rules are the same as for tennis except that, as there is no service line, the server can use the full depth of the court in which to place the ball.

Ball returner

The simple, elasticated ball returner, shown right, can provide a good off-court aid to improving co-ordination.

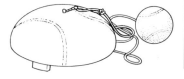

Tournament procedure
The draw

Each player's name is written on a separate card or piece of paper and placed in a box or hat before being withdrawn singly at random. All competitors in a tournament have a right to be present when the draw is made.

When the competitors number 4, 8, 16, 32, 64, or any higher power of two, the competitors can all meet in pairs in the first round. When the number of entries is not a power of two, the players that are left are said to have a "bye" and will not have to play until the second round. Byes will be placed in the first round in numbers equivalent to the difference between the number of entries and the next highest power of two (see chart below). The number of pairs meeting in the first round will be equal to the difference between the number of entries and the next lowest power of two. If there is an even number of byes these will be divided equally between the top and bottom halves of the draw and allotted, as the names are drawn, to positions above and below the pairs. When the byes are uneven, one more bye should be placed in the bottom half of the draw than in the top.

Table of byes for up to 64 competitors

Number of players	64 63 62 61 60 59 58 57 56 55 54 53 52 51 50 49 48 47 46 45 44 43 42 41 40 39 38 37 36 35 34 33
	32 31 30 29 28 27 26 25 24 23 22 21 20 19 18 17
	16 15 14 13 12 11 10 9
	8 7 6 5
Byes	0 1 2 3 4 5 6 7 8 9 10 11 12 13 14 15 16 17 18 19 20 21 22 23 24 25 26 27 28 29 30 31

Seeding

Seeding is a system of separating out the best players, to keep them apart till the latter stages of events. It is carried out by the tournament committee.

The seeding of players is restricted to level (non-handicap) events as follows:

Number of seeds	Number of competitors
2	Not less than 8 entries per event
4	Not less than 16 entries per event
6	Not less than 24 entries per event
8	Not less than 32 entries per event
12	Not less than 48 entries per event
16	Not less than 64 entries per event

The placement of seeds in the draw

2 seeds Number 1 at the top of the top half of the draw. Number 2 at the bottom of the bottom half.

4 seeds Numbers 1 and 2 as above. Numbers 3 and 4 are drawn by lot. The first drawn is placed at the bottom of the third quarter and the second at the top of the second quarter.

6 seeds Numbers 1 to 4 as above. Numbers 5 and 6 are drawn by lot. The first draw is placed at the bottom of the seventh eighth and the second is placed at the top of the second eighth.

8 seeds Numbers 1 to 4 as above. Numbers 5 and 6 are drawn by lot. The first drawn is placed at the top of the fourth eighth and the second is placed at the bottom of the fifth eighth. Numbers 7 and 8 are then drawn by lot. The first drawn is placed at the bottom of the seventh eighth and the second is placed at the top of the second eighth.

12 seeds Numbers 1 to 8 as above. Numbers 9 and 10 are drawn by lot. The first drawn is placed at the top of the fourth sixteenth and the second is placed at the bottom of the thirteenth sixteenth. Numbers 11 and 12 are then drawn by lot. The first drawn is placed at the bottom of the ninth sixteenth and the second is placed at the top of the eighth sixteenth. Remaining entries are drawn as above.

Handicapping

Handicapping is a leveller which provides lesser players with the opportunity of competing realistically against superior match players, while at the same time affording exacting competition for the better player. Known players are allotted a handicap annually that mirrors their competitive results. This handicap must be declared on a handicap entry form when entering for a handicap event, along with recent results. The more information you give to the handicapper of a tournament the more likely you are to receive the handicap that is best for you.

Points are awarded as either received or owed odds in each group of six games of a set, according to your standard of play. Players cannot be given a handicap greater than owe 50, or more than receive 40. But a player cannot receive more than 30 from any opponent in match play, so the opponent might have to make up a full handicap by giving owed odds up to the limit of 50. In this case, two owed points are equal to one received.

Points are received in the even games – as early as possible in the first six games, and repeated every sixth game until the set is won. Points are owed in the uneven games – as late as possible in the first six six games, and repeated every sixth game until the set is won.

Handicaps are described as sixths of 15, 30, 40 and 50 (as there are six games in a set), telling you how many points you owe or receive, and in what games. The two tables, above right, show when you receive or owe odds for $\frac{1}{6}$ to $\frac{5}{6}$ of 15.

For the purpose of matching the handicaps of different handicap players, handicaps are also graded above and below scratch (the handicap of 0), where .1 owed or received equals a handicap of $\frac{1}{6}$ of 15 owed or received. Similarly, a handicap of, say, 15.1 owed or received means that the player receives 15 every game and 30 on the second of each six games, or a handicap of, say, owe 15.3 means that the player owes 15 every game and 30 on the first, third and fifth games of every six games.

When both players are handicapped to receive points or both to owe points, they play on the difference of their respective handicaps. In the case of received odds the player with the less odds goes back to scratch (love) and in owed odds he goes forward to scratch.

Bearing in mind that when players meet with handicaps on either side of scratch, two points owed are equal to one received, the Match Handicaps when a player with an individual handicap of receive 30.5, plays against a player with an individual handicap of owe.1, would be receive 30 and owe 15.5 respectively.

Received odds

	$\frac{1}{6}$ of 15	$\frac{2}{6}$ of 15	$\frac{3}{6}$ of 15	$\frac{4}{6}$ of 15	$\frac{5}{6}$ of 15
1st game				15	15
2nd game	15	15	15	15	15
3rd game					15
4th game		15	15	15	15
5th game					
6th game			15	15	15

Owed odds

	$\frac{1}{6}$ of 15	$\frac{2}{6}$ of 15	$\frac{3}{6}$ of 15	$\frac{4}{6}$ of 15	$\frac{5}{6}$ of 15
1st game			15	15	15
2nd game					
3rd game		15	15	15	15
4th game					15
5th game	15	15	15	15	15
6th game				15	15

Handicap matching table

When matching handicaps, remember that two owed points are equivalent to one received point.

	40.4	40.5	50				
Owed	30.3	30.4	30.5	40	40.1	40.2	40.3
	15.2	15.3	15.4	15.5	30	30.1	30.2
	.1	.2	.3	.4	.5	15	15.1
Scratch	0						
	.1	.2	.3	.4		15	15.1
Received	15.2	15.3	15.4	15.5	30	30.1	30.2
	30.3	30.4	30.5	40			

Rules of tennis

THE SINGLES GAME

1 **The Court** shall be a rectangle 23.77m (78ft) long and 8.23m (27ft) wide.

It shall be divided across the middle by a net suspended from a cord or metal cable of a maximum diameter of 0.8cm (⅓in), the ends of which shall be attached to, or pass over, the tops of the two posts, which shall be not more than 15cm (6in) square or 15cm (6in) in diameter. The centers of the posts shall be 0.914m (3ft) outside the court on each side and the height of the posts shall be such that the top of the cord or metal cable shall be 1.07m (3ft 6in) above the ground.

When a combined doubles (see Rule 34) and singles court with a doubles net is used for singles, the net must be supported to a height of 1.07m (3ft 6in) by means of two posts, called "singles sticks", which shall be not more than 7.5cm (3in) square or 7.5cm (3in) in diameter. The centers of the singles sticks shall be 0.914m (3ft) outside the singles court on each side.

The net shall be extended fully so that it fills completely the space between the two posts and shall be of sufficiently small mesh to prevent the ball passing through. The height of the net shall be 0.914m (3ft) at the center, where it shall be held down taut by a strap not more than 5cm (2in) wide and completely white in color. There shall be a band covering the cord or metal cable and the top of the net of not less than 5cm (2in) nor more than 6.3cm (2½in) in depth on each side and completely white in color. There shall be no advertisement on the net, strap band or singles sticks.

The lines bounding the ends and sides of the Court shall respectively be called the base-lines and the side-lines. On each side of the net, at a distance of 6.40m (21ft) from it and parallel with it, shall be drawn the service-lines. The space on each side of the net between the service-line and the side-lines shall be divided into two equal parts called the service-courts by the center service-line, which must be 5cm (2in) in width, drawn half-way between, and parallel with, the side-line. Each base-line shall be bisected by an imaginary continuation of the center service-line to a line 10cm (4in) in length and 5cm (2in) in width called the "center-mark" drawn inside the Court, at right angles to and in contact with such base-lines. All other lines shall not be less than 2.5cm (1in) nor more than 5cm (2in) in width, except the base-line, which may be 10cm (4in) in width, and all measurements shall be made to the outside of the lines. All lines shall be of uniform color. If advertising or any other material is placed at the back of the court, it may not contain white, or yellow, or any light color.

If advertisements are placed on the chairs of the linesmen sitting at the back of the court, they may not contain white or yellow.

Note In the case of the International Tennis Championship (*Davis Cup*) or other Official Championships of the International Tennis Federation, there shall be a space behind each base-line of not less than 6.4m (21ft), and at the sides of not less than 3.66m (12ft).

2 The **permanent fixtures** of the Court shall include not only the net, posts, singles sticks, cord or metal cable, strap and band, but also, where there are any such, the back and side stops, the stands, fixed or movable seats and chairs round the Court, and their occupants, all other fixtures around and above the Court, and the Umpire, Net-cord Judge, Footfault Judge, Linesmen and Ball Boys when in their respective places.

Note For the purpose of this Rule, the word "Umpire" comprehends the Umpire, the persons entitled to a seat on the Court, and all those persons designated to assist the Umpire in the conduct of a match.

3 **The ball** shall have a uniform outer surface and shall be white or yellow in color. If there are any seams they shall be stitchless.

The ball shall be more than 6.35cm (2½in) and less than 6.67cm (2⅝in) in diameter, and more than 56.7g (2oz) and less than 58.5g (2¹/₁₆oz) in weight.

The ball shall have a bound of more than 135cm (53in) and less than 147cm (58in) when dropped 254cm (100in) upon a concrete base. The ball shall have a forward deformation of more than .56cm (.220in) and less than .74cm (.290in) and a return deformation of more than .89cm (.350in) and less than 1.08cm (.425in) at 8.165kg (18lb) load. The two deformation figures shall be the averages of three individual readings along three axes of the ball and no two individual readings shall differ by more than .08cm (.030in) in each case.

4 **The Racket** Rackets failing to comply with the following specifications are not approved for play under the Rules of Tennis:
(a) The hitting surface of the racket shall be flat and consist of a pattern of crossed strings connected to a frame and alternately interlaced or bonded where they cross; and the stringing pattern shall be generally uniform, and in particular not less dense in the center than in any other area. The strings shall be free of attached objects and protrusions other than those utilized solely and specifically to limit or prevent wear and tear or vibration and which are reasonable in size and placement for such purposes.
(b) The frame of the racket shall not exceed 81.28cm (32in) in overall length, including the handle and 31.75cm (12½in) in overall width. The strung surface shall not exceed 39.37cm (15½in) in overall length, and 29.21cm (11½in) in overall width.
(c) The frame, including the handle, shall be free of attached objects and devices other than those utilized solely and specifically to limit or prevent wear and tear or vibration, or to distribute weight. Any objects and devices must be reasonable in size and placement for such purposes.

(d) The frame, including the handle and the strings, shall be free of any device which makes it possible to change materially the shape of the racket, or to change the weight distribution, during the playing of a point.

The International Tennis Federation shall rule on the question of whether any racket or prototype complies with the above specifications or is otherwise approved, or not approved, for play. Such ruling may be undertaken on its own initiative, or upon application by any party with a bona fide interest therein, including any player, equipment manufacturer or National Association or members thereof. Such rulings and applications shall be made in accordance with the applicable Review and Hearing Procedures of the International Tennis Federation, copies of which may be obtained from the office of the Secretary.

5 **Server & Receiver** The players shall stand on opposite sides of the net; the player who first delivers the ball shall be called the Server, and the other the Receiver.

6 **Choice of Ends & Service** The choice of ends and the right to be Server or Receiver in the first game shall be decided by toss. The player winning the toss may choose or require his opponent to choose:
(a) The right to be Server or Receiver, in which case the other player shall choose the end; or
(b) The end, in which case the other player shall choose the right to be Server or Receiver.

7 **The Service** shall be delivered in the following manner. Immediately before commencing to serve, the Server shall stand with both feet at rest behind (i.e. further from the net than) the base-line, and within the imaginary continuations of the center-mark and side-line. The Server shall then project the ball by hand into the air in any direction and before it hits the ground strike it with his racket, and the delivery shall be deemed to have been completed at the moment of the impact of the racket and the ball. A player with the use of only one arm may utilize his racket for the projection.

8 **Foot Fault** (a) The Server shall throughout the delivery of the service:
  (i) Not change his position by walking or running. The Server shall not by slight movements of the feet which do not materially affect the location originally taken up by him, be deemed "to change his position by walking or running".
  (ii) Not touch, with either foot, any area other than that behind the base-line within the imaginary extension of the center-mark and side-lines.
(b) The word "foot" means the extremity of the leg below the ankle.

9 **Delivery of Service**
(a) In delivering the service, the Server shall stand alternately behind the right and left Courts beginning from the right in every game. If service from a wrong half of the Court occurs and is undetected, all play resulting from such wrong service or services shall

stand, but the innacuracy of station shall be corrected immediately it is discovered.
(b) The ball served shall pass over the net and hit the ground within the Service Court which is diagonally opposite, or upon any line bounding such Court, before the Receiver returns it.

10 **Service Fault** The Service is a fault:
(a) If the Server commits any breach of Rules 7, 8 or 9;
(b) If he misses the ball in attempting to strike it;
(c) If the ball served touches a permanent fixture (other than the net, strap or band) before it hits the ground.

11 **Second Service** After a fault (if it is the first fault) the Server shall serve again from behind the same half of the Court from which he served that fault, unless the service was from the wrong half, when, in accordance with Rule 9, the Server shall be entitled to one service only from behind the other half.

12 **When to Serve** The Server shall not serve until the receiver is ready. If the latter attempts to return the service, he shall be deemed ready. If, however, the Receiver signifies that he is not ready, he may not claim a fault because the ball does not hit the ground within the limits fixed for the service.

13 **The Let** In all cases where a let has to be called under the rules, or to provide for an interruption to play, it shall have the following interpretations:
(a) When called solely in respect of a service that one service only shall be replayed.
(b) When called under any other circumstances, the point shall be replayed.

14 **The "Let" in Service** The Service is a let:
(a) If the ball served touches the net, strap or band, and is otherwise good, or, after touching the net, strap or band, touches the Receiver or anything which he wears or carries before hitting the ground.
(b) If a service or a fault is delivered when the Receiver is not ready (see Rule 12).
  In case of a let, that particular service shall not count, and the Server shall serve again, but a service let does not annul a previous fault.

15 **Order of Service** At the end of the first game the Receiver shall become Server, and the Server Receiver; and so on alternately in all the subsequent games of a match. If a player serves out of turn, the player who ought to have served shall serve as soon as the mistake is discovered, but all points scored before such discovery shall be reckoned. If a game shall have been completed before such discovery, the order of service remains as altered. A fault served before such discovery shall not be reckoned.

16 **When Players Change Ends** The players shall change ends at the end of the first, third and every subsequent alternate game of each set, and at the end of each set unless the total number of games in such set is even, in which case the change is not made until the end of the first game of the next set.

If a mistake is made and the correct sequence is not followed the players must take up their correct station as soon as the discovery is made and follow their original sequence.

17 **The Ball in Play** A ball is in play from the moment at which it is delivered in service. Unless a fault or a let is called it remains in play until the point is decided.

18 **Server Wins Point** The Server wins the point:
(a) If the ball served, not being a let under Rule 14, touches the Receiver or anything which he wears or carries, before it hits the ground;
(b) If the Receiver otherwise loses the point as provided by Rule 20.

19 **Receiver Wins Point** The Receiver wins the point:
(a) If the Server serves two consecutive faults;
(b) If the Server otherwise loses the point as provided by Rule 20.

20 **Player Loses Point** A Player loses the point if:
(a) He fails, before the ball in play has hit the ground twice consecutively, to return it directly over the net (except as provided in Rule 24 (a) or (c)); or
(b) He returns the ball in play so that it hits the ground, a permanent fixture, or other object, outside any of the lines which bound his opponent's Court (except as provided in Rule 24 (a) or (c)); or
(c) He volleys the ball and fails to make a good return even when standing outside the Court; or
(d) In playing the ball he deliberately carries or catches it on his racket or deliberately touches it with his racket more than once; or
(e) He or his racket (in his hand or otherwise) or anything which he wears or carries touches the net, posts, singles sticks, cord or metal cable, strap or band, or the ground within his opponent's Court at any time while the ball is in play; or
(f) He volleys the ball before it has passed the net; or
(g) The ball in play touches him or anything that he wears or carries, except his racket in his hand or hands; or
(h) He throws his racket at and hits the ball; or
(i) He deliberately and materially changes the shape of his racket during the playing of the point.

21 **Player Hinders Opponent** If a player commits any act which hinders his opponent in making a stroke, then, if this is deliberate, he shall lose the point or if involuntary, the point shall be replayed.

22 **Ball Falls on Line** A ball falling on a line is regarded as falling in the Court bounded by that line.

23 **Ball Touches Permanent Fixtures** If the ball in play touches a permanent fixture (other than the net, posts, singles sticks, cord or metal cable, strap or band) after it has hit the ground, the player who struck it wins the point; if before it hits the ground, his opponent wins the point.

24 **A Good Return** It is a good return:
(a) If the ball touches the net, posts, singles sticks, cord or metal cable, strap or band, provided that it passes over any of them and hits the ground within the Court; or
(b) If the ball, served or returned, hits the ground within the proper Court and rebounds or is blown back over the net, and the player whose turn it is to strike reaches over the net and plays the ball, provided that neither he nor any part of his clothes or racket touches the net, posts, singles sticks, cord or metal cable, strap or band or the ground within his opponent's Court, and that the stroke be otherwise good; or
(c) If the ball is returned outside the posts, or singles sticks, either above or below the level of the top to the net, even though it touches the posts or singles sticks, provided that it hits the ground within the proper Court; or
(d) If a player's racket passes over the net after he has returned the ball, provided the ball passes the net before being played and is properly returned; or
(e) If a player succeeds in returning the ball, served or in play, which strikes a ball lying in the Court.

Note In a singles match, if, for the sake of convenience, a doubles Court is equipped with singles sticks for the purpose of a singles game, then the doubles posts and those portions of the net, cord or metal cable and the band outside such singles sticks shall at all times be permanent fixtures, and are not regarded as posts or parts of the net of a singles game.

A return that passes under the net cord between the singles stick and adjacent doubles post without touching either net cord, net or doubles post and falls within the area of play, is a good return.

25 **Hindrance of a Player** In case a player is hindered in making a stroke by anything not within his control, except a permanent fixture of the Court, or except as provided for in Rule 21, a let shall be called.

26 **Score in a Game** If a player wins his first point, the score is called 15 for that player; on winning his second point, the score is called 30 for that player; on winning his third point, the score is called 40 for that player, and the fourth point won by a player is scored game for that player except as below:

If both players have won three points, the score is called deuce; and the next point won by a player is scored advantage for that player. If the same player wins the next point, he wins the game; if the other player wins the next point the score is again called deuce; and so on, until a player wins the two points immediately following the score at deuce, when the game is scored for that player.

27 **Score in a Set** (a) A player (or players) who first wins six games wins a set; except that he must win by a margin of two games over his opponent and where necessary a set shall be extended until this margin is achieved.
(b) The tie-break system of scoring may be adopted as an alternative to the advantage set system in

paragraph (a) of this Rule provided the decision is announced in advance of the match.

In this case, the following Rules shall be effective:

The tie-break shall operate when the score reaches six games all in any set except in the third or fifth set of a three set or five set match respectively when an ordinary advantage set shall be played, unless otherwise decided and announced in advance of the match.

The following system shall be used in a tie-break game.

Singles

(i) A player who first wins seven points shall win the game and the set provided he leads by a margin of two points. If the score reaches six points all the game shall be extended until this margin has been achieved. Numerical scoring shall be used throughout the tie-break game.

(ii) The player whose turn it is to serve shall be the Server for the first point. His opponent shall be the Server for the second and third points and thereafter each player shall serve alternately for two consecutive points until the winner of the game and set has been decided.

(iii) From the first point, each service shall be delivered alternately from the right and left courts, beginning from the right court. If service from a wong half of the court occurs and is undetected, all play resulting from such wrong service or services shall stand, but the inaccuracy of station shall be corrected immediately it is discovered.

(iv) Players shall change ends after every six points and at the conclusion of the tie-break game.

(v) The tie-break game shall count as one game for the ball change, except that, if the balls are due to be changed at the beginning of the tie-break, the change shall be delayed until the second game of the following set.

Doubles

In doubles the procedure for singles shall apply. The player whose turn it is to serve shall be the Server for the first point. Thereafter each player shall serve in rotation for two points, in the same order as previously in that set, until the winners of the game and set have been decided.

Rotation of Service

The player (or pair in the case of doubles) who served first in the tie-break game shall receive service in the first game of the following set.

28 **Maximum Number of Sets** The maximum number of sets in a match shall be 5, or, where women take part, 3.

29 **Role of Court Officials** In matches where an Umpire is appointed, his decision shall be final; but where a Referee is appointed, an appeal shall lie to him from the decision of an Umpire on a question of law, and in all such cases the decision of the Referee shall be final.

In matches where assistants to the Umpire are appointed (Linesmen, Net-cord Judges, Foot-fault Judges) their decisions shall be final on questions of fact except that if in the opinion of an Umpire a clear mistake has been made he shall have the right to change the decision of an assistant or order a let to be played. When such an assistant is unable to give a decision he shall indicate this immediately to the Umpire who shall give a decision. When an Umpire is unable to give a decision on a question of fact he shall order a let to be played.

In *Davis Cup* matches or other team competitions where a Referee is on Court any decision can be changed by the Referee, who may also instruct an Umpire to order a let to be played.

The Referee, in his discretion, may at any time postpone a match on account of darkness or the condition of the ground or the weather. In any case of postponement the previous score and previous occupancy of Courts shall hold good, unless the Referee and the players unanimously agree otherwise.

30 **Continuous Play & Rest Periods** Play shall be continuous from the first service until the match is concluded, in accordance with the following provisions:

(a) If the first service is a fault, the second service must be struck by the Server without delay.

The Receiver must play to the reasonable pace of the Server and must be ready to receive when the Server is ready to serve.

When changing ends a maximum of one minute thirty seconds shall elapse from the moment the ball goes out of play at the end of the game to the time the ball is struck for the first point of the next game.

The Umpire shall use his discretion when there is interference which makes it impractical for play to be continuous.

The organizers of international circuits and team events recognized by the ITF may determine the time allowed between points, which shall not at any time exceed 30 seconds.

(b) Play shall never be suspended, delayed or interfered with for the purpose of enabling a player to recover his strength, breath, or physical condition. However, in the case of accidental injury, the Umpire may allow a one-time three minute suspension for that injury.

The organizers of international circuits and team events recognized by the ITF may extend the one-time suspension period from three minutes to five minutes.

(c) If, through circumstances outside the control of the player, his clothing, footwear or equipment (excluding racket) becomes out of adjustment in such a way that it is impossible or undesirable for him to play on, the Umpire may suspend play while the maladjustment is rectified.

(d) The Umpire may suspend or delay play at any time as may be necessary and appropriate.

(e) After the third set, or when women take part the second set, either player is entitled to a rest, which shall not exceed 10 minutes, or in countries situated between latitude 15 degrees north and latitude 15 degrees south, 45 minutes and furthermore, when necessitated by circumstances not within the control of the players, the Umpire may suspend play for such a period as he may consider necessary. If play is suspended and is not resumed until a later day the rest may be taken only after the third set (or when women take part the second set) of play on such a later day, completion of an unfinished set being counted as one set.

If play is suspended and is not resumed until 10 minutes have elapsed in the same day the rest may be taken only after three consecutive sets have been played without interruption (or when women take part two sets), completion of an unfinished set being counted as one set.

Any nation and/or committee organizing a tournament, match or competition, other than the International Tennis Championships (*Davis Cup* and Federation Cup), is at liberty to modify this provision or omit it from its regulations provided this is announced before the event commences.

(f) A tournament committee has the discretion to decide the time allowed for a warm-up period prior to a match but this may not exceed five minutes and must be announced before the event commences.

(g) When approved point penalty and non-accumulative point penalty systems are in operation, the Umpire shall make his decisions within the terms of those systems.

(h) Upon violation of the principle that play shall be continuous the Umpire may, after giving due warning, disqualify the offender.

31 Coaching During the playing of a match in a team competition, a player may receive coaching from a captain who is sitting on the court only when he changes ends at the end of a game, but not when he changes ends during a tie-break game.

A player may not receive coaching during the playing of any other match. The provisions of this rule must be strictly construed. After due warning an offending player may be disqualified. When an approved point penalty system is in operation, the Umpire shall impose penalties according to that system.

Note The word "coaching" includes any advice or instruction.

32 Changing Balls In cases where balls are to be changed after a specified number of games, if the balls are not changed in the correct sequence, the mistake shall be corrected when the player, or pair in the case of doubles, who should have served with new balls is next due to serve. Thereafter the balls shall be changed so that the number of games between changes shall be that originally agreed.

THE DOUBLES GAME

33 The above Rules shall apply to the Doubles Game except as below.

34 The Doubles Court The Court shall be 10.97m (36ft) in width, i.e. 1.37m (4½ft) wider on each side than the Court for the Singles Game, and those portions of the singles side-lines which lie between the two service-lines shall be called the service side-lines. In other respects, the Court shall be similar to that described in Rule 1, but the portions of the singles side-lines between the base-line and service-line on each side of the net may be omitted if desired.

35 The **order of serving** shall be decided at the beginning of each set as follows:

The pair who have to serve in the first game of each set shall decide which partner shall do so and the opposing pair shall decide similarly for the second game. The partner of the player who served in the first game shall serve in the third; the partner of the player who served in the second game shall serve in the fourth, and so on in the same order in all the subsequent games of a set.

36 The **order of receiving** the service shall be decided at the beginning of each set as follows:

The pair who have to receive the service in the first game shall decide which partner shall receive the first service, and that partner shall continue to receive the first service in every odd game throughout that set. The opposing pair shall likewise decide which partner shall receive the first service in the second game and that partner shall continue to receive the first service in every even game throughout that set. Partners shall receive the service alternately throughout each game.

37 Service Out of Turn in Doubles If a partner serves out of his turn, the partner who ought to have served shall serve as soon as the mistake is discovered, but all points scored, and any faults served before such discovery, shall be reckoned. If a game shall have been completed before such discovery, the order of service remains as altered.

38 Error in Order of Receiving in Doubles If during a game the order of receiving the service is changed by the Receivers it shall remain as altered until the end of the game in which the mistake is discovered, but the partners shall resume their original order of receiving in the next game of that set in which they are Receivers of the service.

39 Service Fault in Doubles The service is a fault as provided for by Rule 10, or if the ball touches the Server's partner or anything which he wears or carries; but if the ball served touches the partner of the Receiver, or anything which he wears or carries, not being a let under Rule 14 (a) before it hits the ground, the Server wins the point.

40 Playing the Ball in Doubles The ball shall be struck alternately by one or other player of the opposing pairs, and if a player touches the ball in play with his racket in contravention of this Rule, his opponents win the point.

Note Except where otherwise stated, every reference in these Rules to the masculine includes the feminine gender.

Index

Page numbers in *italic* refer to photographs

INDEX

Acknowledgments

The author would like to thank the following:
Dudley Cooper MSc, Dip. CC, A. D. Douglas,
Priscilla Douglas, Lisa Downer, I. Gefen BA, Jan
Harper BA, D. M. Jones CChem, FRSC, Jack
Lennard MSF, L. M. Naidoo DOMRO, J. E. Pryor
PTCA, W. B. Robertson DOMRO, Stephanie
Stevens, St Maur's Convent, Molly Woodget
BSc, Cresta Ltd, Chevron Oil (UK) Ltd, Dunlop
Sports Company Ltd, En-Tout-Cas Ltd,
Grassphalte Ltd, The International Tennis
Federation, Jet Enterprises Ltd, The Lawn
Tennis Association, The Lawn Tennis Umpires
Association, Medisport Developments, New
Malden TS&B Club, D. Petri, Polyfreem Ltd,
Robinsons Services to Sport, Rosslyn Research
Ltd, Slazenger Ltd, The Wimbledon Lawn
Tennis Museum, Wingfield Sports.

Dorling Kindersley would like to give special
thanks to the following: Denise Brown, Jean
Cooke, Teresa Cross, Lesley Gilbert, Ann
Kramer, Graham Read (Scholl (UK) Ltd),
Theodore Rowland-Entwhistle, Sandra
Schneider, Dr Anthony Yates MDFRCP.
In addition, valuable help in the preparation of
this edition has been given by:
Apollo Strings, John D. C. Crump, Dunlop
Slazenger International Ltd, Goode Sport
Promotions (Ashaway Strings), Lee Griffiths, R.
C. Haines, New Era Laboratories Ltd, Jane
Newton, Pro-Kennex (UK) Ltd, Jenny Speller
Dorling Kindersley: Derek Coombes, Jemima
Dunne, Kate Fox, Rachel Griffin, Krystyna
Mayer, Alison Melvin, Candida Ross-
Macdonald, Lorna Damms, Camilla Fox and
Rosalind Priestley.

Illustrations
Kuo Kang Chen, Andrew Farmer, Kevin Malloy,
Coral Mula, Jim Robins, Venner Artists.

Reproduction
F. E. Burman Ltd, London.

Typesetting
Dorchester Typesetting Group Ltd, Dorchester
Text Filmsetting Ltd, Orpington

Photography
t = top, b = bottom, l = left, r = right
Allsport 186
Michael Cole Camerawork 20(b), 33(tl), 90(b),
204, 252 Colorsport 2, 18, 33(b), 55, 69, 83, 89(b),
95(l), 118, 129, 177, 181, 183, 184(t), 213, 252
Gerry Cranham FIIP 11, 14, 15, 84, 88, 92, 94(t),
96, 130, 131, 134, 135, 138, 139, 141, 142, 143,
180(b), 184(b), 185, 188, 189, 192, 219
David Lamb 20(b), 33(l), 51, 82, 85, 103, 110,
133(l), 137, 140, 160, 197, 201, 245
Le-Roye Productons 6, 10, 13(b), 16, 17, 59, 72,
80, 86, 87, 94(b), 95(r) 121, 128, 140, 144, 151, 155,
167, 171, 175, 178, 182, 187, 190, 191(r), 227, 229,
236, 249, 250
London News Agency 12
Vision International 180(t)
Sporting Pictures 6, 20(t), 25, 65, 107, 136, 179
Wimbledon Lawn Tennis Museum 8–9, 13
Steve Wooster 91, 127, 132, 133(r), 136, 245